T0288005

THE
DEVELOPMENT
OF
HIGHER EDUCATION
AND SOCIAL CHANGE

THE
DEVELOPMENT
OF
HIGHER EDUCATION
AND SOCIAL CHANGE

AN
ETHIOPIAN EXPERIENCE

TESHOME G. WAGAW

Michigan State University Press
East Lansing, Michigan
1990

All Michigan State University Press books are produced on paper which meets the requirements of American National Standard of Information Science—Permanence of paper for printed materials. ANSI 239.48-1984.

Michigan State University Press
East Lansing, Michigan 48823-5202

Printed in the United States of America

Library of Congress Cataloging-in-Publication Data

Wagaw, Teshome G., 1930–
    The development of higher education and social change: an Ethiopian experience/Teshome G. Wagaw.
        p.   cm.—(African series; no. 2)
    Includes bibliographical references.
    ISBN 0-87013-283-0
    1. Education, Higher—Ethiopia—History. 2. Education—Ethiopia—History. 3. Education, Higher—Social aspects—Ethiopia—History. 4. Higher education and state—Ethiopia—History.   I. Title. II. Series: African series (East Lansing, Michigan); no. 2.
LA1518.W34   1990
378.63—dc20   89-43330
                                                                              CIP

This book is dedicated

To the memory of my parents, Tiroo Kassahun and Wagaw Gebremichael, and to the heroines of the family, Kassaye and Alemnesh Wagaw, who risked career and personal security on behalf of the family at a time of great crisis.

CONTENTS

I
In the Beginning

II
The Guest Models: Importation, Adaptation, Innovation, and Expansion

III
In the Shadows of Revolution

Illustrations

Tables

PREFACE

This book is a study of the development of institutions of higher education and the roles they played in the transformation of traditional Ethiopian society. The study attempts to show that although other modernizing agencies such as a standing regular army, parliament, trade unions, and lower institutions of learning may play significant roles in social and economic change, in Ethiopia the institutions of higher learning, and especially their students, contributed significantly to profound revolution. The study also attempts to show that in the case of Ethiopia these institutions, indispensable as they were to the downfall of the established order, were unable to provide viable political organizations to usher in forms of government that would facilitate progress and the quest for freedom from all forms of oppression, want, and persecution.

In the aftermath of World War II, there emerged a tremendous flood of global awareness of the need for political, technical, and scientific advancement among most of the peoples of the earth who until then had lived under the yoke of European colonialism. As a result, as African nations gained political independence in the 1950s and 1960s, they established new institutions of learning and upgraded, altered, or expanded the few existing ones. For the most part, these institutions drew their models and inspiration from Europe or North America. This borrowing was comprehensive; it included not only the organizational, structural, and substantive aspects, but conventions and traditions as well.

In the African milieu, however, the guest models confronted a multitude of problems that were either not apparent in European and North American institutions or had been resolved a long time ago. These problems included whether, in what ways, and to what extent institutions of higher learning should involve themselves in the application of knowledge to societal concerns such as survival, as opposed to their other central mission which was to discover, modify, expand, and disseminate knowledge. This question did not seem to be an either/or proposition; rather, it sought the appropriate mix of these two broad functional categories. The answer depended on the institutions' relevance and loyalty to the societies in which they existed and from whose material, spiritual, and cultural support they drew their sustenance and strength.

It is given that universities represent a reservoir of highly qualified human and physical resources, developed over a generation at great expense to the respective states, is a given. Therefore, it is obvious that the wealth represented in the higher learning institutions should be tapped in the interests of the wider human communities through teaching, research, consultancy, and outreach programs. It is also axiomatic that in order for these young institutions to merit and maintain their currency in the international forum of universities, they must declare and pursue the quest for truth, objectivity, democracy, and justice in the gathering and dissemination of knowledge.

On the other hand, many African states are governed by regimes which seized power by other than legal means and, therefore, are preoccupied with problems arising from insecurity and a search for legitimacy. Their struggles to obtain such elusive commodities are illustrated by the comical but brutally serious affixations that some heads of government claim for themselves, including "The Redeemer," "The Guide," "The Miracle," "President for Life," and the like. In most such states, there is only one political party—if a party exists at all. Under such circumstances, these totalitarian powers try to manipulate, dominate, and control all instruments of thought and expression. As they attempt to apply policies affecting the institutions of higher learning, the rulers often insist that the colleges and universities respond to the "wishes" of the state, and, of course, the state and the head of its government are one and the same. Usually, conflicts ensue between the politicians and the universities, and the outcome can be disastrous for both.

Consequently, African institutions of higher learning are criticized, sometimes justifiably, for not being relevant or loyal to their societies and for not becoming fully involved in economic and social reconstruction. They are seldom encouraged to become involved or blamed for not being involved in the processes of political development or participation. Indeed, the emphasis is to the contrary. The universities are admonished not to become foci for political opposition against the order established by the "will of the people." In the real world, however, universities and colleges have frequently been drawn into political controversy, perhaps more than any other single sector of organized societal life. When these types of activities occur, the institutions suffer. In the following case study, the political doings of the university precipitated profound, lasting, revolutionary changes. Given prevailing sociopolitical condition on the continent, more change along these lines is likely.

This study argues that in at least one African state—Ethiopia—institutions of higher learning were relevant and loyal to the society, perhaps too relevant for their own good. They were strong factors in the demise of the establishment, but were unable to forge new sets of organizations and institutions to guide, control, and ultimately establish a system that would lead the society peacefully away from its oppressively traditional past toward progress and enlightenment.

This book derives from a larger study conceived and undertaken over two decades ago while the author was still on the faculty of the Ethiopian national university. Over the years, as circumstances changed, the scope, orientation, and direction of the study also changed. Data were updated to take account of recent developments.

Now a word or two about the author. After twelve years of work and study abroad—first in Australia, then in the United States—I returned to Addis Ababa on 11 September 1966. I had held comfortable teaching positions, first at the University of Maryland and later at Howard University in the United States. Although I had no legal requirements to fulfill (I had been almost entirely self-supporting throughout my student days), I felt dutybound to return home and contribute what I could to the development of my country. I arrived from Cairo at 11:00 A.M. and reported to the Ministry of Education in Addis Ababa at 2:00 P.M. the same day. I was ready to start. However, my naiveté gave way to the reality of bureaucratic requirements. It took almost a month to finalize negotiations, and I ended up working for the National University rather than the Ministry of Education and Fine Arts. Still, I was fortunate in that I was able to assume a number of interesting positions that helped me gain a wider perspective of my country and society. I spent the first year as a counselor to university students who were serving a year in rural areas as teachers, technicians, and the like, as part of their graduation requirements. This took me to remote corners of Ethiopia. In retrospect that was the best single year I ever invested in my education.

Between 1967 and 1969 I served as dean of student services to not only the colleges in Addis Ababa but at the Gondar and Alemaya campuses as well. These were turbulent years of student activism throughout the world. Sitting in this position made me feel that given the lack of institutional, political, and attitudinal traditions, ours was the hottest and most volatile position. Full of challenges, at times traumatic, those two years gave me a chance to observe the political thoughts and actions of young people at close range. From 1969 through 1974, I was associate professor and head of the psychology department. These vantage points gave me unique opportunities to observe, record, and later analyze the interactions of young institutions of higher learning and the polity of a traditional society. Throughout the pages of this volume, then, my personal observations are wedded with other oral or documented sources. I hope that the reader will find this useful.

Many people provided me with invaluable assistance in many forms as I developed this book. There is no way that I can list them all, but I say thank you, nonetheless. I would like to single out my friends and former colleagues, Drs. Aklilu Habte (then president of the university who was always an enthusiastic supporter of the project), Mulugeta Wodajo, Akalou Wolde Michael, Aklilu Lemma, and Germa Amare, as well as Professors Dartha and Fay Starr who were most gracious in reading the earlier draft. Thank you, friends, for your encouragements and criticisms. I would like to acknowledge the material assistance provided by the Horace Rackham School of Graduate Studies, the School of Education program in Higher and Adult Continuing Education and the Center for African-American and African Studies of The University of Michigan. I thank the Annenberg Research Institute in Philadelphia for granting me a very valuable fellowship during 1989–90. Special appreciation and gratitude goes to Mary Achatz of the University of Michigan for her meticulous and painstaking editorial work. Her many talents and sharp sense of detail gave full play in the enhancement of the final product of this work. I would like to extend my appreciation to Julie Loehr of the Michigan State University Press for her meticulous care in shepherding the manuscript through the Press. My wife, Tsehi Wolde-Tsadik, was as usual patient and understanding during my long journey and toward completing this work. Thank you, Tsehai. As the final arbiter, any shortcomings in form or substance are the author's responsibilities.

T. G. W.
Ann Arbor and Philadelphia
February 1990

INTRODUCTION

In global, as well as African, perspectives, Ethiopia is one of the oldest states while also being one of the newest nation-states. To provide better insight into the theater in which the drama of the old and new were played in the processes of social transformation, a sketch of the political, economic, and demographic characteristics of Ethiopia as it has been and as it is in the process of becoming, follows.

Political-Historical Setting

Ethiopia, or Abyssinia, as it has sometimes been known,[1] is one of the three or four most ancient states of the world, and certainly the oldest continuous nation-state in Africa, including Egypt.[2] One of the most unique characteristics of Ethiopia as an ancient nation-state is its diversity, which prompted the Italian historian Carlo Conti-Rossini to coin the term "museum of people."[3] The variety of human physical characteristics, languages, ethnicity, religious affiliations or beliefs, societal and family structures, conceptions of self in relation to the national community, modes of earning a livelihood, and general ways of life in this vast and beautiful tract of African land is extremely impressive and fascinating. Some think that this diversity inhibits the rate of modernization or threatens national unity. Others believe that such diversity, if properly guided, could continue to be the unique strength of Ethiopian national identity as it resists the onslaught of European and Asian influences.

Throughout most of its three millennia of history, the country has been ruled by kings and emperors who, since the introduction of Christianity in the fifth century, have usually served as heads of the Ethiopian Orthodox Church as well as heads of government. Two major institutions, in addition to the monarchy, which have represented the social, cultural, economic, and political lives of traditional, feudalistic Ethiopia—the church and the nobility.

As the final authority in all religious and secular matters, the emperor has been, over the centuries, the major unifying factor in Ethiopian life. Without the monarchy, Ethiopia's diversity might well have

1

splintered the nation into irreconcilable factions. Indeed, for the most part the power of the monarch was so absolute that many thought that he would have no problem leading a united country to progress.

Some insight into the claims upon which the Ethiopian rulers based their legitimacy and the attitudes they elicited on the part of the populace is offered by the noted Ethiopian scholar, Blatengetta Mahiteme Selassie. Writing as late as the 1950s, he observed:

> The people consider the Emperor as the representative of God on earth and obey his laws and orders happily. I do not think that a monarch is so much loved and so much revered in any other part of the world as in Ethiopia. The monarch's very name is awesome. There is no Ethiopian who will not keep an appointment or promise after he has promised to do so upon oath saying "Let the king die!" Even in a marriage contract, which is considered as an honourable affair, the last binding word of oath is "Let the king die!" In Ethiopia the orders of the Emperor are very much feared. Thus there is a saying in Ethiopia that if you entreat it to stop in the king's name even flowing water will stop, let alone a man. (This saying, in effect, expresses the great reverence and obedience the people have towards the Ethiopian monarch.)[4]

For their part, the emperors had to fulfill certain obligations to exact this universal obedience and respect. The *Fetha Negest*, for centuries the legal basis of the contract, states that:

> The king you appoint must be one of your brethren. It is not proper for you to appoint over yourself an alien and infidel. . . . And when he sits on the throne of his kingdom, some priests shall write for him the Divine Book, so that he may keep it by his side and read it through his life, in order to learn the fear of God his Creator, to observe his commandments and to practice them, lest his heart become proud (and feel contempt for his brothers).[5]

The obligations of the citizens to the king, on the other hand, were equally clear:

> Everyone of you must be submissive to the authority of your ruler, since a ruler is appointed only by God. And God has appointed all these rulers and given them authority; one who opposes the ruler and revels against him, rebels against the ordinance of God, his Creator. Those who rebel against the rulers secure their condemnation. . . . Therefore, we must be submissive to him not only for fear of his (the king's) anger, but

also in our conscience. It is for this same reason that we give tribute since one who is appointed to keep (public) affairs orderly is God's minister and one who does his will. Give every man his due; tribute, if it be tribute, fear, if it be fear, honor, if it be honor, tithes, if it be tithes.[6]

The exhortation continues:

> For the spiritual and corporal benefits which we derive from the ruler, let us give him tribute and presents in payment for them. This tribute is meant to provide the judges with necessities which they are in need of, since they put aside their own interest and case for the public welfare. Do not say that he has transgressed the law but consider the order obtained by the law. There is no peace if an authority is not constituted: instead, because of the lack of authority, there is great confusion and lack of peace, which leads to the loss of life and existence.[7]

These contractual obligations between monarch and people endured for centuries and were binding even in the Revised Constitution of 1955. Commenting on that constitution, Paul and Clapham point out that "only the Emperor and the people are, under the Constitution, self-sufficient' sources of political power. The establishment of the other elements and institutions of the state is ultimately dependent upon one or other, or both of them."[8]

Thus by sheer legal and traditional force, the power of the monarch remained almost unassailable for centuries. When challenged, it was maintained through personal strength and the frequent application of brutal force. At the same time, the most successful rulers were those who publicly avowed support for such strong institutions as the church and its educational and spiritual activities. For instance, during the last quarter of the nineteenth century, before launching reforms in government and civic affairs, it was necessary for Emperor Menelik II, who was highly respected, loved, and ably supported by his politically astute empress, to go out of his way to convince a significant segment of the Christian populace that he was a staunch, unassailable leader who unflinchingly supported the values of the state religion. It was only after he had accomplished this that he was able to turn his attention to reorganizing the apparatus of government and introducing modern means of communication, administration, and social as well as military services. Even then, he knew the limits of his modernization programs. For instance, during the first decade of this century when he established cabinet posts for the first time in the history of the country, he deliberately left the responsibility for education in the hands of the church, while at the same time he was initiating the

3

infrastructure for a far-reaching system of state supported and controlled secular education. In doing so, he was able to lay sound foundations for the modernization of this conservative nation without unnecessarily alienating important segments of the population, i.e., nobility, the church leaders, and the Christian peasantry, whose support and cooperation were essential to the success of his endeavors.

It is with these political and historical settings in mind that the drama of institutional and generational conflicts that culminated in the 1974 Ethiopian revolution should be viewed.

Demographic and Economic Characteristics

Ethiopia covers an area of 1,183,998 square kilometers (457,142 square miles). Although it is only about eight degrees north of the Equator, for the most part Ethiopia enjoys varying climates which stimulate and support a variety of agricultural and livestock developments. This results from the high elevations of mountains and plateaus, and the influence of the surrounding continental land masses and oceans. The rugged terrain and deep valleys have also contributed to the lack of effective communication among the inhabitants and impeded the rapid spread of education.

A 1984 census—the first ever—indicates a total of 42 million people increasing at a rate of 2.5 percent per annum, which would double the population by the end of the century. An increasing percentage of the population consists of children and young people as a result of the combined effect of rapid population growth and a relative decrease in child mortality.

Since more than 85 percent of the population live in rural communities and depend on agriculture and herding, the Ethiopian economy is essentially a rural one, i.e., agro-pastoral activities are the main contributors to the national gross domestic product. Agricultural production includes such cash crops as cotton, coffee, sugar, fruits, vegetables, oilseeds, and pulses. Other crops (produced primarily for domestic consumption) include *teff* (a type of millet specific to Ethiopia), wheat, maize, sorghum, and millet. The livestock potential of Ethiopia is very promising and is expected to play an even more significant role in the future.

Since 1975, most of the modern sector of the economy (which is relatively young and small) has been brought under state control and management. This sector includes textile mills, mining, food processing, production of beverages, tobacco, sugar, and footwear. National development programs for the construction of rural roads and housing, forestry, settlement, and hydroelectric schemes are expected to accelerate the growth of the modern economic sector.

4

In response to perceived popular demand, economic activities in Ethiopia were altered by the 1974–1976 nationalization and redistribution of all rural lands among the heretofore landless populace; by the reformation of urban lands; by the nationalization of big industries, banks, and insurance; and by the changes in labor conditions. But, as will be shown later in this book, there is a new generation of emerging problems which cast serious doubt on whether these measures have in fact improved the lives of the majority of Ethiopians.

Theme and Organization

This book is a social and historical analysis of the development of institutions of learning in Ethiopia, particularly higher education, and a critical analysis of the role these institutions have played in the transformation of Ethiopian society from a feudal monarchy to a socialist economy dominated accidentally, at least up to the present, by the military.

Higher education is largely a post-World War II phenomenon in Ethiopia. The traditional education system supported and operated by religious institutions had some indirect influences on the tradition of higher education when it finally found itself on Ethiopian soil. However, in terms of structure, approaches to teaching, scholarship, and the relationship of teachers and students to the larger national community, the new, imported secular higher education prototypes were as far from the traditional indigenous models as could be imagined.

Ethiopia has probably undergone more convulsive social and political dislocations than any other African nation in this century. In response to the tremendous global changes following World War II, Ethiopia, having been the first to fall victim to fascist aggression and the first to be liberated, found itself in the 1950s face to face with the challenges of reconstruction. Mussolini's fascist Italy invaded the country in 1935, and among the consequences was the systematic and ruthless destruction of the infant secular public education system. In its place, the Italians established—for the privileged few—a few primary schools with prescribed, strongly pro-Italian curricula. Public education was, therefore, practically nonexistent between 1935 and 1941.

When the national government was restored in 1941, rehabilitation of the educational structure proved difficult. The former teachers were either dead or scattered abroad. World War II was underway in Europe and recruitment of foreign teachers proved extremely difficult. Ethiopia was compelled, therefore, not only to reconstruct and expand the educational system in general, but also

5

to create new institutions of higher learning to train the needed teachers, economists, health personnel, administrators, and technicians. The nation made a concerted effort to train badly needed staff for the civil service and for the business and commercial sectors of national life. In spite of many obstacles, the infrastructure of the education system—from preprimary to college level—was reestablished within a decade.

The practice of sending selected young people to overseas institutions for further training proved slow and expensive. By 1950, therefore, Ethiopia decided to establish a liberal arts college. Within the next decade, eight other colleges embracing the social and physical sciences and technology areas were established. By 1961 a national university system brought most of these colleges under one administrative umbrella though it did not include Asmara University, a semi-private institution, or several other junior or teacher training colleges operated by private or religious organizations.

At about the time the new institutions of higher learning were being established, other modernizing institutions were also emerging: a parliament, a regular standing army and air force, a police force, a national constitution, and the like. While these progressive steps were taken, the traditional institutions, such as the monarchy, the state church, the nobility, and nearly all the conventions, values, and symbols they represented remained in place. The political authorities apparently assumed that modernization could be effected without necessarily altering the traditional personal, economic, or social relationships among the various segments of this pluralistic society. The biblical expression that patching a new piece of cloth on the old will destroy the latter proved to be literally true in the case of Ethiopia.

This book is divided into four major parts: Part I deals with the traditional approaches to politics and learning. Part II deals with the conception and emergence of modern institutions of higher learning and the drama of their interaction with the traditional conventions and institutions. Part III covers the postrevolutionary period (since 1974), highlighting the problems confronted, the gains realized, the upheavals precipitated, and the accommodations worked out or unrealized between the new political realities and the institutions of higher education.

Notes

1. The name Ethiopia comes from the Greek word Aithiops, meaning a country of people of sun-burnt face. The term Abyssinia, or Habesh, means people of mixed race and probably originated in the Middle East among people who were not well disposed toward the country. The citizens prefer the ancient name, Ethiopia.
2. The others are Iran, Japan, and China. See Teshome Wagaw, "Emerging Issues of Ethiopian Nationalities: Cohesion or Disintegration," *Journal of Northeast African Studies* 2, no. 3 (1980–81): 69.
3. See ibid.
4. Mahiteme Selassie Wolde Meskal (Blatengetta), *Zekre Neger* (Addis Ababa: 1962 E.C.), as translated in J. C. N. Paul and C. S. Clapham, *Ethiopian Constitutional Development: A Sourcebook I* (Addis Ababa: Faculty of Law, Haile Selassie I University, 1967), 393.
5. Paulos Tzadua (Abba), trans. *Fetha Negest* (Addis Ababa: Faculty of Law, Haile Selassie I University, 1968), 271.
6. Ibid.
7. Ibid., 272.
8. Paul and Clapham, I:393.

I

IN THE BEGINNING

1

IN THE BEGINNING

1

HIGHER EDUCATION AND SOCIETY IN THE AFRICAN SETTING

Introduction

Africans in general believe that the humiliation that came with the subjugation by foreign powers and the resulting economic retardation were largely the consequences of lack of education, particularly higher education, on the part of the citizenry. Consequently, upon attaining political independence beginning in the early 1960s, politicians, parents, and the youth joined forces to remedy the situation. The result was that over the period 1960–1980 higher education became, in terms of enrollment and resources investment, the fastest growing sector of all levels of education. Since 1983, the fast growth rate has been tamed a little in order to divert some resources to the primary level of education, but it is still growing. At the beginning of the 1960s there were only a handful of colleges offering limited programs of a technical or religious nature in the whole continent. By 1989 there were over 80 full-fledged colleges and universities, offering a wide spectrum of programs. Although it is widely recognized that social, cultural, and economic development cannot succeed without the expansion of human resources that higher education can provide, institutions of higher learning throughout Africa are subjected to increasingly severe constraints in terms of policy and resources that tend to inhibit their ability to contribute maximally to human and social advancement. Before delving into the specific case of one single country, the present chapter (1) seeks to present a brief examination of those constraints and offers a critical analysis of the strengths and weaknesses of the institutions themselves and their contribution to social transformation, and (2) tries to establish the continental social, economic, and educational frameworks for the case of higher education and social transformation in Ethiopia.

The Political and Demographic Setting

Africa is not a huge, monolithic entity whose ambitions, problems, and solutions are identical. To the contrary, the African

9

continent consists of states that are large as well as small; states that are rich in oil and mineral resources and those that are primarily agricultural. Many are landlocked and others have long coastlines; there are countries of the tropical rainforest and those of the semi-arid interior. There are market-oriented economies as well as socialist systems.

However, there is sufficient homogeneity to permit some general observations and conclusions. For example, most of the fifty-one independent countries are one-party states, and as nation-states the majority are young (post-1960). Their economies are small and specialized—agricultural, dependent on the export of two or three primary commodities, and a few minerals. Other similarities include a scarcity of educated people, ethnic diversity, and political fragility.[1]

With an estimated (1980) population of 470 million (10.6 percent of the world population), Africa is one of the largest continents of the world, growing annually at a rate of 2.9 to 3.1 percent. It is projected that by the year 2000 the population will total 853 million, 13.9 percent of the world population. The same projection indicates a population of 822 million, or 13.4 percent of the world total, for Europe and the USSR by 2000; 299 million, or 4.9 percent, for North America; 566 million, or 9.2 percent, for Latin America; 23 million, or 0.5 percent for Oceania; and 2,579 million, or 58.0 percent, for Asia. By the turn of the twenty-first century, Africa's population will be second only to that of Asia.

Demographically, Africa is characterized first by a very rapid population growth which is expected to accelerate further before the end of the present century, exceeding the growth rate of any other region of the world; second, by a preponderance of young people. Of all the regions of the world, only in Africa is the largest proportion of the population under the age of 15. In 1980 this proportion was estimated at 44.9 percent for Africa as a whole as contrasted to 39.1 percent for all other developing regions as a whole, and only 23 percent for the developed nations. A third important demographic characteristic is the preponderance of illiteracy. Despite the fact that Africa has made more progress than any other region of the globe in attacking illiteracy in recent years, still, for those 15 years and older, the illiteracy rate in 1980 was 40 percent (156 million people). Throughout the present century, due to rapid growth, this vexing problem will remain a challenge for planners, policy makers, and educators.[2]

In terms of political history, most of the fifty-one independent states that constitute the membership of the Organization of African Unity (OAU) are just attaining the age of majority—30 years old to be exact. With the exceptions of Egypt, Ethiopia, and Liberia, the now-independent African countries were, until the early 1960s, under the domination of European powers—the United Kingdom, France, Belgium, Portugal, Spain, and Italy.

During the colonial period, African resources, material as well as human, were organized to maximize the interests of the metropolitan powers. When independence was attained, the national governments had to struggle with an economic structure that was limited in scope, alien in orientation, and exclusive in its embrace. Since independence this legacy has been buttressed by a shortage of qualified and trained personnel to restructure, expand, and manage the socioeconomic infrastructures; by narrow, externally oriented economies; and natural disasters such as drought, floods, and the like. Coupled with a rapid growth in population due to decreased child mortality and improved longevity, these factors have contributed to chronic stagnation or even decline in most African economies. Since 1973 the international economic situation (energy crises, "stagflation" in the developed countries, a relatively slow growth of trade in both primary agricultural products such as coffee and tobacco and minerals such as iron and copper) has further contributed to the worsening economic conditions in Africa. As a consequence, in sub-Saharan Africa, the average per capita GNP of U.S. $411.00 is the lowest in the world. On the other hand, most African countries have made substantial progress in the areas of health, education, and transportation.

As a result of educational improvements, most of the civil service, as well as parastatal positions, are filled by trained Africans. Health services, staffed by Africans, are becoming more available to a larger population. Though not yet resolved, many cultural, sociological, and psychological problems related to Africa's development are being debated in national and regional forums.

Planning the Development of Higher Education

The concept of higher education has existed in Africa for centuries. The University of Sankore in Timbuctoo (present-day Mali) prospered in the sixteenth century as a modern institution where law, philosophy, and theology were taught. An institution of Moslem study, Al Azhar University in Cairo, has been in existence for over one thousand years and is still functioning, expanding, and modernizing by embracing other branches of study in addition to its traditional mission. As pointed out in chapter 2, a number of institutions of higher learning have functioned in Ethiopia for

11

centuries, primarily as centers of excellence for the study of Christian theology, law, and philosophy.

In the West African state of Sierra Leone, the Church Missionary Society of London founded the Fourah Bay College in 1827, primarily as a center for religious studies. After its affiliation with Durham University in 1876, it expanded its course offerings to include the sciences and other secular subjects leading to the B.A. degree. It later became a state university. Except for these and a few other examples, most of the institutions of higher learning are of post-World War II vintage.[3]

When the African states were emerging as independent entities, one of their first acts was to get together, under the auspices of UNESCO, to compare notes and plan an agenda for educational development. Meeting in the Ethiopian capital of Addis Ababa in May 1961, the Ministers of Education of the independent African states outlined a 20-year plan for educational development. The Addis Ababa Plan, as it came to be known, set a goal of ensuring that 20 percent of high school graduates would proceed to colleges and universities and by 1980-81, 2 percent of the relevant age groups would find a place in the universities, mostly within Africa. The Addis Ababa Plan, however, was part of an overall plan for the development of education on the continent. As far as higher education was concerned, a more detailed, concrete plan had to wait another year.

In 1962, in Tananarive, Madagascar, UNESCO, in collaboration with the United Nations Economic Commission for Africa, convened a conference on the development of higher education in Africa for the next twenty years. The conference interpreted the mission of the African university as defining and confirming:

> the aspirations of the society which it is established to serve. While aspiring to make its full contributions to the Universal stock of knowledge, African higher education must aspire to give African peoples their rightful place and to cement African unity forever. Towards this end, the African University must regard itself as the cultural centre of the community in which it is placed and the guardian and proponent of its artistic, literary, and musical heritage. It should provide research into this heritage and make available the fruits of this research by sponsoring concerts, plays and exhibitions, and by establishing art galleries and museums. Its library and archives should also be made available to the public.[4]

According to the participants of the Tananarive conference, African institutions of higher education "are at once the main instrument of national progress, the chief guardian of the people's heritage and the voice of the people in the international councils of technology and scholarship. This triple role—progressive, conservative, and collaborative—is an excitingly challenging one.''[5] Like universities everywhere, African universities were expected to advance the frontiers of knowledge through teaching and research and, at the same time, accommodate the unique genius and special characteristics of their respective societies. In addition to the traditional role of providing liberal education, African universities were to respond to the needs of the African world by equipping men and women with the skills, knowledge, and attitudes that would enable them to participate fully and productively in the economic, social, and cultural development of the continent.

These heavy responsibilities assigned to the institutions of higher learning required political and moral support from the societies they were to serve. In particular, the Tananarive conference stressed that African universities must enjoy traditional academic freedom to the fullest extent possible:

> They must have the fullest freedom to teach, to advance the frontiers of knowledge through research, and disseminate as widely as possible the results of their research. Like other universities, African universities must keep these principles intact and consolidate and defend these rights as may be necessary.[6]

Since Africa must, by necessity, emphasize social development and transformation, and since man is the center, the means, and the end of this development, the responsibilities as well as approaches of the institutions must be complete. As the conference document rightly noted:

> For full and complete development and enrichment of the individual, higher education institutions in Africa should become responsible for placing emphasis on moral and spiritual values, developing a sense of social and civic responsibility as well as appreciation for beauty in art, music and ethics. They should endeavour to develop an awareness of local problems and aspirations, cultivate the ability to analyze and seek solutions to problems and help realize national aspirations. Such self-identification of the individual with the great cause of society will awake a loyalty and dedication to Africa and its people and will strengthen the bonds that bind them to the larger human society.[7]

In addition, the conference noted that Africa's higher education institutions must play a positive, significant role in the improvement of the entire education system and prepare young people at all levels for productive citizenship. This positive role could be realized through training, research, and the publication of educational journals as well as other textbooks and teaching-learning materials.

In summary, in addition to the traditional responsibilities and functions of teaching and advancing knowledge, the role of African higher education institutions in social, cultural, and economic development must be to (1) maintain loyalty to world academic standards, (2) insure the unification of Africa, (3) encourage the elucidation and appreciation of African culture and heritage and dispel misconceptions about Africa through research and teaching, (4) prepare the necessary human resources for meeting high-level work force needs, (5) develop the whole person for the task of nation building, and (6) over the years, develop a truly African pattern of higher education "dedicated to Africa and its people yet promoting a bond of kinship to the larger human society."[8]

The Tananarive conference adopted a number of measures designed to facilitate the development of institutions of higher learning. The caliber of the teaching staff was to be of the highest order possible. However, it was acknowledged that due to shortages of local qualified staff, recruitment of expatriates would be necessary for the next eight to ten years. The conference highlighted the importance of students receiving their education in their home countries, and suggested that the number of university students studying abroad from North and Middle Africa be reduced to 5 and 10 percent, respectively. The conference also expressed the wish that by 1980, 60 percent of all university students would be enrolled in the science-technology fields, with 8 percent studying agricultural subjects, and that the number of African institutions of higher learning be expanded to 32.

Subsequent continental and international conferences considered the problems associated with higher education. In 1964 the conference of Ministers of Education held in Abidjan, Ivoire d'Côte, pointed out the need to reduce unit costs in higher education as much as possible. To this end they urged the establishment of close cooperation among existing institutions, especially in areas where costs were highest, e.g., in medicine and engineering. Aware of the importance of strengthening higher education, participants at the 1968 conference held in Nairobi, Kenya, proposed a target of 200 teachers and researchers and ten to fifteen engineers per million inhabitants in Middle Africa and twice that number for North Africa.[9] The Lagos conference of 1976 emphasized the role of the Association of African Universities as an instrument of cooperation among regional and continental institutions in the interest of achieving maximum efficiency and utilization of resources for the benefit of all.

As the universities were established, the African political leadership became very interested and supportive. Following British or French models, the presidents or heads of state of the respective countries became chancellors or visitors of the universities. In their capacities as heads of both governments and the institutions, they became involved in defining the roles and missions that the institutions should play. Julius Nyerere of Tanzania (then Tanganyika), the first chancellor of the now-defunct East Africa University, challenged the staff and students to remain truthful to the world standard of objectivity and the pursuit of truth without at the same time becoming isolated from the community.

> We must, and do, demand that this University take an active part in the social revolution we are engineering. I am not telling the University to become a centre of opposition to the elected Governments. On the contrary, the University belongs to the people, and must serve their wishes. But if the University is to be of any benefit to the people or their government, then it must be a centre of objective thinking; and it must accept all the responsibilities which go with that position.

Nyerere affirmed that the university must stand firm on the principles of truth and objectivity and fight even against political authorities. It must maintain:

> the spirit of truth; it must be as objective and scientific as possible, and must fight prejudice of all kinds, at all times, and at all places. . . . The University must think, and force us to think, in terms of humanity—not any sectoral interests. Its members must guard against their own prejudices as well as ours.

As the faculty and students go about the business of collecting and analyzing data "we ought to want," they must constantly remember that at the same time they "must be the torch bearers of our society and the protectors of the flame, should we [politicians], in our urgency, endanger its brightness."[10]

For Nyerere, the African institution of higher learning was to be a leader in the search for truth, beauty, and enlightenment; a full partner in social development; a critic of public policy and action without being a center for political opposition. These multiple university responsibilities were repeated by Kwame Nkrumah of Ghana, Felix Houphouet-Boigny of the Ivory Coast, Emperor Haile Selassie of Ethiopia, and others.

For Nkrumah, the university "must kindle national interests in the youth and uplift our citizens and free them from ignorance, superstition, and indolence." To carry out these tasks faithfully,

> scholars must be free to pursue the truth and to publish the
> results of their research without fear, for true scholarship fears
> nothing. . . . Without academic freedom. . . there can be no
> higher education worthy of the name, and, therefore, no in-
> tellectual progress, no flowering of the nation's mind. . . . [The]
> University is, and must always remain, a living, thinking, and
> serving part of the community to which it belongs.[11]

As Nyerere and Nkrumah reiterated, the university must not be used
as a center for political opposition.

For Houphouet-Boigny, president of the Ivoire d'Côte, the role
of the university was that of providing leadership for development,
without losing its French cultural orientation. In his words: "Our
university must be an intimate part of the social body of which it
will be the highest cultural expression, that it must support the aspirations of our society and associate itself with the efforts for material
well-being and a better knowledge of the world in which we live."
His enduring ambition was to see the university "award diplomas
equivalent to those of the French universities, thus placing our youth
on an equal plane of knowledge with the youth of one of the most
civilized nations of the world." And, he said, the university must
serve as "a center for the spreading of French culture, an ideal meeting place between countries of the English and French background."[12]

Thus, the broad courses charted, the missions defined, the targets set, the African journey into higher education began anew.

Twenty Years of Challenges

The 1961–1980 development plan period was an era of significant accomplishment in African higher education. The remainder
of this chapter examines the progress made, the challenges confronted, and the results achieved regarding the development of
higher education and its contribution to Africa's development.

The numerical recommendations of the Tananarive conference
were overfulfilled. Enrollments in higher education grew faster than
any other level of education—from 142,000 in 1960 to 1,169,000
in 1980—a more than eightfold increase. The 1980 total represents
3 percent of the relevant age-group instead of the 2 percent anticipated in 1960.[13]

Recent censuses indicate that the number of university students
as a proportion of the relevant age-group in each country was over
1 percent for more than half of the countries in 1980, while in 1970
this proportion was exceeded in only about nine countries. Egypt,
Libya, Congo, Tunisia, and Morocco (except Congo, all are North

African countries) lead the rest of Africa in this comparison with 13.7, 5.8, 5.2, 4.8, and 4.8 percent, respectively.

From 1961 to 1980 the development of African institutions of higher learning, both in numbers, structure, and program complexity, was very significant. By 1980 the number of universities increased from 32 in twenty-three countries to 80 in forty-three countries.[14] Fifty are located in Arabic and English-speaking countries, the rest are found in Francophone and Lusophone (Portuguese) countries.

Because of their recent development, enrollment rates in African universities are very small by world standards. Taking 1965 as the first year of deliberate expansion of university education, the rate of growth since that time has exceeded that of any other region of the world. As shown in Figure 1, the number of university students per 100,000 inhabitants doubled or tripled in two-thirds of the countries over the period 1970–1980. In most of the remaining countries there was no significant change; in four of the smaller countries there was a decline. In terms of regions within the continent, the North African countries, led by Egypt, stand out first, followed by West, Central, and East Africa, in that order. At this writing, eight of the fifty-one African countries do not have universities.[15]

Female Students

The number of female students in African higher education varies from country to country. Although significant improvement has been noticed lately, on the whole the proportion of female students remains low. In the years immediately preceding 1980 (latest figures available), the proportion of women students exceeded 20 percent in only about half of the countries. For the rest, the percentage was between 10 and 20 percent. In addition, female students tended to drop out earlier than men. In terms of field of studies, they tended to concentrate in teaching and the social sciences, followed by the health professions. In the universities that offer both graduate and undergraduate programs, the number of female students at the graduate level is very low.

Distribution of Students by Field

The 1961 plan for African higher education recommended a ratio of 6 to 4 in favor of the technical-science fields, a goal that was not realized by 1982. However, there has been a noticable shift from the social sciences and humanities in favor of the pedagogic sciences. Because of deficient backgrounds at the earlier levels of education

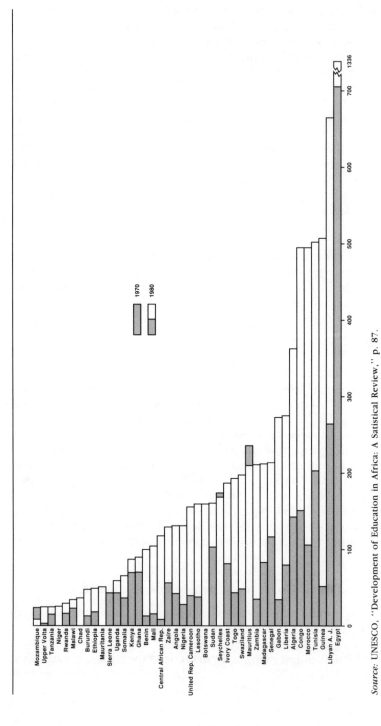

Source: UNESCO, ''Development of Education in Africa: A Satistical Review,'' p. 87.

FIGURE 1

Number of Students in Higher Education per 100,000 Inhabitants, 1970 and 1980

due to lack of science equipment, facilities, and qualified teachers, the natural sciences and engineering still attract relatively few students in most of the countries observed. African states have yet to come to grips with the fundamental causes underlying this problem.

Students Abroad

The Tananarive Plan recommended that, as African universities develop, most students should be trained in their home countries— or at least within Africa. According to that plan, by 1980 only 5 to 10 percent would be studying abroad. However, in 1979–80 an estimated 159,800 students were pursuing their studies overseas. This is a dramatic increase over 1974–75 when the figure was 99,700. Except for Egypt and Zaire, where only 1 and 5 percent, respectively, of the total university enrollment was abroad, the number of Africans studying abroad in 1979-80 represented about a quarter of the total student body, indicating that for a variety of reasons—prestige, better study facilities and academic environment, attractive monetary reward upon graduation, etc.—African students, whether supported by government, international or private organizations, or individuals, continued to proceed abroad. It is interesting to note also that more than 60 percent of these African students in 1979–80 were in Europe and the USSR and 23 percent were enrolled in North American universities. Eleven percent were studying in other African countries, primarily Egypt, which increased its intake of foreign students sixfold from 1974–75 to 1979–80. The remaining 5 percent of African students were enrolled in Asia, Latin America, and Oceania.

Of the seventeen major host countries, France received about 35 percent of the African students, followed by the United States with 21.4 percent, the USSR with 8.3 percent, the United Kingdom with 7.2 percent, and Egypt with 4.4 percent. In terms of country of origin, Nigeria (the most populous state in Africa) led the rest with 23,330 students, followed by the North African countries of Morocco, Algeria, Tunisia, and the Sudan. Some of the smaller countries, with no home university of their own, continue to send students abroad.

The concern of the home governments, as noted elsewhere in this chapter, is whether these students will return home and, if they do, whether they will be overqualified or misqualified to fulfill the urgent development needs of their countries, and whether their training will have long-range political implications. Definitive answers to questions such as these must await further study.

In concluding this section of statistical analysis, it must be noted that, in general, the enrollment growth in African institutions of higher learning, although still low by world standards, has been significant. African states are deservedly proud of their commitments of vast amounts of precious resources to this venture.

Questions of Quality

African institutions of higher learning have been accused of being rigid, unimaginative, and imitative, following the metropolitan models which were designed for other societies at other times and under different socioeconomic and political conditions. These and similar charges contain some element of truth. However, after drawing their initial inspiration from European or North American models, most African institutions of higher learning have built their own traditions, values, and approaches while remaining mindful of their obligation to global standards of excellence in scholarship and the dissemination of knowledge. This is a natural and highly desirable development for, in the long run, the interests of Africa and the world will be better served by African research and teaching conducted by educated Africans rather than perpetuation of the "dark continent" myths that have been spread for centuries by those external to the African conditions.

Nevertheless, the qualitative aspects of higher education should be continually and carefully examined. In the African context, the qualitative question may be assessed by examining the role of the institution in (1) the development of high-level personnel for the various sectors of national life, (2) the development of indigenous science and technology, (3) the safeguarding and expansion of African cultures, and (4) the revitalization of the educational system.

Preparation of High-level Personnel

No matter where they are located, the primary role of institutions of higher learning has always been the imparting of knowledge, skills, and attitudes at the highest level. It is from the resulting pool of qualified people that the political, economic, cultural, and spiritual leadership of most societies has been drawn. In Africa, however, such leadership has for several decades been imposed from Europe by Europeans with little regard for the wishes or interests of the local people. As a result, when most African countries gained their independence there were only 142,000 university students in the whole continent, and many countries had only twenty or so university graduates. As late as 1960 the African universities, which were then often little more than faculties or institutes in the early stages of development, confined themselves to the teaching of the humanities and the law. Even after independence this imbalance persisted for some time, despite accusations that the universities were ivory towers, unresponsive, even irrelevant to the urgent development needs of the respective societies.

In the industrialized countries, higher education developed in step with social and economic evolution, which was accelerated first by the industrial revolution and then by scientific and technological breakthroughs. In most instances, these countries were fortunate enough to find themselves equipped simultaneously with academic training facilities on the one hand, and political, administrative, and socioeconomic infrastructures and production potential on the other. So, for the most part, the primary question for these countries was, and still is, matching training needs to socioeconomic requirements or correlating the needs of the production sector with the educational system. For African institutions of higher learning the problem of correlating the production sector with education is more complex and problematic.

As far as training is concerned, the institutions of higher learning must not only ascertain the whole range of African development needs, based on solid knowledge of local and national environments, but also that their educational programs correspond to development goals that help communities solve their basic and practical problems. The aim, then, of the universities and other institutions specifically designed to address practical problems is to develop a new breed of high-level personnel which breaks away from the traditional and primarily academic education inherited from the colonial past. At the same time, African institutions of higher learning realize that requirements of Africa do not absolve them from their obligation to maintain their fair share of the world currency of excellence in the creation and dissemination of knowledge.

What are the uniquely African primary developmental needs to which the institutions of higher learning must respond? An exhaustive list of these needs will not be presented here, but it may be instructive to consider some illustrative examples. About 80 percent of African people live in rural areas, making their livelihood from subsistence farming and cattle raising. Most of the population is young (up to 60 percent are under 30 years of age). African economies are largely based on the exchange of primary goods, though some have reliable mineral deposits. The commercial and industrial infrastructures are limited in range and young in age. The captains of industry and banking are still mostly non-Africans.

African institutions of higher learning must address these issues as they attempt to develop high-level work forces, and they have begun to respond. Though the number of such institutions totals about eighty, this number does not reflect the full range of centers and institutes that have been established as part of existing

21

institutions or independent of them (for example, as part of other governmental or parastatal departments) to address specific development needs. In fact, because the older colleges and universities have been slow to respond to urgent training needs, the governments have passed them by to create numerous postsecondary, subuniversity level institutions, in an attempt to give higher education greater relevance and participation in the development process. In the meantime, the need to link these activities to the traditional tasks of a university—advancing and disseminating knowledge, providing intellectual stimulus at the highest level, and producing high-level managerial personnel—remains ever-present.

Rural development requirements call for the preparation of local people with a wide range of skills, including farm management, agricultural engineering, home economics, maintenance and repair of farm equipment and tools, health service, animal husbandry, and extension work. Other modernizing sectors of the economies, such as public administration, industry, trade and small business, tourism, commerce, transport, telecommunications, energy and mining, public works, and teaching require appropriately trained personnel. Institutions of higher education are best equipped to impart the wide range of expertise required for such responsibilities, and they ought to respond.[16]

Especially in Africa, institutions of higher education must also provide continued lifelong education through in-service training, workshops, and seminars for people in government and industry. As existing knowledge and skills become obsolete, the demand for continuous upgrading and retraining increases. Many of Africa's administrative and other personnel gained high positions at relatively young ages, when they were inexperienced and not well educated. To keep pace with the fast-changing tempo of modern times, they need to be retrained in order to continue to function adequately. The importance of these retraining activities is properly recognized by African higher learning institutions, and it is being addressed on most campuses.

The Development of Science and Indigenous Technology

As most of Africa responds to the challenge of reestablishing its identity, its traditional values and institutions, it must also keep pace with the tremendous changes wrought by science and technology. Science is, or ought to be, value-neutral and universal in its ramifications. Technology is value- as well as environment-dependent. As an applied science it must be made to fit the values and needs of specific societies. Many developmental problems,

especially those associated with nutrition, health, and the environment, can be altered through the appropriate use of technology.

African societies decided at the 1962 Tananarive conference that,
to prepare the requisite quality and number of specialists in the various fields of national life, their institutions of higher learning should
work toward and maintain a 6:4 enrollment ratio in favor of science
and technology. This, however, has proved insufficient. Since the
foundations of the skills and attitudes that may lead students to
choose these fields are laid in the grade schools, and since most
of these schools are destitute of sufficient facilities, equipment, and
qualified teachers, the goal of preparing enough engineers, technicians, and other technical specialists remains elusive.

Unfortunately, it is not possible to manage the present problems
of Africa—its population explosion, energy shortages, droughts,
floods, diseases—without the requisite technology and skills. But
the technology must be appropriate to African needs. As a 1982
UNESCO publication aptly pointed out, inasmuch as development
is a global process—social and cultural no less than economic and
technical—and the improvement of science teaching in African
countries is inseparable from the need to strengthen its indigenous
character, it is necessary to not only emphasize priority development needs but also provide courses in the social and human
sciences. Technology is:

> a sector of values which derive from a cultural model and bring
> about radical changes in ways of life. These are the considera-
> tions that those responsible for scientific and technological edu-
> cation in Africa have in mind when they speak of endogenous
> development of science and technology. . . . Imported tech-
> nologies are not relevant to the needs, values and aspirations
> of the people of the countries concerned."[17]

Recognizing that technology can be a tool for the betterment of
the quality of human life, African societies have urged their universities to provide well-trained people who can translate the social
need for appropriate technologies to reality and develop Africa's
scientific and technological potential. The basic need is to realign
research to emphasize the solution of African problems, thus end-
ing the technological dependence brought about by the adoption
of foreign technology without the necessary precaution of considering its impact on the host society.

Hence, African institutions of higher learning face a dual challenge: to undertake a considerable amount of research in technology geared to the development requirements of communities and
based on solid knowledge of such communities on the one hand,

and to expand basic research, which alone can give them full equality with other universities in the world on the other. So far, efforts to meet this dual challenge remain the weakest link in African higher education. The universities, and the financial and moral forces of the respective societies, must rise to this occasion and respond valiantly.

The Development, Safeguarding, and Promotion of Culture

As centers of excellence in teaching and research, African universities have been called upon to commit themselves to the proposition that Africa, to remain true to itself and contribute maximally to the well-being of the global society, must anchor itself on its true identity. Among other things, this effort requires a vast amount of research and dissemination of the results thereof. However, cultural work of this kind faces a number of basic obstacles, particularly language.

The international languages—English, French, Portuguese, and Arabic—remain predominant in African education. However, research into the development of some of the indigenous languages is being carried out. For example, in Tanzania, Somalia, parts of Nigeria, Mali, and a number of other countries, considerable efforts have been made to research, codify, and popularize local languages. More needs to be done in this area. "African languages as languages of instruction . . . are the vectors of values, thought processes and perception . . . [hence, they] constitute the child's and the adolescent's natural bond with the environment of his birth."[18] It is vital that this work in codification, standardization, grammar, and textbook production proceed. Until such work in African languages reaches an adequate level, the efforts of African states to foster the utilization of African mother tongues and national languages, and the preservation and promotion of cultures and traditions will remain elusive.

A number of African universities are now collecting oral histories, folklore, artifacts, theater, painting, and other cultural treasures. Some stage exhibits, conduct workshops and seminars, and encourage members of theatrical groups to travel and perform. In this way, African governments and universities have attempted not only the preservation of African cultures but also their incorporation into a design for a living and dynamic reality.

The Revitalization of the Educational Systems

Because of their position at the apex of the educational system, the African universities have an obligation to contribute to the effectiveness of the whole system of education, from kindergarten to the tertiary levels. Most of them attempt to do so through teacher training, retraining, curriculum research, program evaluation, and the like.

The African universities employ a variety of approaches to teacher training. Some relegate this function to nonuniversity units, such as institutes of education, while in other cases it is assumed by a department or a college of education within the major university. Whatever form the training functions take, the universities must be charged with the ultimate responsibility of providing the school systems with adequately prepared instructors at all levels.

Further research on African languages, sociology, anthropology, and history would help to make teacher training more interesting and more relevant. Studies of the African child—stages of development, ways of learning, behavior, etc.—are awaiting discovery and understanding. Delineation or articulation of educational objectives and facilitation of the understanding necessary between the schools and the communities also fall within the purview of institutions of higher education.

Some African universities have demonstrated not only their capabilities, which are presumed, but also their willingness to lead in the continuous renewal of the educational apparatus. Others are only just beginning to recognize their responsibilities in this area.

The Universities and Politics

The relationship between national politics and the universities is one of the most sensitive questions facing African societies. Although the progressive political leaders of the early 1960s, such as Nkrumah of Ghana and Nyerere of Tanzania, urged the institutions to remain true to the objective pursuit of truth regardless of political consequences and added that they would provide all necessary material and moral support, they also emphasized that universities must not be used as centers of opposition against the legally-elected government of the people. Much has changed since those words were enunciated. In the aftermath of economic and social crises, the character of many of the governments of Africa has changed. A number of countries are now governed by military dictatorships which, in many cases, came to power by force. Most of the countries under civilian rule have become one-party states to avoid the politically uncomfortable position of being challenged or constantly criticized by an opposition party. Under such circumstances, an increasing number of intelligent university students and faculty members find it difficult to remain aloof from politics.

At the same time, African universities have undergone significant changes. Their numbers have grown, enrollments have increased eight- to tenfold, faculty and staff have been effectively Africanized and, more and more, current history and politics are being incorporated into the curricula and closely studied and scrutinized in and out of classes.

In the past, colonialism served as a lightning rod for critical analysis of the ills of society. Now, a generation after independence, with many social problems worsening, the usual retreat to blaming colonialism is no longer sufficient. Students and intellectuals are now holding those in authority accountable for success or failure. Members of the university communities now discern discrepancies between methods of government, official corruption, incompetence, and authoritarian rule on the one hand, and the need for dramatic improvement in the lives of the rural and urban masses of the people on the other. Especially students who have studied how the governing bodies and the governed should relate to one another, but who are not yet tempered by experience in the "real" world, are aggrieved at the discrepancies they observe in society. Hence, they assemble, demonstrate, and confront the authorities in power. In addition to Ethiopia, students have been in the vanguard of political agitation in recent years in such countries as the Sudan, Somalia, Ghana, and Kenya, to mention a few. (In one West African state, the chancellor, who is also the head of state and government, goes to the campus to award the annual diplomas only after most students are gone on vacation.) When demonstrations occur, the police or the army usually take steps to forcefully restore order. When this happens, the sanctity of the university is defiled and the search for truth, wisdom, and objectivity is mortally wounded.

Summary

Since they began to proliferate in the early 1960s, African institutions of higher learning have, by and large, responded well to development needs in Africa. The evolution of higher education and its role in social and cultural development has been remarkable. Still incomplete, however, is the task of guiding these universities to become fully African in terms of their loyalty, orientation, and methods of carrying out their appointed missions. To be successful, this process requires increased financial as well as moral support from the peoples and their governments. Because African universities are struggling to resolve so many difficult problems, they do not need added political antagonism. But, if present trends are any indication, they may be drawn even closer to the position of being used as centers of political activism, which in turn may render them vulnerable to the wrath of political authorities. The challenges and opportunities for future expansion of the role of institutions of higher learning in the transformation of African societies will be determined by how willing all segments of the respective societies are to work for accommodation, understanding, and flexibility.

The number of African institutions of higher learning has expanded rapidly since the early 1960s. Qualitatively, they have shown significant progress, especially in the preparation of high-level personnel for the various segments of the economy, including government and quasi-government organizations. They have been instrumental in providing the requisite environment for critical thinking, dialogue, and discussion of the enormous problems facing African countries.

Due primarily to fiscal, political, and attitudinal constraints, however, they have yet to develop the crucial understanding and loyalty of the masses of people as well as the political and business leadership, without whose moral and financial support they will not survive as entities capable of discharging their critical roles in social development. They have yet to convince those in political authority that the quest for objectivity in research and the dissemination of knowledge require freedom from fear of persecution by those in power, whose current views, political or otherwise, may not be supported by academic inquiry. The cultivation and nurture of a tradition of tolerance, understanding, and support for universities requires sustained effort on the part of those who are in a position to render it—the members of the academic community as well as the political authorities. Where efforts have begun in this direction, the future is full of promise.

In the case of Ethiopia, although the country was not colonized by foreign European powers (except for the brief Fascist interlude during 1936–1941), the emergence of modern, as contrasted to traditional, indigenous, and religious education is also a phenemonon of the post-World War II era. Hence, Ethiopian higher education shares with other sister African institutions of higher learning in terms of being relatively young, and in drawing its models from the European and North American prototypes. The major differences are in the areas of traditions (Ethiopia had a tradition of higher education as shown in the next chapter) and tutelage. While many of the other African institutions drew their personnel and other resources from their erstwhile respective colonists during the period of growth, Ethiopia had to shop around for the same commodities while at the same time trying to avoid political entanglement with foreign powers. Achieving such seemingly conflicting political and development goals, as we will see presently, was not an easy matter and heavy prices were paid.

Notes

1. For a brief discussion on African development during the past two decades and prospects for the next two, see *Accelerated Development in Sub-Saharan Africa: An Agenda for Action* (Washington, D.C.: The World Bank, 1981), 1–132; the specific sections referred to in this part of the analysis are found on page 12.
2. These projections were made in 1980 by the United Nations. For demographic characteristics, see UNESCO, *Education and Endogenous Development in Africa: Trends, Problems and Prospects* (Paris: UNESCO, 1982), 12.
3. For a very informative outline of higher education development, refer to Davidson Nicol, "Politics, Nationalism, and Universities in Africa," in *Education and Nation-Building in Africa*, ed. L. Gray Cowan, et al. (New York, Washington, London: Frederick A. Praeger, 1965), 281–90.
4. UNESCO, *The Development of Higher Education in Africa* (Paris: UNESCO, 1963), 12.
5. Ibid., 13. See also UNESCO, "Conference of African States on the Development of Education in Africa," May 15–25, 1961, *Final Report* (Paris: UNESCO, n.d.), 3–27.
6. UNESCO, *The Development of Higher Education*, 12.
7. Ibid., 18.
8. These and other objectives were elucidated further by the various speakers at the conference. Ibid., 18–19, 91–213.
9. According to UNESCO classifications, Middle Africa constitutes the independent sub-Saharan African countries minus the Union of South Africa. Information for this section is based on UNESCO's report of "The Conference of Ministers of Education and those Responsible for Economic Planning in African Member States," (Harare, 28 June-3 July 1982, ED82/MINEDAF/REF.5), 73–90.
10. Julius K. Nyerere, "An Address by the President of Tanganyika at the Inauguration of the University of East Africa," in *Education and Nation-Building in Africa*, ed. L. Gray Cowan, et al. (New York: Frederick A. Praeger, 1965), 309–13.
11. Kwame Nkrumah, "The Role of the University," in *Education and Nation-Building in Africa*, 314–16.
12. Felix Houphouet-Bigny, "Our Students Must Participate in the Development of the Country," in *Education and Nation-Building in Africa*, 317–21.
13. This section benefits from a UNESCO document prepared for "The Conference of Ministers of Education and Those Responsible for Economic Planning in African Member States" (Harare, 1982), 73–80.
14. This number does not include the other numerous post-secondary, sub-university institutions that developed in response to research or training needs in the various countries of Africa.
15. Statistical information is based on UNESCO, *Development of Education in Africa: A Statistical Review* (Paris: UNESCO, 1982, ED-82/MINEDAF/REF. 2), 84–112.

16. The recognition of requirements for African institutions of higher learning in the process of development is documented in the resolution of the Assembly of African Heads of State and Government Second Extra-Ordinary Session, *Lagos Plan of Action* (Addis Ababa: Organization of African Unity, 1980, ECM/ECO/9, XIV, Rev. 2), 38–90.
17. UNESCO, *Specific Aspects of Educational Development in Africa* (Paris: UNESCO, 1982, ED-82/MINEDAF/REF. 5), 73–90.
18. Ibid., 83–84.
19. Ibid., 85.

2

ETHIOPIA'S INTELLECTUAL LEGACY

For centuries the church school system was the principal core of cultural, spiritual, literary, artistic, and scientific life in Ethiopia. This educational system, organized and supported by the Ethiopian Orthodox church, originated in the Aksumite Kingdom after the introduction of Christianity from the Middle East in the fourth century. From its inception until the twentieth century the system grew and adapted itself to the local realities. As the Aksumite Kingdom of Ethiopia expanded to the south and southwest, Christianity spread. The new churches and monasteries that were founded became important centers of learning as well as spiritual life.

In theory, church education was open to all children, male and female, of members of the Ethiopian brand of the Christian faith. However, passage through the school system was arduous and exacting. The first level, *Nebab Bet* (School of Reading), generally took two years to complete. Few students pursued studies at the higher levels—*Qeddase Bet* (School of the Holy Mass); *Zema Bet* (school of Hymns); *Qine Bet* (School of Poetry and the beginning of the understanding of the deep subtle meanings of the Ge'ez language); and the highest level, *Metsahift Bet* (House of Books or Scriptures), which had several subdivisions. It took about twenty-eight years to reach the apex of the educational pyramid. A very few of those who did reach *Metsahift Bet* excelled in more than one branch of study. For those who did, additional years of study were required. The latter were known as *Arat-Ayna* (Four-Eyed Ones). They were sought after by scholars as masters of the art of traditional instruction and scholarship.[1]

Every important church and monastery in Ethiopia maintained at least one such school. Scholarship and research were carried out at these advanced centers. In these centers of advanced learning, the custodians of traditional cultural values and national heritage received their instruction, and many precious manuscripts, art works, and medicinal studies were secured and maintained for the edification of posterity. Most of the scholars, artists, religious leaders, teachers, and the educated class of state functionaries were, until World War II, products of these schools.

31

Church Hierarchy and Scholastic Organization

The hierarchy of ecclesiastical administration in Ethiopia was clear. However, within this hierarchy local or regional churches or monasteries were granted limited power in matters of discipline, traditional support of the clergy, and scholastic organization in their respective congregations or communities.

The reigning monarch assumed quintuple responsibility as head of the church, state, the armed forces, the judiciary, and the government. In the spiritual and educational arenas, the *Abun* was supreme after the emperor. For centuries this ecclesiastic position was filled by a monk appointed by the See of St. Mark of Alexandria, Egypt. Usually, the *Abun* was sent to Ethiopia for life. The quality of the individual *Abun* varied from time to time. Some had been of high religious and intellectual qualities (though the prospect of lifelong exile in a foreign country sometimes failed to attract the best candidate). However, after Ethiopia regained its independence, a long and involved negotiation ensued between the Ethiopian government, Ethiopian church, and the See of St. Mark of Egypt. Finally, autocephalous was achieved which enabled the Ethiopians to appoint their own church leader independent of Egypt. As head of the church, the *Abun* annointed his assistant bishops and priests, and officiated at important ecclesiastical and national ceremonies. He was usually in close communication with the reigning monarch. The *Abun*'s responsibilities, assisted by the *Etchegue*, were primarily to promote the spiritual well-being of the people and set the tone of theological teachings. He did not involve himself in the specific activities of individuals or institutions. That work was delegated to the individual churches or, most often, to the monasteries.

Third in the hierarchy was the *Etchegue*. His importance was paramount in terms of understanding the language, culture, and political order of the society as well as the political idosyncracies of the monarch. He was, as a rule, a highly learned, pious, and trusted Ethiopian. At the highest level, he was the link between the populace and the rulers, and the church leaders and the laity. His other duties included supreme administrative control over officials such as the *Liqe Kahinat* (Chief of the Clergy), and the *Nebure'edoch* (ecclesiastical heads of the famous church of Aksum and the one at Addis Alem in Shoa established by Emperor Menelik II to rival the one in Aksum). To the extent that he commanded the trust of the reigning monarch and the respect of the monks, he was able to carry out his functions effectively. Since the fifteenth century, the *Etchegue* has also been the abbot or chief prior of the most famous monastery of Debre Libanos which is located some 120 kilometers north of the capital city of Addis Ababa.[2]

Below the *Etchegue, Liqe Kahinat*, and *Nebure'edoch* in the hierarchy were the *Menkusewoch* (monks), various abbots of the monasteries and the *Aleqa* (chief) of the churches who were responsible for the day-to-day affairs of their respective charges. In almost all cases, the material needs of these monasteries and churches were supplied locally from either land taxes or the proceeds of communal farming. As far as relations with the state and established church were concerned, there were definite rules and criteria for the training and promotion of the intellectual and religious elites. For monks, the requirements included ritual purity, renunciation of the world, ascetic piety, and traditional learning. For the priests, while ritual purity, piety and learning were required, the depth of these traits was limited; the same applied to the *debtrawoch*. At the discretion of the monarch, members of all three of these groups were eligible for promotion to higher secular-religious offices. Thus, the *Etchegue* was always a monk; the *Aqabe Sat'at* was a *debtera*, and the title *Aleqa* (chief, learned one) could be bestowed upon a number of any of the three groups. A lay person could become a monk at any time of his life if he decided to renounce the world and meet certain other requirements in addition to learning.[3]

State-Monarch-Church Relations

On most occasions, in at least the past sixteen hundred years, the Ethiopian (Abyssinian) state, monarch, and church have collaborated to achieve harmonious prosperity in politics, religious studies, and the arts. As long as this trio of institutions worked together harmoniously—recognizing their need for one another and compromising when necessary—they exemplified the best that can be said in favor of such a union. When they did not, the result was most often disastrous for all parties concerned.

The ascendance or decline of philosophy, literature, religious studies, and the arts varied directly with the ascendance of power or decline of the geographical regions under a particular dynasty or group of rulers. Thus, for the first seven centuries of the Christian era, or perhaps even earlier, the Aksumite Kingdom in northern Ethiopia prospered. During that period Ge'ez (Ethiopic) was developed and made the language of church and state, the famous castles and stelae were built, and some of the best literature was produced. Under the attack of the Jewess Gudit (Judith) in the tenth century, Aksum eclipsed. Lalibela became the center under the Zagwe ("of the Agew" clan or tribe) dynasty. The Christian tradition continued. During this period the eleven rock-hewn monolithic churches at Lalibela—one of the wonders of the world—were built and other church-related edifices were constructed in the area which to this day bear testimony to the great achievements of that era.

33

As might be expected, some of the best kings and emperors were not only warriors and statesmen but also religious leaders, priests, philosophers, and patrons of the arts and literature. The medieval king Zare Yakob, for example, authored books, endowed churches and monasteries, and otherwise encouraged the development of the arts and literature. Yohannes I (the Pious, reigned 1667–1682) was a man devoted to the advancement of religious studies and literature. He is credited with having built a library to house religious manuscripts, and two beautiful churches in the city of Gondar. As Levine notes of this ruler:

> [he was] possessed of an unusual decorative bent, he had the walls of the library covered with yellowish plaster and raised designs in stucco, and he himself painted miniatures on some of the manuscripts. His queen, Sebla Wangel, sponsored the translation of works from Arabic. Among these were the *Laws of the Kings*, a collection of civil and canon laws which became the official basis for judication, and a penitential manual, *Spiritual Medicine*, the last major production in Ge'ez literature.[4]

The emperor-priest-philosopher Yohannes I also pursued the traditional avocation of Christian emperors and kings of purifying the church against heresies and sponsored the convocation of a synod in Gondar to discuss the nature of the Holy Spirit in Christ.

Iyasu I (the Great, reigned 1682-1706) followed the example of his great mentor to consolidate the city of Gondar as the "most important center of religious culture in Ethiopia. To this end he brought outstanding priests and learned men together from all over the country to his capital. . . . The number of teachers in Gondar in his time exceeded five hundred; there were one hundred and fifty at his church Debre Berhan Selassie alone. It was under Iyasu I that the classic subject matter of the higher religious studies in Abyssinia—*Zema* (religious chant'), *qine* and *tergum* (interpretation')—is said to have received its definitive organization."[5]

As an illustration of the full involvement of Iyasu I in things artistic, the following is cited:

> The king used to stand at the window of his palace . . . and listen from his tower on high to the singing of the priests and learned men, to their gentle hymns which moistened the bones by their exceeding tenderness; when their offerings pleased him greatly he was pierced with affection for them and drawn by the harmony of their heavenly peace. For this reason . . . he would prepare them dinners filled with delights, and bid them eat with him in his royal chambers ornamented all about with

the beauty of pure gold and wrought silver. He would take off his gold necklace and present it to them. He adorned them with garments of purple and of staffs interwoven with gold from the treasury of his Kingdom. . . . None of the kings before him had done such as he, and none of the clergy of yore had been treated as were his priests and learned men. After the dinners, the king and his priests together sang hymns of joy and jubilation all night long in the palace . . . in their time of pleasure, in the sweetness of divine ministry.[6]

The tastes of some of these kings were highly sophisticated and refined. It is reported that Iyasu II (reigned 1730–1755) cultivated extensive gardens and orchards. He built churches and palaces and took personal interest in the decorations.

A number of Christians who had fled from Smyrna took refuge in Gondar, and the king employed them to decorate his palace with filigree work. The upper parts of the walls of the throne room were covered with three rows of Venetian mirrors set in gilded copper frames, and their lower parts . . . with slabs of ivory. The roof was made of painted cane mosaic, the work of the Falasha, but the room was never finished, owing to the king's death. Iyasu II spent his days with the workmen, and himself learned to do some of the work under the direction of the Greek workmen.[7]

This artistic splendor has survived. According to Levine: "Gondar is the only city in Ethiopia with charm and character expressive of Amhara culture. Even today, despite modern accretions, the remnants of its castles, walls, bridges, and sanctuaries transmit a stately calm, redolent of past nobility and African grandeur."[8] Iyasu II also gathered and sponsored Ethiopian and foreign scholars in the pursuit of his goals.

In the eighteenth century, the momentum and ferment of religious as well as literary studies continued in Gondar. More churches were built. One of these, Bete Mariam, later became one of the most famous centers for the teaching of *aqwaqwam* (religious dance) and in its heyday boasted of 276 maters. Another church, Abi Egzi, became known for instruction in *tergum* (interpretation) and is still the leading center for such studies.[9]

Even as the reputation and power of the monarchy grew dim, "that of the town, as a center for religious studies continued unabated. Gondar was the most famous place in the country for instruction in art, music, dance, poetry, and the great books of the Ethiopian Church, and young men continued to travel great distances to drink at such sources."[10] Even the descendants of royalty made their contributions. In the middle of the last century they were found making paintings and illuminating manuscripts.

Despite the growing political turmoil in the second half of the nineteenth century, the work of learning and creating went on in Gondar for some time. Gondar continued to excel as a center for teaching in *aqwaqwam* and *tergum,* while Gojam, to the south, began to excel as a center for the study of *qine.* Other sites in Gojam and Gondar, as well as in Lasta and Tigre, were the hub for the study of *zema.*

As political conditions continued to deteriorate, the teaching-learning activities in Gondar suffered. By 1866 the new emperor, Tewodros II, who, because of his humble origin had difficulty legitimizing his accession to the throne, came into direct conflict with the clerics in Gondar. In retribution, the emperor precipitated the destruction of villages in Gondar. Many artistic and literary treasures were damaged or destroyed. Some manuscripts were carried to the emperor's new capital at Debre Tabor. He later transferred the manuscripts to the new church and library he built for them at Magdella. The result was severe civil disorder. Many of the people from Gondar fled the city for the countryside and other provinces. As they left, Muslim Dervishes from Sudan overran Gondar and completed the process of destruction begun earlier. Once again, the people of the region turned to one of the kings for deliverance by invoking the sentiments of religion and nationalism, concepts which have always played significant roles in the annals of Ethiopian history. Levine records the message delivered to Emperor Yohannes IV of Tigre, who had succeeded Tewodros, by the Gondares:

> Oh master! The heathen have come into thine inheritance; thy holy temple have they defiled; they have laid Gondar in heaps. The dead bodies of thy servants have they given to be meat unto the fowls of the heaven, the flesh of thy saints unto the beasts of the earth. Their blood have they shed like water round about Dambiya; and there was none to bury them.[11]

As would be expected, the emperor responded affirmatively and valiantly. During the ensuing conflict Yohannes IV lost his life. The dervishes were expelled, but Gondar never fully recovered its preeminence as the citadel of study and scholarly productivity. The torch was passed further south to the hitherto unimportant province of Shoa. Menz in Shoa province assumed the mantle of Gondar. However, in terms of intellectual excellence, it never approached the achievements of Gondar. In this modified and reduced form, the traditional collaboration of the church, monarch, and state in the realms of instruction and scholarship continued until 1974.

Philosophy of Education

The church system of education rested on a well-developed philosophy regarding the nature of man, the essence of nature, the nature of God, and man's relationships to God, nature, and himself. This theocentric approach provided for an elaborate and profound understanding of the intentions or the meaning of God in relation to man's good, man's end.

In Ethiopic literature and teaching man is thought to be made of two entities or domains—a body and a soul—each with its distinct set of characteristics. The bodily domain consists of four elements: water, fire, earth, and air. This makes man part and parcel of the material world, which is *gizuf* or visible and concrete, *wussin* or finite, limited in time and space. The body has desires of its own, *fekade sigga* (literally, will of the flesh). These desires are earthly, temporal, and limited. The needs or desires of the body conflict with the desires of the soul. The soul is spiritual and therefore higher and eternal.

The soul is inspired into the body of man by God, the Creator, at the time of creation. Although it is an entity within the body, it is not *of* the body. The soul is *requiq*, invisible or abstract, lacking the quality of the material body; it is abiding and eternal; it is part of God. The soul has three additional characteristics: *hiawit* (immortality), *libawit* (understanding or cognition), and *nebabit* (speech or prophecy). The desires of the soul are spiritual and directed toward the eternal, heavenly life. Given that the spiritual soul is superior to the earthly body and the main purpose of life is to fulfill the desires of the soul, and since the claims of the body are in conflict with the mandates and aspirations of the soul, human existence is explained as a perpetual struggle between these two conflicting sets of desires. It is therefore incumbent upon the true Christian to subdue his bodily desires to those of the soul so that ultimately the soul will rule supreme over the body. As a means of training the body for this end and freeing the soul for higher spiritual activities, fasting, hardship, and torture are prescribed.

Since learning is a higher level of spiritual activity involving all human faculties, including the mind or consciousness, as well as cognition, feeling, memory, and the like, and since such activities are abstract and invisible, they are functions of the soul; they are of God. In contrast, thoughts or acts of personal comfort, appearance, and other forms of earthly pleasures are to be shunned since they devote time and energy to things that are temporal and material

37

in nature. In the educative process, therefore, it is the duty of the teacher to administer (at the lower levels, at least) discipline—even for minor infractions of rules and regulations—on the ground that such measures would liberate the soul from the importunities of the body and thus make learning possible. It was the duty of the learner to submit to these repressive measures. As we shall see in chapters 7 and 8, this traditional student-teacher relationship was severely criticized and flaunted by students in the 1960s and 1970s.

There are additional imputed factors of the soul and its relationship to learning. As a replica of the image of the omnipotent God, man is at birth endowed with certain inborn properties such as *tsegga habitat* (intellectual grace and riches), and unmerited rewards or gifts. One of these gifts is *yetefetro ewket* (inate or natural knowledge). *Aemro* (the mind) is considered a container of this kind of knowledge. The mind also has the ability to derive from without, thus facilitating the act of learning, which in turn awakens the hidden treasures within the soul of man. In this respect, the learning process is compared to a key that opens a closed room containing a treasure of knowledge. Knowledge itself is compared to a live coal buried under the ashes of a stove. The power of God is needed to release knowledge from within. In this respect, knowledge, skill, eloquence, and the gift of prophecy are acquired by the soul through the Spirit of the Almighty. It follows, therefore, that in the act of learning the teacher plays a vital role as intermediary between the Spirit of God and the learner. The teacher's position as a guide, interpreter of wisdom, and an authority are all unquestioned. He is feared, revered, and even loved. He is addressed as *Yeneta* (Master) by his students.[12]

The main thrust is that God is the center of all activities—both temporal and spiritual. Since God has instilled certain intellectual or physical qualities in the individual, it is the responsibility of the individual, through the medium of the teaching process, to cultivate and expand these treasures, and put the outcomes to work in the realm of the metaphysical. The individual is a conduit for the fulfillment of the grand design of the supernatural.

The Traditional Higher Education System

The creators of the Ethiopian intellectual legacy were most often products of the traditional higher education system, the *Zema Bet* and beyond. The *Nebab Bet*, which was theoretically open to all children, and the next level, the *Qeddase Bet*, which was designed to train the altar priests, did not provide scholarly training. The priests were the only ones qualified to administer the mass and sacraments, to serve as *Yenefis Abat* (father-confessors for the people), to baptize children, and to perform burial rites or ceremonies. They were trained to guide the faithful in their day-to-day lives. The priests were seldom expected or called upon to function as teachers or scholars at the higher levels. Teaching tasks were delegated to the graduates of the higher levels, the *Zema, Qine,* and *Metsahift Bet.*

The first stage of higher education, the *Zema Bet,* (School of Hymns) was divided into at least three disciplines, each led and taught by a specialist. The first branch within this school, the *Degwa Bet,* contained most of the songs and hymns of the church for a year, except the mass and the horologium, which were contained in the *Qeddase* and *Sat'at* books. *Degwa* study was the longest and most challenging branch of the *Zema Bet.* Most *Degwa* students took time to carefully seek out a distinguished *Degwa* school or professor from among the many centers of excellence scattered in the northern, northwestern, and central parts of the country.

In the *Qine Bet,* the second level of higher education, students were trained in the techniques, methods, and skills of poetry making and were introduced to the deep meanings of Ge'ez literature. *Qine Bet* study was demanding, arduous, and long. To undertake this course of study, a student had to be well motivated, in good health, and of acute mind. There were many forms or models of *qine* composition. Students were led step by step, following the sequence of well laid out study schemes, until mastery was achieved. At this stage, students experienced for the first time relatively personal freedom and were considered mature by their mentors.

The final stage, *Metsahift Bet,* was the apex of learning. It consisted of several broad branches of study: the *Bluey Kiddan* (the forty-six books of the Old Testament), the *Haddis Kiddan* (the thirty-five books of the New Testament), the *Liqawint* (the writings of the Church Fathers), the *Fetha Negest* (canon laws) as well as the *Bahere Hasab* (the science of computing time and calendar), and finally, the *Menekosat* (the school of commentaries on monastic life and literature). In these specialized branches of the *Metsahift Bet,* the student learned the traditions of the church, its history and law, and the subtle shades of biblical interpretations rendered by the various schools of thought. The method of study was didactic, and the contributions of the student at this stage were well recognized. He was treated as a mature co-scholar by his mentors. As I pointed out elsewhere: "the *Metsahift Bet* was in essence a university where the whole approach to learning, including the qualifications of the professors, methods of teaching and learning, and the popular attitude toward the leadership of the community of scholars, reflected maturity of mind and the ideal(s) of democracy in action."[13]

Scientific and astronomical branches of learning did not receive their due share of scholarly attention. As Wallis Budge, a noted historian, observed, "Works of science do not exist in Abyssinian literature. As the heavens and the earth are ruled by God all inquiries into the working of the heavenly bodies and the laws of nature were and are regarded as sinful."[14]

Monks and Monasticism

In Ethiopian history, monasticism played a vital role in the spiritual and intellectual life of the national Christian community. This institution entered Ethiopia in about A.D. 480. According to legend, during the reign of Al-Amida nine monks arrived in Ethiopia from Syria as missionaries. Their purpose was to reform Ethiopian Christianity which had reportedly become isolationist, intolerant, and somewhat fanatical. In addition to founding the liturgy and liturgical music, these nine monks translated the Greek-Syrian gospels into Ge'ez. Their death assumed a significant role in Ethiopian hagiography.[15]

The monasteries were, in some respects, part of the church; yet in that they followed strict ethical and religious principles and renounced the world they were also separate from it. In the religious hierarchy they ranked fifth: the *Abun, Etchegue, Liqe Kahinat, Nubure'ed, Menkusewoch* (monks), *Kesoch* (priests), and *Debtrawoch* (deacons). For their financial support, the monasteries traditionally relied on the income from vast tracts of land. Since 1975, when all lands reverted to government control, monasteries lost this source of support. To date, no alternative system of financial support has been identified.

There were two major orders of monasticism in Ethiopia. The first was named after Tekle Haimanot who led a great missionary effort in the regions of Western Shoa and Damot and is perhaps the most famous Ethiopian saint. He is considered the "Benedictine of Abyssinia." Fifty-seven years after his death the famous monastery of Debre Libanos was named in his honor. This order was headed by the *Etchegue.* The second major monastic order was known as Ewostatewos. It had no vicar-general.[16]

In some of the monasteries, such as Debre Bizan in the north, the monks lived frugal, isolated lives "forgetful of the world and the world forgotten."[17] Access to the monasteries was through the aid of ropes. No woman, or even female animals, were permitted inside. For both their piety and religious studies, monks enjoyed the highest respect and esteem in the country. According to Levine, "Monks have exerted a great influence on the thinking and behavior of the people. Itinerant hermits have harangued the people to live more pious lives. The counsel of monks has been to help the rulers in time of trouble. The prophecies of monks have been influential in setting the pattern of hopes and fears about the future."[18]

In the annals of Ethiopian history, of the numerous monasteries found scattered in the northern and northwestern parts of the country (traditional Abyssinia), perhaps the two most famous are the centers of excellence at Debre Damo in Tigrai province and Debre Libanos in Shoa. Other monasteries of various sizes are located in the districts of Waldeba and Gaint in Gondar, in the Lake Tana Islands in Gojam, and in Tembien in Tigrai. Most of these monasteries are semi-independent in relationship to one another and from Debre Libanos in the sense that they are not governed under any major administrative umbrella. They set their own rules and establish scholarly and communal requirements and procedures. Each scholar-monk is relatively free to pursue ascetic ideas and intellectual challenges in his own way without subjecting himself to institutional discipline. Indeed, some monks do not belong to any community at all.[19]

Some of the most highly educated and productive scholars, including the *Arat-Ayna* (Four-Eyed Ones), who have reached the summit of intellectual achievement, have lived and worked in monasteries. Buxton notes, "The great monasteries, like those of medieval Europe, have been centres of art and learning throughout Ethiopian Christian history."[20] The monastic institutions and the monks have been instrumental in preserving the intellectual and religious freedom of individuals, in recording and expressing their views, dogma, and observations and to composing and preserving works of art and literature. In addition, they have provided safe havens for the many treasures of art and literature in times of peace and prosperity as well as during political and social upheavals.

Throughout Ethiopian Christian history, the sacredness of the monasteries has been immutable. Even criminals, if they took refuge in one of the *geddams* (monasteries) and renounced their deeds, were provided not only protection from arrest, but also fulfillment of their temporal and spiritual needs as long as they stayed within the confines of the monastery. No agent of the state dared touch them, not even the monarch.[21]

In addition to the monks who associated themselves with the established monasteries, there were itinerant monks known as *bahitawi* (hermits). They wandered from place to place and sought shelter in isolated hilltops, in caves, and in the peripheries of villages. Sometimes they built their small temporary huts in lonely forests or wedged them between the mountains in the northern areas of the country. A few others lived in haunted' huts in the churchyards near the tombs. Usually, the *bahitawi* enjoyed the utmost freedom to express their ideas regarding justice, sin, repentence, and any other subject they felt inspired to address. Since they were thought to convey revelations from God, they were respected or feared by citizens and officials alike. Some functions of these hermits are well described by Buxton.

> The hermit is the messenger of God, and at times will appear by night to cry aloud, "A mighty tribulation is coming upon you! Repent!" and will disappear like a puff of smoke. He may be known by his hair, which is uncut and shaggy with butter rubbed upon it. . . . If God shows him aught in a dream, he will cry it aloud to an officer, saying, "Such-and-such a dream have I seen! Take heed and give alms to the poor and set prisoners free!"[22]

The *bahitawi*'s uninterrupted tradition of expressing their convictions publicly and freely without fear of intimidation by politicians, and their reputation as men of integrity, self-denial, and messengers of truth and justice have been major contributors to the Ethiopian intellectual legacy. If there has been a single group of people in Ethiopian history who have escaped official corruption and remained unintimidated by rulers and their surrogates, it is this group of ascetics. Alas, in the past three decades their numbers are few and their appearances in cities and villages have become less frequent. It may be that the long arms of self-serving rulers are reaching out to silence and perhaps eliminate them.

The Debtrawoch

Another class of Ethiopian ecclesiastics and scholars was the *debtrawoch* or scribes. As a group they were very well educated in the arts, music, calligraphy, and interpretations of the mysteries of holy books and legends. Although they were not ordained as priests to serve in the churches, they were an intimate part of church activities. They were among the best singers, dancers, and guardians of tradition. They may or may not have been authors of original works, but they copied the most valuable manuscripts by hand with great care and meticulous dedication. Faithful copying was crucial, for a little carelessness might seriously damage the intellectual heritage of the society—an act that was tantamount to treason to faith and scholarship.

To become a *debtera*, one had to study beyond the level required for priests. The *debtera* had to master *aqwaqwam* (religious dance), Ge'ez grammar, *qine* (poetry), *qine mahilet* (choir), *zema* (chanting), and the study of numerous religious works. This course of study might consume twenty to thirty years. It was also required that the *debtera* master the knowledge and skills of writing, parchment making, and preparation of magic formulae.

The *debtrawoch* were learned men who were thoroughly familiar with Ge'ez and well acquainted with the scriptures in much the same way as scholars in Medieval Europe were familiar with Latin. Without them, no liturgical dance or rhythmic accompaniment of drums and sistra during the numerous church festivals was complete. The *debtrawoch* also composed and sold amulets or spells which were often ordered by an individual whose name was cited in the text. Buxton describes the *debtera*'s expertise in these matters:

> The amulets take the form of narrow parchment strips [*Kitab*] about two meters long which may be tightly rolled (and worn in decorative metal cylinders made for the purpose) or folded in zig-zag fashion with wooden covers like a small book. These amulets, which protect their owner against the evil eye, blindness, and various diseases, contain magico-religious prayers invoking the deity; ostensibly Christian, they clearly have a pagan background.
>
> Other *debtrawoch* are expert herbalists, willing to prescribe natural drugs against various ills. Still others make a reputation as soothsayers and sorcerers trafficking, it is sometimes said, with the powers of darkness.
>
> The *debtrawoch*, then, with their erudition, their wide knowledge and special skills, but lacking as they do the mystic and unworldly office of the ordained priest, form a kind of link between laity and clergy in this religiously ordered society. Whatever magic arts they may be thought to practice, they are highly respected citizens, whose multifarious services are indispensable to the church and people alike.[23]

Perhaps Bent summarizes the essence of their importance best when he notes that the *debtrawoch* "are lay assistants in all the [church] services, acting as singers and performers in all the church ceremonies; they are the scribes, advocates, and doctors of Abyssinia, and are certainly the most instructed and intelligent people we came across."[24]

Commenting on the clever convention that allowed the *debtrawoch* to function as they did in society, Levine notes: "With its characteristic forebearance toward human frailty, Amhara culture has established in the *debtera* a religious vocation in which special knowledge is required but holiness is not expected."[25] The *debtrawoch* have been and continue to be a vital force in the medicinal, spiritual, and literary aspects of Ethiopian culture.

Manuscripts

All known Ethiopian manuscripts of earlier periods were written on either skin or papyrus (a paperlike material which came into use toward the end of the eighteenth century). Whether the translations of the scriptures during the fifth and sixth centuries were written on papyrus or skin cannot be ascertained. The vellum used in Ethiopic manuscripts was made either of goatskin or sheepskin. The goatskin was supposed to be the preferred medium in terms of quality and durability. However, the cost must have been prohibitive because one medium-sized manuscript required scores of goats. Once the book was made, extreme care was taken to assure the safety of this precious possession.

> Among the Abyssinian people generally a book was regarded as a priceless treasure, and service-books and Psalters especially were provided with stout cases. . . . Such a book was regarded as an *amulet*, and the pious caravan man provided the case for his book with straps so that he could hang his Psalter round his neck, or carry it on his back under his cloak. It was to be read morning and evening and thus it was carried even during long caravans or journeys.[26]

Perhaps as a result of contact with Italian and Portuguese missionaries in the seventeenth century, Ethiopian authors and artists discovered or rediscovered the art of decorating manuscripts with colored pictures. This was an excellent period for Ethiopian literature. Some of the extant manuscripts of that period display sophisticated approaches to the production of beautifully executed manuscripts with colored illustrations and decoration. The Ethiopian artists drew inspiration from both the local scene and imported models. The subjects of these manuscripts were, as usual, biblical figures, saints, scenes from the Nativity, Baptism, Ascension and Configuration, the entry of Christ into Jerusalem, and the like. Local plants and animals were also depicted. As Wallis Budge comments:

> When the Abyssinian artist illustrated an event which had taken place in his own country, e.g., a local miracle, he copied accurately the people and objects that he saw round about him, and pictures of this kind are valuable records. But in all the other pictures we see the influence of Byzantine painters and architects, and the artists must have drawn their inspiration from manuscripts which came from Jerusalem, the home and source of their religion, and from Egypt.[27]

In one manuscript, according to Budge, the palaces represented are those of southern Europe; the churches of Constantinople, Italy, and Spain; the dress of the Virgin Mary is similar to that of a European nun; Christ is seen wearing a crown like that of the emperor of Constantinople; angels and archangels seem to be copies of the mosaics and frescoes found in Italy and Spain. But often, Christ and the Virgin are represented as Ethiopians. The colored figures of animals and plants that decorate the margins of this Bible might have been copied form manuscripts written between the ninth and twelfth centuries. Here, as in other realms of artistic or scholarly endeavors, the Ethiopians seem to have been open to external influences as well as internal inspiration based on the local environment; but in all cases the end product had to conform to or support the perceived Ethiopian realities.

Ge'ez Literature

The origins of Ethiopia's classical literature are diverse. The early Egyptian raids into the country's West Lake area under the twelfth and eighteenth dynasties probably had no influence on the civilization of Ethiopia. Hence, Ethiopic writing owes nothing to Egypt. However, it is possible that some of the hieroglyphic inscriptions on the temples and in the tombs of Napata and Mero were done by Egyptian scribes and engraved by Egyptian workmen imported for this purpose.

Recent research clearly indicates that the early Ethiopians borrowed the fundamental parts of their letters from the Semites of Arabia, who brought to Ethiopia a form of writing that was superior to that found locally. This might have taken place about 1000 B.C., but some maintain it happened several centuries later. The Ethiopian syllabary of today still bears some resemblance to the alphabets in use among the Mineans and Sabaeans between 200 B.C. and A.D. 400. However, while the Minean-Sabaean inscriptions are read from right to left like Hebrew, Syriac, and Arabic, the Ethiopians wrote from left to right, like the Babylonians and Assyrians. It is probable that this practice was influenced by the Greek way of writing which was familiar to the Ethiopians from the time of the Ptolemies. The inscriptions of Ezana (about A.D. 350), the first Ethiopian king converted to Christianity, are written from left to right. Legend has it that the converted king decreed that writing should be modified to emulate the methods of Christian writing.

The Minean-Sabaean alphabets were entirely consonated. The reader was forced to supply his own vowels to give sense to the words he was attempting to understand. This was no easy task. The

45

Hebrews, Arabs, and Syrians invented a series of signs, dots, and strokes and placed them above and below the consonants to serve as vowels. In Ethiopic, this problem was overcome by attaching minute circles and dots to the consonants to express vowels. This development transformed the alphabet that the Ethiopians had derived from the Sabaeans into a syllabary which was superior to that of the Babylonians and Assyrians (which, in turn, was an improvement over the Minean-Sabaean form).[28] Each of the thirty-one letters of the Ethiopian syllabary has seven forms. Although the Ethiopians had used some system of numbering in their bartering and other business transactions and had signs that expressed figures before they came in contact with the Greeks, some scholars assert that the signs for Ethiopian numbers were borrowed from the Greeks.

The factors that eventually determined the character of Ethiopian literature are many. First, it appears that the immigration of the Semites from southern Arabia inspired the inscriptions on stone. Greek influences can also be discerned in some early epigraphic documents. Other sources, including Egyptian, Hellenistic, and Byzantine, may have affected either the form or substance of Ethiopian literature.

The major pre-Christian literary evidence includes the inscriptions of Yeha, the Akkel Guzay, and the trilingual prescriptions of King Ezana which were written in Sabaean, Ethiopic, and Greek. During his reign, King Ezana added further inscriptions which glorified his military campaigns and expressed his gratitude to his newly found God. However, the primary literary achievement of the Aksumite period (as the period from the fifth to seventh century is known) was the translation of the Holy Scriptures. The original translators might have been Syrian monks who originally came from Greece and found refuge from the Byzantine persecutions of the monophysites in Ethiopia. The Old Testament was rendered from the Septuagint (the Greek version), though it is impossible to ascertain if all the books of the canon of the Old Testament were from the same source. The New Testament was translated from the Lucianic version which was current in Syria. Ecclesiastic Ge'ez dates from this period and although the imprint of the Syriac script is discernible "it has been so completely absorbed that it has become a characteristic part of the Ethiopic linguistic patrimony."[29]

Ethiopian literature, which includes chronicles, legends, history, religious, and medico-magico writings, can be divided into four periods: (1) from the fifth century through the seventh; (2) from the eighth century to about 1250 or 1270; (3) from the restoration of the Solomonic Dynasty in 1270 to about 1420; and (4) from Zere

Yakob's reign in the Middle Ages until about 1620 (a period of two hundred years).

The translation of the Bible included all the canonical and apocryphal books, as well as some pseudo-epigrapha that are accepted in Ethiopia as genuine. Among the latter are the Jubilees, the Ascension of Isaiah, and the paralipomena of Baruch. With regard to these works, it is recognized that the Ethiopic texts are of utmost importance. Indeed, in the case of the book of *Enoch*, the Ethiopic version is the only complete extant text. Another work that belongs to the Aksumite period is *Rules of Pachomius*, which derives its origin from Egypt but was significantly modified to accommodate the special needs of monastic life in Ethiopia. Yet another work is the *Kerillos* which is a collection of writings about Christ whose authorship is attributed to several of the church fathers. Mention must also be made of one more famous work, the *Physiologus*, a type of natural history on animals and plants, which was apparently very much in evidence during the Middle Ages in Europe. This work was translated and expanded from the Greek text. While the influence of this work waned in the Oriental and Western languages, it retained its appeal in Ethiopia for a long time. Since there is only one copy of the Greek manuscript remaining in Europe, the Ethiopic version is considered of great importance for text critique.

With the introduction of Christianity in the fifth century, the new religion became the arbiter of morality, the moving force and central focus of literary expression. As Ullendorff aptly points out, "it was also the filter through which every facet of thought, old or new, had to pass—to be accepted, rejected, or modified. How much was suppressed and lost in this process can never be known."[30] Along with Christianity came political and literary alliances with Syria and Egypt. Later, the adventurous Ethiopian community in Jerusalem established relations with the eastern Mediterranean region and parts of Europe. Despite all external influences and intellectual cross-fertilization, however, "Ethiopic literature always maintained its Christian character, the peculiar bent of its indigenous monophysitism, allied to the Abyssinian state, the Court, and the person and institution of the *Negusa Negest* [King of Kings]."[31]

In literature, as well as in other aspects of Ethiopic intellectual life, scholars have not hesitated to borrow from, to influence, or be influenced by, outsiders. A number of works of Hellenistic, Oriental, and southeast Asian origin have been imported, translated or adapted. Nevertheless, the emphasis has always been on incorporating the imported materials into Ethiopian realities as perceived and understood by the scholars and scribes of the time. Some of these works, such as the *Fetha Negest* (Judgment of the Kings), were subjected to such profound rethinking and modification that in some cases they lost their resemblance to the protoptyes. As Ullendorff stresses, the relationship between model and reproduction, translation and pattern, has become so complicated that all the minutiae of research have been employed to disentangle it.[32]

Beginning in about the first part of the eighth century, a dark cloud settled over Ethiopia. As Christianity was accepted, pacts were made with the Byzantine emperors to defend it against nonbelievers. As a result of these alliances, the Aksumite government weakened. Colonial territories in southern Arabia asserted their independence from Ethiopia. The Persians overran the Red Sea coasts against the Roman Empire and, by association, other Christians. The new religion, Islam, mounted its own onslaught against the Red Sea littoral and expanded further south. At about this time, the legendary Queen Judith (Gudit—also known as the monstrous one) led some of the original Agew people in an uprising against the monarchy. In her wake, many churches, monasteries, and documents were destroyed and the creation of literature must have nearly ceased. Ethiopia looked inward and used the occasion to consolidate its form of Christianity and to gain converts in regions further south. It was probably during this turbulent period that true indigenization of the principles of imported Christianity, that is to say, monophysitism, took place. The remnants of Judaic and pagan practices and beliefs were incorporated to give it a truly national and peculiarly Ethiopian character. As Ullendorff rightly reflects, "The transformation of Christianity, its moulding in the image of the religious and cultural syncretism of the country, probably received its most notable accession of this period [tenth century]."[33]

Beginning in about A.D. 1137, the Agew dynasty, which Ethiopian tradition considered usurpers of power since they were not of the King Solomon-Queen Sheba (Makda) line, assumed power. The Agew kings, in spite of fears to the contrary, were not only converted to Christianity but also became active proponents and built a series of marvelous churches carved from living rock at Rhoa (renamed Lalibela), which to this day stand as monuments to unrivaled achievement. They ruled until 1270 when the Solomonic dynasty was restored.

It would be rash to consider the period from the eighth to the thirteenth centuries as an era of complete intellectual sterility. Nonetheless, for five hundred years, literary development stagnated, mostly as a result of the destruction and suppression of intellectual materials. One scholar suspects "rigorous censorship and inquisition that were aimed at disposing of all evidence of an un-Solomonic and unorthodox past,"[34] but destruction by external forces and internal disorders contributed as well.

In A.D. 1270, the Solomonic dynasty was reestablished by Yekuno Amlak. With the assistance of *Abuna* Tekle Haimanot—the favorite Ethiopian saint—he ousted the last of the Agew monarchs. He claimed descent from the ancient kings of Aksum who traced their line to King Solomon and the Queen of Sheba. This new Solomonic dynasty ruled Ethiopia until 1974. Yekuno Amlak's ascension was celebrated by the composition or translation of the *Kibre Negest* (Glory of the Kings), which traced the dynasty's lineage from Adam to Solomon and the Queen of Sheba down to its own time, and enjoyed a long tenure as Ethiopia's national epic. With this resurgence of national consciousness, Ge'ez, as a literary medium, was in full bloom.

Numerous chronicles, collections of laws, treatises on folklore, medicine, and natural sciences, miraculous stories of the Virgin Mary, prayers to her, and the like were produced after the restoration. Even as Ge'ez reached its zenith as a literary medium, a new language, Amharic, emerged. In A.D. 1270 it became the official language of the country. Though it eventually gave way in speech to Amharic,[35] Ge'ez remained the language of literary and intellectual discourse until well into the latter part of the eighteenth century.

Perhaps as a result of renewed interaction with European scholars and the revitalized determination of Ethiopian scholars to incorporate new approaches, the quality of the materials on which the manuscripts were written, the calligraphy, and the art of manuscript production approached perfection between the fourteenth and eighteenth centuries. The best manuscripts, written on expensive goatskin, were produced for the court, the monasteries, and influential churches.[36] They were bound with thick wooden tablets, usually covered with leather, and placed in leather or cloth straps designed to be slung over the neck and shoulder.

Among the great Ethiopian works that have been published and found in Ethiopia or abroad and identified, edited, and catalogued is *The Chronicles of the Wars of Amde Sion*. This work is an eyewitness account of the life of King Amde Sion (reigned A.D. 1314–1344), Yekuno Amlak's grandson, who provided stability during a long period of political and social upheaval. The emphasis is on the king's wars against the Muslims who were entrenched in eastern Shoa.

Another product of this period, the *Kibre Negest*, is perhaps the most important single literary work in Ethiopian history. The *Kibre Negest* is the legendary saga of the union of King Solomon of Jerusalem and the Queen of Sheba (or Makda) of Ethiopia which resulted in the birth of Menelik I, the first Solomonic ruler of Ethiopia and the one with whom most of the subsequent 225 kings or emperors identified themselves. It also describes how the original Ark of the Convenant was spirited away form Jerusalem by a group of clergymen and was deposited at the famous Church of Zion at Aksum. Whether this tale has some factual basis is a moot question; what is important is that the work was believed by the leaders and the led alike, and provided guidance and served as the foundation for legitimizing the beliefs and actions of state, monarch, and church until recent times. Whether it is consciously recognized or not, the *Kibre Negest* has had a profound effect on religious, political, and social life in Ethiopia. Few students of Ethiopian history would disagree with Edward Ullendorff that "the *Kibre Negest* is not merely a literary work, but—as the Old Testament to the Hebrews or the Koran to the Arabs—it is the repository of Ethiopian national and religious feelings, perhaps the truest and most genuine expression of Abyssinian Christianity."[37] Although some of the foundations of the *Kibre Negest* were of south Asian origin, the substance of the story must have been pervasive in Ethiopia for a long period of time before the document's arrival.[38] Both from the literary as well as the historical point of view, it was a great achievement of Ethiopian genius of the fourteenth century.

Other significant works of the Amde Sion period include the *Meshafe Gizret* (Book of Burial), a collection of ancient burial rites, and *Meshafe Sat'at* (Book for Timekeeping), originally based on Coptic-Arabic works, but later incorporating Ethiopian material. Another popular and typical work in the annals of Ethiopic history is the *Wuddase Maryam* (Glory to the Virgin Mary) which contains a collection of hymns and laudations dedicated to the Virgin. It is still used today in liturgical services.

Still other important Ethiopic works are based on the lives and deeds of martyrs and saints: *Gedle Sematat* (Works or Acts of Martyrs); *Gedle Hawariat* (Works of the Apostles); and the *Senkssar* (Synaxarium), a vast compilation of saints' lives which are read in the church on their name days. This last work is one of the most fundamental achievements of Ethiopic literature.

This very productive literary period was enhanced not only by the restoration of the Solomonic dynasty, but also by the arrival of Coptic archbishops from Alexandria which facilitated Ethiopia's intellectual interactions with outsiders. This vigorous intellectual climate was primarily the legacy of King Amde Sion, who, as Conti-Rossini has pointed out, was the real founder of the dynasty's might and power and created the Ethopian state by widening its frontiers through intelligently planned and brilliantly executed campaigns.[39]

Following the death of Amde Sion, there was a period of unrest and degeneracy that persisted until King Zere Yakob (Seed of Jacob, reigned 1434–1468) assumed the throne. Zere Yakob surrounded himself with able monks for spiritual consultation and scholarly activities which increased interaction between the church and the monarch, enhanced the age-old role of the monarchy as a focal point of the religious and political life of Christian Ethiopia, and as Taddesse Tamrat notes, made the court the focal point of a growing sense of independence from Alexandria.[40]

Ge'ez literature reached the pinnacle of its development during the Zere Yakob period. The king not only actively encouraged literary productivity, but also personally engaged in producing works of a politico-religious nature. He zealously (sometimes brutally) forbade pagan worship, reorganized the administration of church and state, and authored, or caused to be authored, such works as *Meshafe Berhan* (Book of Light) and *Meshafe Milad* (Book of Nativity). These works dealt with the central questions of the ecclesiastical reforms he inaugurated; the refutation of heresies, magical practices, and idol worship; and his requirement that the Sabbath be observed on both Saturday and Sunday.

Another significant work of the Zere Yakob period was *The Mysteries of Heaven and Earth*, which dealt with the secrets of the creation of the world, the rebellion of the angels, and the mystery of the Godhead. A major type of literary work was the *Tamir* (Miracle) genre. There are many manuscripts that contain the stories of the miracles of Jesus, the angels, the saints, and the Virgin Mary. *Tamre Maryam* (Miracle of Mary) is one example. Religious pamphlets and hymns to the Virgin Mary gushed forth during this era. Zere Yakob himself is credited with writing *Egziaheber Negese* (God Reigns), and *Arganona Maryam* (Organ of the Virgin Mary).

Another major collectino of hymns, invented in the sixth century by Saint *Abuna* Yared and revised in the fifteenth century, is the famous *Degwa*. Several beautiful *Degwa* manuscripts containing words and musical notations to be sung during the liturgy can be found today in Ethiopia and abroad. This work, beautiful when performed well, still remains the backbone hymnody of the Ethiopian Church.

There are only a few rulers in Ethiopia's long history who have attained such distinguished and, on balance, human achievements in politics, military science, and religious dogma and letters as King Zere Yakob. As Ullendorff has observed: "He [Zere Yakob] was unquestionably the greatest ruler Ethiopia had seen since Ezana, during the heyday of Aksumite power, and none of his successors on the throne—except only the Emperors Menelik II and Haile Selassie—can be compared to him."[41]

With the end of Zere Yakob's reign, literary, social, and political development slowed once again. Under Zere Yakob, a large empire was created, the harmonious union of church and state was cemented, and the administration was centralized,[42] but his successors were not able to consolidate and maintain these gains. The situation was complicated by the Muslim invasion of Ethiopia under the leadership of Ahmad ibm Ibrahim (Gra&mcén, the left-handed), and Ethiopia's alliance with a Christian European power—Portugal. The Muslim invasion initiated a period of turbulence which resulted in material, intellectual, and spiritual destruction in Ethiopia. There was looting and deliberate destruction of church properties, art works, manuscripts, and paintings, resulting in the irretrievable loss of some treasures created during the preceding ten centuries.

In 1529, Grañ defeated the forces of the Ethiopian king, Lebna Dengal. Two years later, he succeeded in invading most of highland Ethiopia, burning churches and monasteries and forcibly converting people to his religion. Ullendorff notes:

> The holocaust enveloped most parts of Ethiopia and brought in its train misery and murder, ruin and devastation. Much of the literary and intellectual heritage of Abyssinia was irretrievably lost, and the barbarism and brutality had an effect for transcending that age. To Ethiopians a good deal of their hard-won civilization was destroyed; while to the historian and *Ethiopisant,* precious documentation and irreplaceable evidence perished forever.[43]

Eventually, with the cooperation of the Portuguese, and at great cost to Ethiopia, Gra&mcén was defeated. The Portuguese assumed that in return for their assistance, the Church of Ethiopia would submit to the Church of Rome. Among the one hundred or so Portuguese who remained in Ethiopia following Gra&mcén's defeat were some Jesuit priests who proceeded to reorder the Ethiopian Church and convert the king, Susenyos, to Catholicism. With time, these activities aroused the indignation of the Ethiopian people; Jesuits were persecuted and eventually expelled and efforts were made to restore the indigenous religious system.

For the first time, pamphlets in Amharic began to appear in large quantities. A number of important documents for and against church doctrines were produced in that language. Such Amharic works as *Fekkare Malakat* (Exposition of the Divinity), *Mashafe Felasfa Tebeban* (Book of Philosophers), *Sawna Nefs* (Humanity and Soul) and *Haimanot Abaw* (faith of the Fathers) defended the Ethiopian version of Christianity against Roman Catholicism.

Another controversial work (authorship uncertain), *Mazgebe Haimanot* (Treasure of the Faith), was composed during the heat of the Monophysite-Catholic controversy. Because it contained bitter attacks on Catholic doctrine, this work drew many replies not only from the Jesuits but also from King Susenyos, who was struggling to persuade Ethiopians to accept the doctrine of the Roman Church.

In the seventeenth century there was another outpouring of hymnography and prayer books including the *Wuddase Amlak* (Laudation of God), and *Mazgebe Qine*, a collection of poetic hymns. The *Qine* is a uniquely Ethiopian form of poetry that has its own regulations and standards regarding meter and rhyme. In Ethiopian tradition, one particular *Qine* form, *Semina Worq* (Wax and Gold),[44] is well known and appreciated for its richness in expressing the depth of one's perceptions of the universe without, at the same time, betraying the true meaning of that expression. This form of poetry was often put to music, and *Mazgebe Qine* is one of the most sublime examples of its creative potential.

Another fundamental work of the seventeenth century is the *Fetha Negest* (Legislation of the Kings), originally compiled by Ibn al-Assal for Christians living in Islamic Egypt. In Ethiopia the work underwent drastic transformation by Ethiopian reductionists until it conformed to local requirements. It deals with penal legislation and civil as well as canon laws. Much of Ethiopia's present penal code is based on this work, and its influence continues. There are many other works from this period, such as historiography, history, historical legends, biographies, and chronicles, which are sources of information for the student of Ethiopian literature and history.

Although Amharic was recognzied as the language of the court as early as A.D. 1270, and there are some Amharic manuscripts from the fourteenth and seventeenth centuries, it was not until the reign of Emperor Tewodros II (reigned 1855–1868) that Amharic literature achieved full recognition. Under Tewodros' rule, Amharic was given the greatest impetus and encouragement as a language of literature and national unification. Despite the fact that Amharic is associated with a particular ethnic group bearing the same name, this policy has continued up to the present.

Ethiopia's first printing press was imported by Emperor Menelik II (reigned 1889–1913). It produced the first regular periodicals, pamphlets, and newspapers, as well as some original literary and historical works, philosophical and religious treatises, and hymnals and chronicles. Added impetus was given to publishing during the reign of the late Emperor Haile Selassie I (reigned 1930–1974) and, despite traditional conventions, censorship, and conditioned inhibitions on the part of Ethiopian authors, literature has flourished up to the present time.

As increasing numbers of Ethiopians graduated from the modern secular education system, and as printing presses became more available to both government and private groups, Ethiopians wrote extensively. Understandably, most of this writing was in Amharic, which has led non-Ethiopians to rely predominantly on non-Ethiopian scholars (limited by unfamiliarity with the language and culture) for their understanding of the Ethiopian essence, traits, and conditions. Since the 1974 revolution, increased attention has been paid to the production of some literature in the several other Ethiopian languages, in addition to Amharic.

Libraries

The earliest libraries were collections of manuscripts assembled by the ascetic Christians who lived and worked in the various monasteries found in the northern and northwestern parts of the country. Many of these centers may not have possessed much beyond the Old and New Testaments and the liturgy. Since the monasteries were often raided and looted, precious manuscripts were guarded with meticulous care. They were often hidden in holes made for that purpose in walls, or buried in earthen vessels. In the larger monasteries such as Debre Libanos and Debre Berhan, special rooms with shelves were built and functioned as libraries, and, as in the libraries in Egypt, Syria, and Mesopotamia, the scribes whose duty it was to write the service-books of the church must have kept some sort of catalogues. The number of works collected in this way is unknown, but it must have been considerable. Independent of the monasteries, Ethiopian rulers established centers of learning supported by excellent libraries. Iyasu the Great (reigned 1682–1706) made the city of Gondar a center not only of theological learning but also of secular excellence and culture by attracting to his court outstanding scholars from various parts of the realm. It is reported that during his reign over five hundred scholars lived in Gojam, in central Ethiopia. The Church of Debre Berhan Selassie in Gondar had a famous library of 981 religious manuscripts and books.

The type or number of extant Ethiopian manuscripts is not known. One thing that is known is that monasteries, larger churches, and private individuals possess many invaluable mansucripts that deal primarily with religious and medicinal subject matter. The monks, hermits, and priests guarded the manuscripts very carefully and were not always willing to make them available. Until the establishment of the Ethiopian Studies Institute in the 1950s it was not possible to bring many of these manuscripts together. Even now, the task of collecting, cataloging, and editing within Ethiopia is in its infancy.

Ethiopic manuscripts that have been well preserved, identified, cataloged, edited, and published are those which for one reason or another found their way into European museums, libararies, and private collections. Although ferreted from Ethiopia, until recent times these were the only works that were readily accessible to scholars for further study and analysis.

From time to time, far-sighted emperors tried to establish libraries of significance. One such recent attempt was made by Emperor Tewodros (Theodore II, last half of the nineteenth century). As he tried to move his capital from the ancient city of Gondar to a more receptive Debre Tabor to the east, he took a large collection of manuscripts with the hope of placing them in a library adjacent to a church which he planned to build. When he decided to move on to Makdela he took the manuscripts with him. When the British stormed the castle in 1868 and the emperor died, they carried some four hundred works to England; individual soldiers looted undetermined numbers; and the rest were distributed among the local people.

The number of Ethiopic manuscripts which found refuge in the various parts of Europe and elsewhere is still undetermined, but it must be considerable. Conti-Rossini made a list of thirteen hundred, but he did not claim that his list was exhaustive. The Italian, Portuguese, and Spanish priests took collections of manuscripts to Europe. Many other travelers such as Bruce, Salt, Parkyns, and Rupell took others. One of the greatest collectors was d'Abbadie who secured many ancient and rare works. In addition, some five hundred Ethiopic manuscripts are located in the British Museum; the Bodelian Library contains at least thirty-five; other mansucripts can be found in the Cambridge University Library and the Royal Library in Windsor, England; and it is reported that scores of manuscripts are held privately—primarily in the collections of families and relatives of officers and soldiers who served in the Napier Expedition of 1868. There are also Ethiopic collections in Berlin, Frankfurt, Paris, Vienna, Rome, Jerusalem, the Vatican, and Leningrad. During the 1936–41 occupation it is believed that the Italians looted additional Ethiopic manuscripts. In terms of numbers, the Bibliotheque Nationale in Paris possesses the largest collection; quality-wise, the British collection is the richest. There are still more uncataloged manuscripts in private homes in Britain. Most of these volumes contain several compositions by different Ethiopian authors. Very few of these manuscripts date back to the fourteenth century, approximately a half dozen belong to the fifteenth century, manuscripts of the sixteenth century are rare, and all the rest belong to the seventeenth, eighteenth, and nineteenth centuries.[45]

Art, Architecture, and Music

Although a definitive study of Ethiopian art, architecture, and music is yet to be realized, there is no doubt that cultural and environmental factors furnished the inspiration for Ethiopian artistic accomplishments. No civilization or artistic achievement is created in a void. There must be some antecedents on which subsequent endeavors are built. These antecedents then continue to influence the forms, biases, and styles of those that follow. This seems to be true in the case of Ethiopia.

As in other areas of intellectual endeavor, artistic expression in Ethiopia revolved around religious themes; Ethiopian artists readily borrowed, as they were willing to share, from Coptic, Byzantine, Hellenistic, Syriac, and later from southern European sources. They were always careful, however, to ensure that the borrowed forms, styles, or inspirations conformed to the exceptions and perceived realities of Ethiopia. Materials were systematically worked and reworked to achieve an integrated body of Ethiopian artistic expression. While it is true that some of the works of art and architectural design can be traced back to their original imported sources, the results are uniquely Ethiopian. As Jean Doresse, the French author who carried out extensive archeological studies in Ethiopia, observed: "Early Ethiopian Christianity had to borrow extensively from foreign sources in acquiring a traditional [ceremony], organized monasteries, scared music, ecclesiastical architecture and decorative design; but out of all these influences there emerged an integrated system whose pattern was distinctively Ethiopian."[46]

Commenting on the importance of religion in the artistic traditions of Ethiopia and the Byzantine Empire, Ullendorff noted:

> Byzantine art and the indigenous Ethiopian tradition were deeply transfused with Christianity, which imbued the two civilizations with an almost unparalleled exclusiveness and dominance of religious matter. Literature, art, music and most facets of organized expression were virtually wholly ecclesiastic, and the religion of the state determined the scope of all artistic creation. Christianity was thus not only the source of Byzantine and Ethiopian art, but it also moulded it and prescribed its task and purpose.[47]

The earliest known specimens of pictorial art in Ethiopia are the rock carvings found scattered throughout the northwestern portion of the country. These works are of mixed quality, from crude incisions to beautiful and delicately executed color paintings of human or animal figures. The age of these works has not yet been determined, but they probably existed before the oldest painting in manuscripts for they "belong to a completely different type of art form and to a mode of contemplation that is far removed from anything else that is known to us of Abyssinian pictorial representation."[48]

Painting on canvas, calligraphy, and manuscript illumination are the most representative and important branches of the Ethiopian visual arts. At various times, each of these branches achieved exceptional excellence in artistic expression. Of Ethiopian manuscripts Ullendorff writes:

> The beautifully shaped letters, distinguished by attention to minute detail, reached, in the fourteenth and fifteenth centuries, a standard of perfection that has never been surpassed; they are a delight to the eye—even to an eye unfamiliar with Ethiopic writing. Colour and illumination were often generously applied, ornamentation and vegetable design and borders give free reign to the imaginative powers of artists.[49]

The painters, like the writers of the manuscripts, were monks, *debtrawoch* (cantors), and priests. Their artistic endeavors decorated the interiors of thousands of churches and illuminated or illustrated many more manuscripts. Their subjects were the numerous saints, the Virgin Mary, Christ, the Apostles, and many other biblical figures and themes.

Scenes of martyrdom were also the subjects of artistic expression. Usually such scenes were depicted with great directness and vigor. Toward the end of the last century, nonreligious themes such as scenes of battlefields, secular holiday celebrations, and, most importantly, the then-fashionable traditional scenes of King Solomon and Queen Makda (Queen of Sheba) were introduced. This latter scene is usually vulgar, highly commercialized, and produced with the foreign tourist in mind.

In ancient times Ethiopian artists relied on their skills not only to render art, but also to create their own instruments and materials. Brushes, parchments, and colors were prepared by the artists themselves following established standards of quantity and quality, as well as the right blend of ingredients. The painter—as well as the manuscript scholar—who needed, for instance, black ink, had to obtain nine different herbal ingredients and ferment them for at least three months. Likewise, the production of parchments from sheep or goatskins involved making and using at least ten different tools. The fact that many ancient paintings are still relatively fresh and unfaded is testimony to the patience and care of these dedicated, skilled artists.

The professional artists of Ethiopia were men who commanded respect both at home and in the community at large. Many were granted the title *Aleqa*, though this high honor was not bestowed on all outstanding artists. Often their rewards were generous: money, livestock, dairy products, clothing, grain, and land.

There were, of course, significant obstacles to conventional artistic endeavors. In traditional painting, the creative urge of the artist did not always enjoy free expression. In many instances, conventions and rules governed the execution of certain works of art which tended to stifle creativity and encourage repetition and rigidity. By tradition, any figure painted with only one eye showing was an evil person, Satan, one of those responsible for the crucifixion of Christ, or the enemy. On the other hand, saints, the Virgin Mary, and Christ were always shown full-face with both eyes visible. In addition, the order in which the lines were drawn and the figures painted, as well as the colors to be used, were dictated by conventions which had to be strictly followed. Different media had different sets of rules. The illumination of manuscripts and books, the decoration of margins and covers, and the production of full-page illustrations, at first delicate and exquisite, gradually fell into the same stifling and sterile conformity. Even the placement of paintings in the churches was prescribed. For instance, pictures of the life of the Virgin Mary were always hung on the south wall; pictures of Christ and the Apostles had to be placed in the east corner. Some of the greatest masterpieces of Ethiopian art were produced by artists working within these established conventions. There is no doubt that had such restrictive requirements been absent, even greater achievements would have been realized.[50]

The arrival of modernity and the encroachment of secular painting tended to diminish the vigor and might of traditional painting. Professor Chojnacki, a noted critic and curator of Ethiopian art for many years at the Ethiopian National University, states: "In the past paintings were exclusively of a religious nature, art was permeated with faith and the paintings were prayer in colour."[51] Regarding the modern painting, including the King Solomon and Queen of Sheba variety, Professor Chojnacki feels that they are no match for the traditional paintings. "They have lost the spiritual depth of the old paintings, exchanging it for the triviality of a production turned out for worldly amusement."[52] Nonetheless, these paintings may be considered a bridge between the past and the present, and in this sense they have value. For the ". . . transformation of traditional art has served some modern painters as inspiration in their search for and rediscovery of their national artistic heritage."[53]

At the turn of the century, a new generation of Ethiopian artists began to emerge. Some of the most promising were sent to Europe for further studies. For some time after their return, despite their training to the contrary, they continued to draw their inspiration from the traditional paintings. One noted, "Their attitudes still reflected the traditional ways of thought." An artist who was caught between the traditional ways of thought and the modern, secular demands of Ethiopia in the 1950s was Afework Tekle. Educated in Addis Ababa, London, and Paris in the post-World War II era, he tried to blend the old and the new. However, his work and his values developed at a critical time in Ethiopian history, when the new piece of cultural cloth was threatening to slough off the old. Professor Chojnacki provides a portrayal of this dilemma:

> Afawarq certainly draws from the old Ethiopian traditions. His subjects often represent the old ways of life, legends or handicrafts of Ethiopia. Of necessity he paints religious scenes, and seems much taken by the pomp of the ritual of the Ethiopian Church. . . . Afawarq's art has deep roots in Ethiopia's situation in the 1950s, and eloquently expresses this particular moment in the country's history, the last moments of a fading past. Afawarq is a painter of traditionally minded, self-contented old Ethiopia, and his art is always in harmony with what is currently called the Establishment. Yet Ethiopian society, and especially the coming generation, have changed dramatically in the 1960s. Their attitudes and aspirations, actions and sometimes violent reactions, represent the opposite of what Afawarq's careful art stands for. It is significant to remember that the supreme moment of his career, the acceptance of the Haile Selassie I Prize in Art, also apparently marked his swan song in the role of a modern Ethiopian painter. Afawarq shows no eagerness to communicate with new Ethiopia, which is obviously alien to him. Since 1961, the year of his last exhibition in Addis Ababa, he has shown no works to the public, with the exception of his murals at the official opening of the new St. Paul's Hospital. Let us hope that this inactivity represents only a temporary lull.[54]

During this time more art schools were opening in the country and other artists were returning from studies abroad. Their work continued to reflect the supreme confusion and uncertainty that Ethiopia was experiencing. In the meantime, the patrons of the arts were less the church and state, and more the growing new intelligentsia—perhaps indicating that better times were ahead for the arts in Ethiopia.

With few exceptions, Ethiopian architecture is ecclesiastic in conception as well as in function. There are differing opinions regarding the underlying reason for this. Some scholars feel that since the civilization was theocentric, the architecture was consonant with the beliefs of Ethiopians. Others feel that because Ethiopian kings moved around from place to place for so many centuries, the construction of lasting secular palaces was unnecessary. The exceptions to this rule are found in the stelae and royal and judicial thrones of the Aksumite period (third century B.C. to the seventh or tenth century A.D.); and the amazing number of stylish palaces, administrative offices, and churches that were built in Gondar in the seventeenth and eighteenth centuries (most of which are still in relatively good shape). However, the kings who ruled Gondar were different in many ways from other rulers before them. "The Gondarine ideal even in the period of that empire's strength," notes David Mathew, was "a power that was remote, instinct with dignity, spiritual in the widest sense, religious, sacrosanct."[55] Aside from these few exceptions, no royal castles or secular buildings of note have survived.

Some of the earliest architectural remains are to be found in the temple at Yeha, an important town of the pre-Aksumite period (perhaps of fifth to fourth century B.C. vintage). The style of these remains shows some affinity to the pattern of architecture then found across the Red Sea in the southern Arabian peninsula. A gap appears in architectural continuity between the earlier period represented by the buildings of Yeha and the architecture of the Aksumite Kingdom which assumed prominence during the first century of the Christian era. It is still difficult to delineate how many of the techniques represented by the buildings of the Aksumite Kingdom were invented locally and how many were imported. What is important here is that whatever might have been derived from beyond the Red Sea was adapted to the local milueu with the result that the architectural styles of the Aksumite period assumed uniquely Ethiopian characteristics.

Scholars describe the characteristics of early architectural styles as consisting of the use of stone and wood in alternate layers. This style was used in the ancient Aksumite buildings, in the numerous early medieval churches such as Debre Damo in Eritrea, as well as in modern structures. Some analysts of early architectural styles and materials have even suggested that the man responsible for the construction of the Ka'aba at Mecca (now Saudi Arabia) in A.D. 608, must have been an Ethiopian by the name of Embakom due to "the close resemblance to the characteristic Abyssinian style scarcely stressed."[56]

The most famous architectural achievements of the Aksumite period are, of course, the several great stelae located in and around the famous city of Aksum. Of pre-Christian origin, it is possible that the simulated stelae were constructed to serve as gravestones and memorials for important personages or kings. As Ullendorff notes,

"The perfection reached by the largest of these monoliths is expressed not only in the immense technical skill required in working, moving, and erecting these colossal single blocks of granite, but especially in their beautiful sculpturing and rich decoration as well-proportioned multi-storeyed towers."[57] Many of the obelisks have fallen and broken to pieces; one of them—which is twenty-four meters long—was stolen by the Italian Fascists in 1937 and now stands in the center of Rome. The one in Aksum, which is still standing and in relatively good condition, has a height of about twenty-one meters. The largest, though now fallen and broken into several pieces, measures some thirty-three meters and is thought to be the largest monolith in the world.

The one still standing at Aksum has sunk some eight or nine feet into the ground. Both sides are covered with relief designs. The back is blank, except for small eccentric circles enclosed by a larger one near the top of the stone. On its lower front, the obelisk has the image of a door—complete with lock. Over the door are found nine stories, and between each story are five round imitation beams or so-called "monkey heads." The famous church of Debre Damo—located on the summit of a high mountain and accessible only by rope—shows similar building characteristics, suggesting that the architectural styles of the pre-Christian Aksumite period continued to influence later, post-Christian thinking.

Though hardly architectural monuments, the stone thrones of Aksum also deserve mention. Though in poor condition, a number of these still exist in Aksum. Their function is not precisely known, but it may be safe to assume that they served as ceremonial seats for kings and some of their important subordinates during public festivals, church ceremonies, or coronations. A number of recent kings traveled to Aksum to mark the solemnity and legitimacy of their ascension by sitting on one of these ceremonial thrones during their coronation. Whatever purpose these stelae and thrones served, either as memorials to great monarchs or as abodes for their spirits, they, together with the most beautiful and ancient church of Debre Damo, form a partial record of contemporary architecture of the highest order.

Commenting on the great church architecture and decoration that flourished in the earlier part of the Middle Ages, one student of Ethiopian history notes that when one examines beautiful churches like Debre Damo or Debre Libanos and observes the beautifully executed animal designs, floral and geometric patterns, and delicately carved crosses on the walls and ceilings, one is reminded of the Byzantine and Coptic influences, but, he adds: "this connexion cannot detract in any way from the rare and superb craftsmanship of the Ethiopian woodcutters who produced such exquisite beauty in so remote and inaccessible a place [and] displaying an elegance and delicacy quite untypical of the main current of Abyssinian art."[58]

A different kind of church architecture, altogether marvelously beautiful and without doubt one of the great wonders of the world, is the famous group of rock-hewn churches at the village of Lalibela in a remote part of the region of Lasta. These churches were built by the most unlikely rulers of Ethiopia, the Zagwe (or Agew) dynasty that ruled until the tenth century. Their founder, Gudit (the monstrous one), who overthrew the first Solomonic dynasty and destroyed churches, monasteries, and their contents, was of Agew origin (some say she was a Jewess or Falasha). Yet her descendants proved to be zealous Christians and the greatest of them, King Lalibela, built the churches which were named after him. After his death he was canonized and became one of the revered saints in the Ethiopian church tradition.

All eleven of the churches at Lalibela are carved from the living mountains that form a part of the region. The largest, *Madhane Alem* (Saviour of the World), measures 110 feet by 77 feet and is 35 feet high; the others display a remarkable variety in design and styles of architecture and decoration. Five of the churches are completely detached from the rocks; the rest form part of the rocks. Construction of these edifices was ingenious. Large trenches were dug on all sides of a rectangular form, thus isolating a large chunk of granite. This huge rock was then worked and shaped from outside as well as inside to achieve a harmoniously balanced and well-proportioned masterpiece. The workmanship of the decorations, carvings, and pillars exhibit great delicacy of the highest standard.[59] In addition to the rock-hewn churches at Lalibela, others of similar design, though not of the same architectural perfection, can be found in Tigrai province and at other sites in Lasta. They were created later and incorporated the forms and styles of the Aksumite period.

A cursory survey of Ethiopian traditional architecture must also include the group of secular buildings built in the city of Gondar. The Fasiladas' buildings (named after the seventeenth century emperor who was responsible for most of their construction) were different in conception as well as execution. They include secular palaces and administrative buildings as well as one church. Like the monarchs who ruled from Gondar for a period of time, this series of strong, spacious, and unique structures lies outside the mainstream of Ethiopian architecture known up to that time. They represent another departure, another attempt to diversify from tradition, to experiment, to recreate a different approach to conventional architecture.

Ethiopian musical traditions are secular and religious, vocal and instrumental. The invention of Ethiopian ecclesiastical music is traditionally attributed to Yared (sixth century A.D. who later became an *Abun* and still later was canonized), whose memory is still cherished. The ecclesiastical music is by far the most demanding in terms of skill and knowledge required for production. Composers, vocalists, and instrumentalists received intensive training over a long period of time. In fact, the *debtrawoch* (scribes or deacons) who were usually the most qualified singers or instrumentalists, were among the most highly educated and esteemed church functionaries. At its best, Ethiopian church music is ecstatically inspiring and uplifting. As one scholar notes: "When the priests and deacons sing as they have learnt from Yared they do it to the point of complete exhaustion, until sweat bursts from their pores, until their limbs are out of control . . . until their throats are hoarse, until their hands, with which they clap while they sing, are raw."[60]

The fundamental collections of most of the compositions of ecclesiastical music are contained in the *Degwa*. This collection of church hymns with musical notation is also attributed to Yared but it is most likely that additional notes and compositions have been incorporated over time. The musical notations are dots and letters indicating melody, meter, mode, transposition, and the like. There are additional signs and notations indicating the season and circumstances for which various passages are appropriate.

There are three types of ecclesiastical hymns: Ge'ez (also the name of the ancient language), which is appropriate for weekdays and other ordinary occasions; *ezel*, which indicates low-voiced and dignified singing appropriate for such occasions as fasts, vigils, or funerals; and the *arary*, which indicates light and gay moods and is usually reserved for great festivals of a secular or religious nature.[61]

Religious music makes use of a variety of instruments. Among the most important ones are the *tsenstsil* or sistrum; and the *kabaro* or drum, also known in its modified form as *negarit*. These instruments are indispensable and ubiquitous in church services; without their accompaniment, the celebration of many religious feasts could not be imagined.

Ethiopian secular music, on the other hand, embodies many forms and styles depending on the particular region of the country. The traditional highland music, in contrast to religious music, is seldom reduced to writing and is usually played by the *azmari* (wandering minstrel) who is "the nearest approach in the modern world to the troubadours and minnesingers of the Middle Ages."[62] The *azmari*'s music celebrates the human condition and its manifold rhythmic cycles: sowing, threshing, harvesting, childbirth, initiation, marriage, love, death, and the like. The *azmari* travels from place to place, appearing at important functions such as wedding feasts or other joyous occasions, flattering, cajoling, and goading the people into dancing, laughing, and giving money, or, making full use of the ingenius subtlety and indirectness of the Amharic language, insulting high and low. To this day, no important occasion, whether in the city or the countryside, is complete without the presence of an *azmari* with his *masenko* (a single-string musical instrument that produces pleasing, melodious music of limited range and tone). The *masenko* is ubiquitous with the *azmari*. One cannot imagine the presence of one without the other at weddings and other festive public or private occasions.

In addition to the *masenko*, there are a number of secular musical instruments in Ethiopia, including the *imbilta*, a single-note flute-like instrument; the *malaket* (trumpet), usually used to herald the approach of important personages; the *washint* (flute), a five-note bamboo stick with four holes played by experts and amateurs alike with equal musical benefit; the *kirar*, a five-stringed instrument used to play light music; and the *begna*, a very noble eight- or ten-stringed instrument usually played on very highly dignified or somber occasions. Traditinally, the last instrument more than any other has attracted young students of high as well as low birth; the others are usually adopted by people of lower social status (if they play to earn a living or as a profession). Ethiopian tradition has it that the *begna* descended from the biblical harp of David, making it especially respectable.

This very limited presentation of the musical life of traditional Ethiopia is only an indication of its prominent role in the life of the nation. Whatever its origins, this music continues to inspire, encourage, and otherwise give expression to the joys and dilemmas of life, love, and death.

Summary

The central force of the intellectual and cultural life of Ethiopia has been, until recent time, the organized church. As an institution, the church itself has passed through a number of metamorphoses, gathering strength from the Judeo-Christian as well as the African traditions to become a truly national institution. The church tradition has nurtured the Ethiopian essence and has given it the tremendous psychic and spiritual energy necessary to effectively withstand adversarial assaults from without and within; not only to survive but to flourish as well.

As a partner in the state apparatus, the influence of the church was wide and pervasive. However, its effect on education was relatively narrow and conservative. Education was reserved primarily for the male progeny of the membership and was perceived as essential for the few leaders of church and state; it was never intended for the common people. The philosophies, curricula, and approaches of education in general emphasized the centrality of the Almighty and the supremacy of the human soul over temporal bodily needs. Teaching, scholarship, artistic creation, modesty, humility, and dedication to the pursuit of thoroughness in one's undertakings were emphasized. Seldom did an author announce his name on the front cover of his work. He might begin his work by invoking the help of the Almighty and, if he lived long enough to see his work through, he acknowledged gratitude to God for granting him health and life to accomplish the work.

As the twentieth century progressed, this metaphysical view of man in relation to his environment and himself tended to lag behind emerging concepts of "modernization" and technological progress, with their often vulgar overemphasis on the economic man. The criteria of education became technical skills and numbers. The emphasis shifted to how many students had enrolled, graduated, and were employed. At this juncture, traditional liberal education parted company with "modernism." Ethiopia's traditionally independent education institutions looked elsewhere for new inspiration, for new models for a new era. Whether those who initiated these educational changes foresaw the social and political consequences of their actions is a moot question. But the effect of the action was nothing short of revolutionary.

Subsequent chapters in this volume examine how, through the instrumentalities of imported guest models, the colleges, for good or ill, effected profound, fundamental psychosociological, political, and economic transformations in all of Ethiopia's traditional institutions.

Notes

1. For a more complete discussion of the various branches of study and curricular requirements, see Teshome Wagaw, *Education in Ethiopia: Prospect and Retrospect* (Ann Arbor: The University of Michigan Press, 1979), 10–21; and Aleka Imbakom Kalewold, *Traditional Ethiopian Church Education* (New York: Teachers College Press, Columbia University, 1970), 1–41.
2. See David R. Buxton, *The Abyssinians* (London: Thames and Hudson, 1970), 73–75.
3. For further detailed analysis, see Donald N. Levine, *Wax and Gold: Tradition and Innovation in Ethiopian Culture* (Chicago: University of Chicago Press, 1965), 168–69.
4. Ibid., 24–25.
5. Ibid., 25–26.

6. Carlo Conti-Rossini, ed. and trans., "Iyasu I, Re d'Etiopia E Maritire," *Revista degli studi orientali*, xx, 107, quoted in Levine, *Wax and Gold*.
7. See Sir E. A. Wallis Budge, *A History of Ethiopia*, vol. 2 (London: Methuen and Co., Ltd., 1928), 453. Also see Levine, *Wax and Gold*, 26.
8. Levine, *Wax and Gold*, 21.
9. Ibid., 26.
10. Ibid., 27.
11. Ibid., 28.
12. See Haile Gabriel Dagne, "Education Magic in Traditional Ethiopia," *Ethiopian Journal of Education* 4, no. 2 (June 1971): 3–12; and Wagaw, *Education in Ethiopia*, 1–21.
13. Wagaw, *Education in Ethiopia*, 1–21.
14. Budge, *A History of Ethiopia*, 574.
15. See John Spencer Trimingham, *Islam in Ethiopia* (London: Oxford University Press, 1952), 40.
16. Ibid., 27, 65–66.
17. James Theodore Bent, *The Sacred City of the Ethiopians* (London: Longmans, Green, and Co., 1896), 51.
18. Levine, *Wax and Gold*, 171.
19. See Buxton, *The Abyssinians*, 77–78. Also see Budge, *A History of Ethiopia*, 611.
20. Buxton, *The Abyssinians*, 77.
21. Bent, *The Sacred City*, 169.
22. Buxton, *The Abyssinians*, 78.
23. Ibid., 79–80.
24. Bent, *The Sacred City*, 161.
25. Levine, *Wax and Gold*, 171.
26. Budge, *A History of Ethiopia*, 558–59.
27. Ibid., 595–60.
28. Ibid., 550–54.
29. Edward Ullendorff, *The Ethiopians: An Introduction to Country and People*, rev. ed. (London: Oxford University Press, 1965), 102, 139.
30. Ibid., 137.
31. Ibid., 138.
32. Ibid.
33. Ibid., 62.
34. Ibid., 140.
35. The British Library, *The Christian Orient* (London: British Museum Publications Ltd., 1978), 46–47.
36. Ullendorff, *The Ethiopians*, 144.
37. Ibid.
38. Ibid.
39. Ibid., 67.
40. Taddesse Tamrat, *Church and State in Ethiopia, 1270–1527* (Oxford: Clarendon Press, 1972), 243–45.
41. Ullendorff, *The Ethiopians*, 69.
42. Ibid., 70.

43. Ibid., 73.
44. Levine, *Wax and Gold*, 5.
45. Budge, *A History of Ethiopia*, 561–62.
46. Jean Doresse, *Ethiopia: Ancient Cities and Temples*, trans. Elsa Coult (London: Elek Books; New York: Putnam, 1959), 85.
47. Ullendorff, *The Ethiopians*, 159.
48. Ibid., 165.
49. Ibid., 165–66.
50. Wagaw, *Education in Ethiopia*, 17–18.
51. Stanislaw Chojnacki, "A Survey of Modern Ethiopian Art," *Sonderausgabe* (Addis Ababa, 1973), 84.
52. Ibid.
53. Ibid.
54. Ibid., 86.
55. David Mathew, *Ethiopia: The Study of a Polity, 1540–1935* (London: Eyre and Spottswoode, 1947), 206.
56. Ullendorff, *The Ethiopians*, 159–60.
57. Ibid., 160.
58. Ibid., 162.
59. Ibid., 163. See also Buxton, *The Abyssinians*, 103–6; and Ruth Plant, "The Ancient and Medieval Architecture of Tigre Province in the Light of Present Evidence" in Robert L. Hess, ed., *Proceedings of the Fifth International Conference on Ethiopian Studies* (Chicago: University of Illinois at Chicago Circle, 1978), 315–27.
60. Buxton, *The Abyssinians*, 154.
61. Ibid., 155–56.
62. Ibid., 157.

II

THE GUEST MODELS:
IMPORTATION, ADAPTATION, INNOVATION AND EXPANSION

3

FOUNDATIONS OF THE COLLEGES

In recent history there seems to have been a direct cause-effect relationship between external aggression against Ethiopia and Ethiopia's increased awareness of the need for self-renewal through education. At the battle of Adwa in 1896, Italy attacked Ethiopia and the former was soundly defeated. This victory over a major European power attracted great attention among the European nations, most of whom subsequently besieged Addis Ababa for accelerated diplomatic and commercial relationships. In the process, Ethiopia became acutely aware of her lack of expertise in foreign languages, technology, and the diplomatic arts. The resulting embarrassment eventually led to the establishment of a "modern" school which was fashioned after the European model, independent of traditional educational institutions.

This trend continued on a modest scale until 1935 when Fascist Italy once again attacked Ethiopia. This time, with the use of modern and advanced technology, Italy won and the Ethiopian emperor, his family, and most of the nobility sought refuge in Europe, the Middle East, or East Africa. These traumatic experiences profoundly affected thinking at all levels regarding Ethiopia's conditions vis a vis other powers. Upon its restoration in 1941, the Ethiopian government set out to rehabilitate and expand the educational structure.

Since the nineteenth century, some young Ethiopians, under the sponsorship of government or private organizations, have traveled abroad to secure higher education. With the progress of events at the national as well as international levels, the concept of founding a college within Ethiopia, which had been anticipated as early as 1928, was revived. Within a decade after restoration, the education system was rejuvenated and the colleges that were to serve as foundations for a national university system were established.

It is important to remember that although the structures and conceptual frameworks for higher education were imported, there is ample reason to believe that they were not grafted onto a clean slate and absorbed completely into the minds and value systems of the host society. Trudeau's assertion that "these church schools and monasteries which were the centers of religious studies did not influence the modern educational system or constitute a real foundation for the present system of higher education. . . . their history and development is not a part of [the] study of higher education"[1] seems too extreme, but there is some element of truth in it. As will be shown in subsequent pages, it is impossible to think that higher education in Ethiopia was not influenced by what existed prior to World War II.

The Immediate Background

With the steady increase in the number of secondary school students following World War II, the practice of sending a large number of them abroad was proving expensive.[2] In June 1949, twenty-six students took the London Matriculation Examination. In January and June of 1950 an additional sixty to seventy secondary school graduates became eligible. To accommodate the growing number of graduates, three institutions were already making plans to offer college-level courses. The first "modern" secondary school, Haile Selassie I Secondary School, was one that made known its wishes to start a college on its campus; General Wingate Secondary School, under British Council control, organized tutorial classes for its graduates preparing to sit for advanced level examinations per British university entrance qualifications; and Tafari Makonnen School planned a postsecondary school on its campus to take care of the thirty or more students who were expected to graduate in January 1950. In light of these developments, the Ministry of Education sought a unified plan of action to establish advanced studies in Ethiopia.

A committee on the founding of a university was appointed by the vice-minister of education and between October 1949 and January 1950 various proposals were considered. Eventually, the committee adopted a two-year program for academic preuniversity study and a vocational curriculum to prepare high-level technicians, clerks, teachers, and administrators. The two-year program was to prepare those secondary school graduates who had passed the London Matriculation or the Intermediate Level Examinations of the University of London, as well as other students who would follow the vocational programs. The successful candidates of the first group were to be sent abroad for further studies, while the second group would receive a professional diploma and join the civil service. This two-year program was officially approved by the Board of Education in December 1949. At the same time, the Ministry of Education, anticipating the opening of a college-level institution, requested that a group of secondary school graduates be given advanced instruction, especially in science, history, and philosophy. This program started in January 1950 at the Tafari Makonnen School under the direction of Dr. Lucien Matte, who had been serving as principal of the school since 1945.

Dr. Matte and his Jesuit colleagues played a vital role in the development of higher education in Ethiopia. Following the Italo-Ethiopian war in 1941 the decision was made to rehabilitate the education system. Teaching and administrative personnel were recruited from Europe, North America, and Asia. Those recruited to rebuild the Tafari Makonnen School (Emperor Haile Selassie's favorite, which he founded in 1925 under his precoronation name) were Canadian Jesuits led by Lucien Matte. Though the Jesuit tradition of scholarship and professional dedication is well-known, given Ethiopia's conflicting relationship with Jesuits in the past it is not clear why the emperor dared to invite them to assume such influential positions. In the early part of the sixteenth century, Ethiopia had requested help from the Portuguese government to resist a Muslim invasion. The Portuguese responded affirmatively and dispatched arms and men, including some Jesuit clerics. At the conclusion of the war, the Jesuits stayed in Ethiopia and attempted to bring about drastic, forcible reforms in the Ethiopian church. Over a period of more than one hundred years, the Jesuits' activities led to the death of one king, the abdication of another, and a large measure of civil strife. As a result, to this day in highland Ethiopia, the word "catholicism" is associated with anti-Ethiopianism, which in turn means anti-Christian. Yet despite these earlier negative experiences with the Jesuits, the emperor invited the Canadians to Ethiopia.

One reason that Haile Selassie recruited Jesuits may be that as a young boy in Harar he was tutored by both French and Ethiopian Catholic priests. Indeed, one of the people he fondly recalled was his teacher, Aba Samuel, a Catholic priest who lost his life while saving young Tafari's life in a boating accident. This childhood association may have played a part in his decision to invite the Canadians. He may have also known that the Jesuits put great emphasis on obedience, discipline, and hard work—all qualities that the emperor valued. Finally, since Ethiopia had just disentangled herself from Great Britain—her erstwhile ally which was still a feared colonial power—and since the United States was only dimly on the horizon of world power, the choice of a nonpolitical group of educators from a nonmajor power might have been very attractive.

At any rate, when the invitation was received the Jesuit headquarters chose young Lucien Matte to organize an educational assistance group for Ethiopia. Dr. Matte was energetic, academically well-qualified, and had extensive experience in teaching,

71

administration, and institution building, albeit under the umbrella of the Jesuit organization.[3] The Jesuits took charge of the rebuilding of Tafari Makonnen School in 1945. The emperor visited the school frequently, obviously pleased with what he witnessed. There was trust based on actual accomplishment, so Dr. Matte was the natural choice to head the founding of a college.

The University College of Addis Ababa

On 20 March 1950 the emperor called Dr. Matte and asked him to organize a two-year institution of higher education which was to be named Trinity College. Dr. Matte was appointed president of the new institution. Eight months later the name was changed to University College of Addis Ababa (UCAA). It was stated that "the aim of the UCAA was to provide the youth of Ethiopia with a sound academic background in the fields of Arts and Science, leading to further professional studies abroad."[4]

Three weeks after the announcement of the new college, Dr. Matte left for Europe and North America to recruit staff since none were available in Ethiopia; and, presumably, to consult with others. While abroad, the president also purchased all the educational materials needed for teaching and research, including textbooks, library books, equipment, and supplies.

On 11 December 1950 classes began at UCAA. "It was a humble beginning," noted Dr. Trudeau, adding:

> There was a staff of nine teachers, the principal included. There were twenty-one students, all men, who had completed high school. The students, all boarders, and some of the staff members were living together on campus, in the building that used to be the Commercial School and was still partly occupied by students of this school. Dormitories, dining-hall, library, classrooms and laboratories were accommodated in this one building. It was simple and poor, but sufficient.[5]

One of the first students, Aklilu Habte, who later became president of the National University, added:

> University College was then almost a family affair: everybody knew everybody. Staff and students intermingled freely; the same kitchen served them all. The same lecturer dealt with many subjects, and the deans and the librarian had a heavy teaching responsibility in addition to their administrative duties.[6]

The educational purpose and programs were explained to the students by the president on the morning of 11 December 1950.[7] The programs of the first two years were to lead students to the Higher School Certificate in Arts and Science. The level of studies was equivalent to postmatriculation at the University of London. Qualification for entry was, initially, the passing of the Ethiopian School Leaving Certificate Examinations. "Students having succeeded in London Matriculation Examinations (or hoping to complete this examination) have of course a better chance for longer higher studies."[8] The courses of studies, methods of examinations, and grading systems were all prescribed.

On 27 February 1951, with the emperor presiding, the official inauguration of UCAA took place. In his official opening speech, the vice-minister of education noted:

> On this red-letter day, fortunate are the students who have been able to get their names enrolled as the first batch of students of this college. They are lucky to receive their education, board and all they require free of charge. . . . The opening of a college today initiates the first page of a chapter in the history of education in [modern] Ethiopia.[9]

The Pursuit of Identity and Status

Even before the opening of the college, the choice between affiliation with a foreign university or independent status was debated. The fact that the college was Ethiopian in name and in substance was contrasted with the problem of obtaining recognition by outside institutions of higher learning, primarily for the purpose of getting places abroad for the graduates of the two-year programs. The emperor suggested that Dr. Matte visit the University of London to discuss possible affiliation with that institution. In a letter sent on 29 June 1951 to the Inter-University Council for Higher Education in London in anticipation of his own visit, Dr. Matte wrote: "We are anxious . . . to associate the College with the English University system for purposes of examinations, adjustment of syllabuses, recognition of degrees, etc."[10] Dr. Matte further inquired whether it was possible to establish a special relationship with the University of London as had been done with other colleges of the British colonies, although he was fully aware that in the case of Ethiopia, a nonmember of the British Commonwealth, such an arrangement would require special procedures. He also asked whether the syllabi drawn by the college would be equivalent to the appropriate syllabi of the University of London, adding,

> If the above would be technically impossible, we should like
> to know the procedure for taking external examinations. . . .
> We realize that the intermediate and final examination for B.A.
> or B.Sc. will have to adhere as closely as possible to the Lon-
> don University standards in either case.[11]

Dr. Matte visited London in the summer of 1951. Upon return
he recommended to the vice-minister of education that "a special
relationship status" be worked out between the two institutions.
Accordingly, the University of London was invited to send a visiting team to assess UCAA programs. Although the invitation was sent
in December 1951 it was not until March 1953 that the visiting team
arrived. A number of procedural problems on both sides, including the rejection of one of the two members of the visiting team
by the Ethiopian government, contributed to the delay. The visitors, Mr. Michael Grant, professor of humanities at Edinburgh
University, and C. H. Paterson, assistant registrar of Oxford University, stayed nine days in Addis Ababa. At the end of April 1953 they
submitted their report.

The report opened with laudatory remarks and then listed its
recommendations. In part, the recommendations endorsed:

> the strengthening of the teaching of English, the raising of the
> standards of administration, the teaching of a more eclectic sys-
> tem of philosophy, the establishment of a system of external
> examiners for closer control of the final examinations by the
> British universities, [and] the establishment of a committee in
> England that would maintain contact between British univer-
> sities and the Ethiopian system of higher education.[12]

Obviously, the visiting team imagined an affiliation analogous
to that existing between the British and other African colleges which
were then beginning to develop. They believed that the British
university's active involvement in UCAA's development was essential. Another way of saying this was that for UCAA to be worthy
of its name it had to faithfully replicate the conditions, requirements,
and means of evaluation of the University of London. This, if accepted, would have entailed a heavy additional financial burden
for the new college and an unhealthy dependency on a still-feared
colonial power. The college officials and the Ethiopian government
abandoned the idea of affiliation forthwith in favor of independence
and so informed the University of London.[13]

Meanwhile, UCAA continued to expand in physical size and program diversification. Soon after inauguration the Commercial School
left for new premises, leaving its one building (to be known as the
Science Building, built during the occupation) entirely to the college.

At this juncture (October 1951), in anticipation of the federation of Eritrea with Ethiopia, the college was also instructed to set up a special two-year course in port administration.

The School of Law was established as a part of UCAA in January 1952. On 22 January the Board of Education also declared that UCAA should become a senior college. At about the same time, the Faculty of Arts initiated new courses in administration (internal service; foreign service), and in education; the Faculty of Science program began to prepare students for engineering and biology. The Ministry of Education asked that UCAA take over the administration of the Ethiopian School Leaving Certificate Examination (ESLCE), which was replacing the Cambridge Examination, with the president as director.

In April 1952 construction started on two student residences of forty-eight rooms each and a dining hall with a capacity of three hundred seats. Leveling of sports fields also began. In October a former cinema hall (Cinema Cinque Maggio), located at the corner of Miazia 27 Square (Arat Kilo), was turned over to the college. After some repairs and the installation of a new floor, the hall was used as a temporary gymnasium and theater.[14]

As another step toward maturity, the college published its first official bulletin in March 1953. In July the first commencement exercise took place. At the commencement one student obtained a certificate in engineering, five received diplomas in engineering, and three received diplomas in biology. Most of the graduates went abroad to continue their studies.

In October 1953 the Faculty of Arts added a fourth and final year to their program; UCAA was now a complete four-year college. Library facilities, the physical plant, and the museum continued to expand.

Charter

As the first group of students entered their fourth year in 1953–54 the question of legitimacy became crucial and the college asked the government for a civil charter. A draft charter prepared by the college was reviewed by two committees appointed by the vice-minister of education. Apparently there was still some disagreement among committee members as to whether the college should have its own charter, be affiliated with a foreign university, or wait until Haile Selassie I University, which was still at the conceptual stage, was established as a chartered national university, in which case UCAA would then form one of its constituent colleges. Time was running short. The first group of young people, having gone through a four-year training program, expected to be rewarded with the

75

promised degree. Dr. Matte's memorandum addressed to the would-be graduates provides some insight into the acute problems faced by the college during the summer of 1954. In a one-page note of July 1954, he advised students that examinations would terminate on 13 July, that commencement would take place on 27 July, and that the college charter was already published (although actually, it was not).[15]

More than a month later in another note, the president advised the future graduates of the probable commencement dates. He assured the graduates (who were by now very anxious) that the charter was at the printers and that the date of the document was known to him, so that he could take the necessary steps for the students to enter various foreign universities. Interestingly, at that time a first degree was not considered sufficient for a graduate to begin working in a country starving for a skilled work force. In the meantime, graduates were advised to acquire the necessary travel documents.[16]

At last, the UCAA Charter was published on 28 July 1954.[17] Commencement exercises had been held two days earlier on 26 July. "For the first time in the history of Ethiopia," observed Dr. Trudeau, "Ethiopian students received university degrees granted by an Ethiopian degree-granting institution. It was also a milestone in the history of African Higher Education."[18]

At the graduation ceremony, the president of UCAA noted that, along with other achievements, after four years of activity the college had now reached maturity. With its four hundred students enrolled in the Faculty of Arts, the Faculty of Science, the Law School, the Arts Faculty, Extension Department, and the Berhanih Zare New Institute (Your Light is Today, an adult education unit which had recently transferred from the Ministry of Education to the Faculty of Arts), the UCAA had become an institution "adapted to the special needs of the country and always open to further development."[19] Understandably, the mood in Addis Ababa was festive on the part of students, faculty, and the public at large.

The charter granted to the college was liberal and provided all the usual powers and privileges required for an academic institution of its kind. It was undoubtedly "the cornerstone of higher education in Ethiopia, its first foundations. As of that day, Ethiopia took its place in the academic world of colleges and universities."[20] In both conception and practice, UCAA was primarily an undergraduate liberal arts college. The value of such a college at this stage of the country's history may seem questionable, but in retrospect it was a wise and courageous decision.

Other Colleges

The founding of UCAA was but one step toward the realization of a national university. As mentioned above, in June 1951 the vice-minister of education appointed a committee to "consider certain propositions for the establishment of Haile Selassie I University in Addis Ababa." The committee's terms of reference were to advise the Board of Education in regard to:

(a) some general principles involved in the development of university education in Ethiopia; (b) the courses which it is considered desirable to include when planning the first stage of construction of the Haile Selassie I University in Addis Ababa; (c) questions of accommodation arising from the above.[21]

The committee held twenty-one meetings between 19 June 1951 and 11 March 1952 and produced a report. In the foreword of the committee report to the Board of Education, the vice-minister, Akalework Habte Wold, aptly expressed concern regarding the importance of technical education for a developing country—a concern which the committee had so far failed to consider. He observed:

[T]he programme of the Ministry of Education has been carefully planned to provide an integrated training at each stage, and in this training, the development of manual and technical skills is closely associated with instruction in the academic subjects. The aim at all levels is to equip the students for life in Ethiopia. It is clearly understood by the Ministry that any system of schooling which ignored the agricultural background of the majority of the nation's children would be sadly misconceived. The schools have a great part to play in developing the nation's resources by the dissemination of old skills and the introduction of new ones.[22]

Then, acting on behalf of the Board of Education, the education vice-minister nominated two more committees, including representatives of other ministries and departments of the government, to study the questions of technical and agricultural education. It was these two committees that laid the foundations of technical and professional education at the tertiary level.[23]

Engineering College

Previously, only technical and vocational schools at the secondary level had prepared technicians for the vocational trades (mechanics, carpenters, masons, plumbers, electricians, and the like). Some graduates of these schools were rendering useful services in the construction industry and in other areas, but their qualifications were not sufficient to meet the growing need for engineers. Aware of this need, the Haile Selassie I University Committee recommended that "a College of Technology be founded, teaching a four-year course and providing professional training for students in engineering."[24]

The director of the leading technical school in Addis Ababa, Mr. Robert L. Lewis, had been the dynamic force in organizing and drafting the proposals and reports for the Technical Education Committee set up by the Board of Education. His 1951 proposal to the committee was recommended to the board after careful study and some revision. The proposal called for the establishment of a College of Technology as a four-year institution with programs as follows:

1. The first two years to be common to all students and planned to prepare the best qualified students for admission, with advanced undergraduate standing, to engineering colleges and universities abroad, as well as furnishing a sound foundation of basic mathematics and science for those students who will continue their training in the College of Technology.

2. The third and fourth years to consist of separate branches in Civil and Industrial Engineering; and students completing the course will be qualified to serve as engineering assistants almost at once.[25]

The new institution was considered a first step toward the creation of a full-fledged College of Engineering within the proposed Haile Selassie I University. As the committee's report stressed: "In the new University, training in Engineering should be specialized to train a limited number of young men with the best possible preparation in at least four branches of engineering."[26]

The Board of Education accepted the recommendations of the committee and approved the establishment of a College of Technology on the same premises as the Technical School in Addis Ababa. The director of the Technical School, Mr. Lewis, was appointed dean of the new college and instruction began in September 1952. The institution changed its name to College of Engineering and was placed under the Department of Higher Education of the Ministry of Education and Fine Arts. Unlike UCAA, it did not receive a charter until it was integrated with the structure of HSIU in 1962.[27]

The Engineering College began instruction with a two-year certificate program for students who had completed the ESLCE. In

1954, the curriculum was extended to a four-year program. At the beginning of 1959, a fifth year was added so that students would be able to complete the requirements of the B.Sc. degree in civil, mechanical, and electrical engineering. The five-year program adequately covered the areas of instruction needed to train engineers for Ethiopia.[28]

College of Agriculture

The Haile Selassie I University Committee also considered agricultural education at the college level. At its meeting of 11 March 1952, having first carefully reviewed the facts placed before it, the committee recorded the following resolutions:

1. An Agricultural College, providing training on the university level, should be established in Ethiopia;
2. It is clearly desirable that the Agricultural College should be located outside Addis Ababa, but that it should be counted as a constituent part of the Haile Selassie I University.[29]

The Board of Education set up an Agricultural Education Committee soon after the university committee presented its general recommendations. The new committee was charged with preparing more detailed plans and recommendations for the Board of Education "concerning the development of agricultural education at all levels in Ethiopia, and in particular the establishment, equipment, staffing, and curricula of an Agricultural College."[30]

At the time the Ministry of Education was taking these steps, the Ministry of Agriculture, in consultation with the U.S. Technical Cooperation Administration and United Nations experts from FAO, was also considering the establishment of a College of Agriculture. Without waiting for the reports and recommendations of the committee, the governments of Ethiopia and the United States concluded an agreement on 15 May 1959 for a cooperative agricultural education program. From then on, the Ministry of Agriculture, in cooperation with the USAID mission, became responsible for the development of agricultural education.[31]

In Article II of the U.S.-Ethiopian agreement, the objectives of the joint venture in the development of education in agricultural and mechanical arts in Ethiopia were specified:

1. To promote and strengthen friendship and understanding between the people of Ethiopia and the United States of America and to further their general welfare.

2. To aid the efforts of the people of Ethiopia to develop their agricultural and related resources, to improve their working and living conditions to further their social and economic progress.
3. To this end, to facilitate the development of agricultural and mechanical arts education activities in Ethiopia through cooperative action, and
4. To stimulate and increase the interchange between the two countries of knowledge, skills, and techniques in the field of agricultural and mechanical arts education.[32]

Article III provided for the establishment of an "Imperial Ethiopian Agricultural College Fund" as an independent agency of the Ethiopian government. The director of the fund would be appointed by the United States with the approval of the emperor of Ethiopia. The emperor would also appoint a vice-minister as special representative of Ethiopia to consult with the director on all operations of the fund.

Article IV stipulated that the fund should establish, direct and administer the college, which would conduct "instruction, lectures, demonstrations, research, experimentation, extension service and other education activities to promote the development and use of agricultural and mechanical techniques among the people of Ethiopia."[33] The director would serve as president of the college. He would also, in agreement with the special representative, determine the general policies and administrative procedures and have overall authority over the fund's activities, including employees and assets.

The most significant aspects of the agreement, as far as the college was concerned, were the following stipulations: The president of the college, after having been appointed in accordance with the provisions set forth above, would:

> plan, direct and be responsible for all operations and activities of the college, including the admission of students, establishment of curricula, conduct of examinations for the measurement of attainment in learning and conferring of suitable certificates, honors, diplomas and degrees of the college; the disbursement of an accounting for funds, incurrence of obligations, the purchase, use, inventory control and disposition of property of the colleges; the appointment and discharge of personnel of the college and the terms and conditions of their employment, and all other administrative matters.[34]

A clause establishing a Board of Trustees was provided in the agreement. The responsibilities of the board were to consult with

and advise the president of the college on matters of general policy, and otherwise offer recommendations that were designed to
enhance the effectiveness of the college's programs. The board,
then, was intended to be an advisory group. As set out in the agreement, "the advice and recommendations of the Board shall be given
full consideration by the President of the College in directing its
curriculum and activities."[35] The board was to be appointed by the
emperor and comprised of members with broad experience. The
vice-minister, serving in the capacity of Ethiopia's special representative, would be the designated chairperson.

Thus, most powers were vested in the director and the president (who proved to be one and the same person). The Board of
Trustees had only advisory powers. Trudeau later observed:

> This was an unusual type of Ethiopian institution, almost fully
> controlled by the Director of the Fund, a civil servant of the
> United States Government, who had powers that . . . would
> be found in the hands of a Board of Trustees. The Director of
> the Fund and President of the College could appoint their own
> staff and discharge them. . . . This was a new type of college
> structure in Ethiopian higher education.[36]

That so much power was to be vested in one individual was an
alarming prospect, especially in view of the Ethiopian political and
social tradition regarding foreigners, the importance of agricultural education for Ethiopia, and the problems that a non-Ethiopian
president might encounter in a totally different culture. Fortunately,
as it worked out in practice, this concentration of power did not
hamper the progress of the institution. Perhaps the fact that the
president-director was recruited from Oklahoma State University,
who in turn recruited most of the academic staff from among
people he knew and trusted, forestalled potentially disruptive
problems.

According to the agreement (Article VI, Section 3), the government of Ethiopia was to provide sufficient land as a site for the college. The land was provided, and the U.S. government signed a
contract with Oklahoma State University that gave the university
full control over the operation of the college.[37]

College classwork began in September 1953 at the Jimma Agriculture Technical School in southwestern Ethiopia. This arrangement
continued until 1956, when the students transferred to the new
campus at Alemaya in the province of Harerge. The new campus
of eleven *gashas* (440 hectares) was beautifully located in fertile
fields adjacent to Lake Alemaya in the Ogaden region. The official
dedication of the college took place on 16 January 1958. On that

occasion, the emperor presented diplomas to the first recipients of Ethiopian B.Sc. degrees in agriculture.[38]

The 1961–62 *Bulletin* of the agricultural institution defined the tasks of the college as helping to promote overall objectives "by educating young men of Ethiopia so that they will be in a position to guide the agricultural development of their country."[39] The college's obligations were to be carried out through four channels:

1. Resident teaching, directed toward agricultural education, with due consideration given to other studies, so that the student may have both an opportunity to prepare himself for a gainful occupation in the service of his country and an experience of educational enlightenment that will enrich his life.
2. Research, directed toward the solution of problems which confront the people of Ethiopia and particularly the farmers of this country.
3. Extension services, directed toward the dissemination through the country of the results of research, for the benefit of all.
4. Public service, directed toward furnishing technical advice on agricultural problems to the general public.[40]

The establishment of the Ethiopian College of Agricultural and Mechanical Arts, which followed the conceptual framework of American land-grant universities, was another solid element in the final development of the national university.

College of Public Health

The College of Public Health, situated at Gondar, was a joint venture of the Ministry of Public Health; two United Nations agencies, WHO and UNICEF; and the United States Operations Mission in Ethiopia. The college became operational on 4 October 1954 with three types of public health programs—one at the college level and two at the secondary level.[41] A two-year laboratory technology program was added later.

The mission of the College of Public Health was to prepare workers for Ethiopia's provincial public health centers. For admission, the four-year program required satisfactory results on the ESLCE. Grade 10 graduates or more advanced students could enter the college for a two-year program which trained them as community sanitarians, otherwise they could enter a three-year course to become community nurses.

Graduates of the four-year course in health and preventive medicine were put in charge of provincial health centers and worked with a staff of community nurses, sanitarians, and laboratory technicians. They were "taught to consider health and disease as intimately related to social, educational and economical development in the home, the marketplace, and the churchyard, as well as in the clinics."[42] During training, student teams worked in nearby villages, applying their classroom work to practical situations. These students traveled to their work sites on mule-back or foot, carrying their own tents and provisions. For the most part, they were effective and well-received.

A 190-bed provincial hospital with wards for surgical, medical, obstetrics, gynecology, and pediatric patients was located on the college campus. The Gondar Provincial Hospital cooperated with the college in service and training activities on the main campus as well as in other centers scattered throughout the province.[43] A survey team that visited the college in 1959–60 stated: "It is a praiseworthy effort, though a costly one in manpower and in money. Obviously, it has not yet achieved its full potential."[44] Subsequent field observations revealed that cooperation among all groups of students and their approach to village health care was exemplary.

Institute of Building Technology

Founded on 13 October 1954 through a bilateral agreement between the Ethiopian and Swedish governments, the aim of the Institute of Building Technology was to "assist in the improvement and development of building activities in Ethiopia."[45] These aims were to be achieved through three departments:

1. *The Building College*, a post-secondary technical college for training building contractors and engineers, which prepared students for work as contractors, foremen, designers, surveyors, supervisors, etc. The first group of students entered the college in October 1955. The initial program was a three-year course leading to a diploma in Building Engineering. In 1958 a fourth year was added for those candidates qualified to receive a B.Sc. degree in Building Engineering.
2. *The Building Institute* was devoted to the study of traditional Ethiopian housing and building methods. An important aspect of its functions was conducting experiments to "discover new techniques for the better utilization of building materials available in Ethiopia."

3. *The Building Materials Testing and Research Institute*, which had as its aims "the testing of the quality of local as well as imported building materials to contribute to the raising and maintaining of the levels of quality . . . in Ethiopian constructional work" and to give advice and information regarding building materials in Ethiopia.[46]

With departments largely staffed by Swedish personnel, the two research institutes started in 1956.

In 1959–60 an international survey team found that, although instruction in the Institute of Building Technology was of good quality, the existing curriculum was not sufficient to warrant the awarding of a B.Sc. degree to students who successfully completed a four-year program. The team therefore recommended that, for the time being, the Building College not grant degrees. The team advised that "in order to standardize basic fundamentals of education leading to the B.Sc. degree in all institutions of higher education, consideration should be given at an early date to integrating the Building College with the Engineering College; to strengthening the degree curriculum and extending it to a five-year programme; and to the development of an Architectural Engineering Curriculum within the College."[47]

Theological College

An elementary school for the instruction of church leaders was founded in 1942 by the emperor and supported by his personal funds. Its purpose was to upgrade and provide sound religious instruction and secular education for the clergy and other functionaries of the Ethiopian church. This elementary school was later expanded to include secondary-level instruction designed to prepare students for a special grade 12 leaving examination which was equivalent to the ESLCE.

With the establishment of Haile Selassie I University on 18 December 1961 (see chapter 4), the elementary section of the church school was discontinued and the Theological College of the Holy Trinity, as it was named on 5 October 1960, became one of the chartered units of the national university. It was empowered to grant diplomas and the degree of Bachelor of Theology.[48]

The Six Colleges: Progress Between 1950–1960

In the following review of the progress made by the six colleges between 1950 and 1960, the University College of Addis Ababa (UCAA) is emphasized for the following reasons: (1) it was the mother institution and the only chartered college; (2) relatively more information is available on UCAA; and (3) it contributed the most in the way of number and variety of programs as well as number of graduates during this decade. The organization, administration, academic programs, staff, and students of each of the other colleges will also be considered, but in less detail.

Organization and Governance

From 1950 to 1960 the administration, control, and organization of higher education varied from one college or faculty to the next, depending on how each began and under which government department it fell. With the exception of UCAA, each was either subordinate to one of the government ministries or was governed by joint agreement between the Ethiopian government and a friendly foreign government. No single national body was charged with guiding and coordinating the establishment and operation of higher education in Ethiopia. Although it is true that in 1956 the Ministry of Education established a special department to coordinate and supervise the functions and development of special schools and institutions of higher learning, in practice the department was more concerned with Ethiopian students going abroad for higher studies or returning home, and with advising and approving the general policies and activities of the engineering and building colleges which were directly controlled by the Ministry of Education.[49] The special department might have served as a coordinating agency of all the colleges, but it did not do so, primarily for lack of a clear mandate, shortage of qualified personnel, and inability to conceptualize the roles of the various colleges in relation to national needs.

Figure 2 shows the organizational structure of the colleges. The colleges were entirely independent of each other. As a University of Utah survey team was to point out later,

> Various, somewhat independent units in the field of higher education had been developing steadily their own individual plans, and had acquired both staff and facilities at separate locations. This resulted in some duplications and some friction, and was therefore more expensive in both effort and funds than necessary, and certainly more expensive than could be afforded in terms of the economy of the nation.[50]

Each of the colleges developed its own programs regardless of the national need or similar programs offered by other institutions. "In fact," says Trudeau, "an unhealthy competition for qualified students, for new programmes and for financial support from the

	University C. of Addis Ababa	College of Engineering	College of Agriculture	Public Health College	Building College	Theological College
Controlling Agency	Chartered	Education Ministry	Agriculture Ministry	Public Health Ministry	Education Ministry	Church & Education Ministry
Governing Body	UCAA Board of Governors	Education Ministry	Ethio-American Fund	Joint Board of IEG WHO & UNICEF	Education Vice-Minister and Swedish Ambassador	
Chief Executive	President of UCAA	Dean of the College	Director of Fund & President of the College	The President	The Director of the Institute	
Councils	UCAA Council	None	None	None	None	
Executive Officer in charge of the Faculty or College	Dean of Arts Dean of Science Dean of Law Dean of Students	Dean of College	Dean of the College	Dean of the College	Dean of the College	
Academic Commission	Faculty Academic Council for each Faculty	None	Academic	Academic Commission	The Council Commission	

FIGURE 2

Organizational Chart of the Colleges

Source: Adapted from Trudeau, "Higher Education in Ethiopia" (1964), p. 53.

same Ethiopian Government had been noticed on some occasions."[51] Reporting in 1953, the Public Administration Service of the U.S. Operations Mission to Ethiopia, itself hardly a nonpartisan party, sounded the alarm:

> University College has recently been granted a charter which has the effect of endowing this institution with almost complete autonomy from the Ministry of Education; the only provision made in the charter for coordinating its programme with the programme of the Ministry is one requiring that the annual budget of the College be submitted to the Council of Ministers "through the Minister of Education." Fortunately, this will permit the Minister to review and suggest modifications to the budget in the interest of a coordinated educational programme. The granting of the charter to University College appears to be representative of a general inclination to give an autonomous status to all institutions of higher learning; it is felt that this tendency should be resisted in the future. By placing such institutions outside of the Ministry it will become increasingly difficult to plan and execute a coordinated programme of educational services for the entire nation; there will be not one but two or more agencies of government each proceeding more or less independently. Primary, secondary and higher education are integral parts of a total educational process, each building upon or keyed to the others; means must be devised to effect the needed coordination, especially during the present period in which the educational system is being rapidly developed and expanded. The Ministry of Education is the logical agency in which to centre responsibility for the over-all planning and execution of the nation's total educational programme. At a somewhat later date, when the pattern of the educational system is finally decided and firmly established, consideration might be given to the creation of some such agency as a Board of Higher Education to direct the nation's higher education programme.[52]

This was sound advice. Had it been followed, it could have saved much energy and money. On the other hand, the eventual development of higher education in Ethiopia might not have been possible. The traditions and foundations of higher education needed to rest on entirely different grounds, so that it could develop a tradition of independence and academic freedom by drawing on a wide variety of experiences.

In the first three years of its existence, UCAA was not sure where it actually belonged in the administrative structure. During those early years, the Board of Education of the ministry set out the broad policies and general directions the college was to follow.[53] However, the college charter published on 28 July 1954 provided for the formation of a College Board of Governors, a University College Council, and a Faculty Council. The charter specified that the emperor would be chancellor and the president as a member of the Board of Governors.

The charter provided:

> there shall be a Board of Governors of the College of Addis Ababa, consisting of at least six members appointed by Us and of the president of the University College, who shall serve at Our pleasure. When the University College shall have two hundred graduates or more, one additional member of the Board shall be elected by them from among the graduates. . . . The Board of Governors shall have power and authority to exercise in the name and on behalf of the University College any and all the powers, authorities, and privileges of the University College as a body corporate as enumerated in Article 3.[54]

In a letter written on 11 December 1953 the vice-minister of education, Akalework Habte Wold, informed Dr. Matte that in accordance with the college charter the emperor had appointed a chairman and five other people to serve on the Board of Governors of UCAA. In view of the historical role they played in the life of UCAA, the names of the first board members are listed below. Except for the president, all were Ethiopians:

Blatta Merse Hazen Wolde Qerqos: chairman
Lt. Colonel Tamrat Yigezu: member
Ato Bellete Gebre Tsadiq: member
Lij Mikael Imru: member
Dejazmach Zewde Gebre Selasie: member
Ato Ketema Yifru: member
Dr. Lucien Matte (ex officio, as President of the College)[55]

Of the first board members, three were Oxford University graduates; two had received some education abroad or at home (not at the university level); one, Merse Hazen Wolde Qerqos, was a distinguished scholar in the traditional schools of Ethiopia; and one was an author and a former teacher. They all held high positions in the government, as did their successors on the board. Because qualified Ethiopian academicians were in short supply following the Italo-Ethiopian War, the recruitment of non-Ethiopians to run the college was inevitable. Ethiopia was fortunate to attract and retain, on the whole, a distinguished group of foreigners to assist in its educational development. Nevertheless, the Board of Governors must have realized the inherent limitations of non-Ethiopian administrators, for it rightly insisted on close involvement in the formulation of policy for the operation of UCAA. Writing in retrospect, Dr. Trudeau states:

> The University College owes a lot to its Board members who took great interest in their institution and, in general, showed a remarkable sense of identification and participation with this young and growing institution of higher learning. In the seven years of its existence, the University College Board of Governors—as a corporate body—kept its total independence from any serious political pressure. It held eighty meetings in seven years, much more than the minimum of two regular meetings a year required by the charter.[56]

After noting that the two most important matters discussed by the board were those of personnel and budget, Trudeau added that throughout the seven years that it was in existence "the Board always did appoint the proposed new members of the teaching or administrative staff." Typically, the candidates selected by the president and his advisers were presented to the board for appointment. However, the board often resisted a simple rubber-stamping procedure and asked for a list of possible candidates with their complete curricula vitae. Indeed, the board members were meticulous in discharging their duties.

> They might have been afraid of religious influence, or national bias, or just simply wanted to express their deep sense of responsibility. *De facto*, the Board always approved the names presented to them, and the relationship between the President and the Board was a very healthy one. . . . The Board studied, at its meetings, all the memos presented to it. There were no committees. The Board was its own committee on staff appointment, on budget and on all other business. The President was both the informant of and the intermediary between the administrative or teaching staff and the Board. It was surely an institution where the President, backed by his Board, had tremendous power in the execution of various aspects of the institution's life. There were shortcomings, but these were compensated for by the efficiency of the whole organization, for the good of the institution, the students and the staff. A similar concentration of authority would not probably work the same way in a much larger institution. In a small institution, personal leadership and team work are the most important factors of success.[57]

Fortunately for the young institution, the working relationship between the board and the president must have been a very pleasant and rewarding one. The board, as a corporate body, effectively discharged its responsibilities in setting general academic policy. It required that general education be given to both arts and science students and insisted that the last two years of the four-year program be devoted to the fields of specialization which would lead to a B.A. or B.Sc. degree. It also insisted that Ethiopian studies be taught to all students and that considerable research on Ethiopian languages and culture be conducted. To these ends, it approved the establishment of a graduate faculty, two institutes, a school of social work, an observatory, and thirteen departments.

The board supported the president in his negotiations with the United States Agency for International Development (USAID or Point IV) regarding the establishment of a department of education. The Americans had agreed to help initiate and operate the department, but they also wanted to run it. The president demanded that it stay within UCAA and be considered part and parcel of that institution, like all of the other twelve or so departments. Backed by the board, the president prevailed—at least for the time being.

However, the board did not always support programs initiated by the college. It also wanted to be actively involved in originating programs and bringing them for study and elucidation to the president, the University College Council, or the Faculty Council. Almost always, the board insisted that the programs and activities of the college remain faithful to the aspirations of the Ethiopian nation. For instance, at the first meeting of the board, which was held on 21 December 1954 in the president's office, they elected Dr. Matte to serve as temporary secretary until the appointment of a permanent secretary who could record the minutes both in Amharic and English; even at this early date, the minutes were to be recorded in the two languages.[58] In reality, however, Dr. Matte became the permanent secretary and there is doubt as to whether any of the minutes were ever recorded in Amharic. Nonetheless, the board's intentions attest to the deep concerns of those in charge that the institution conform to its mission. At another meeting, the board wanted to channel college students to various fields based on the national needs for a high-level work force. However, the president convinced them that such things were not traditionally decided at the college level.[59] The matter seems to have been dropped there. Yet a decade later, and to this day, programming students according to national work force needs became common practice.

There were other occasions when the board asserted its independence of the college administration. This is elucidated as follows:

Before deciding on academic matters, the Board always asked for a written report from the University Council. In fact, most of the projects for the opening of a new department, of a new school, or for the establishment of an institute originated with the University Council and were then presented to the Board. The Board acted upon recommendations sent upwards from the Council. In some instances, though, such as the creation of a faculty of law, the preparation of a new scholarship system for boarders that was to replace the free education system, greater coordination between the existing colleges, the creation of a university or the integration of all other colleges with the University College—in these instances and in others the initiative came from the Board. In such cases the Board sent their proposal to the Council for study and for comments and recommendations.[60]

Under the Board of Governors, the president was the executive officer who was responsible for the proper management of the college. He was assisted by the University College Council, the vice-president and the Faculty Council. The charter empowered the University College Council to legislate on most important academic matters. The membership of the council was drawn from academic officers and staff representatives. The Faculty Council legislated on academic matters at the particular faculty level. The deans and the department heads in the various faculties functioned as executive and administrative officers, executing academic and administrative programs.[61]

As stipulated in the UCAA charter, the University College Council was composed of the academic officers and one member from each of the constituted faculties. This council was vested with the power "without any control from the Board of Governors, to establish chairs and courses of instruction, and to grant degrees, diplomas and certificates of proficiency."[62] Consistent with its responsibilities, the University College Council zealously guarded the academic growth of its institution. For instance, recommendations for a new school or institute were emulated by other colleges and later by the national university.

The Engineering College

The College of Engineering was directly under the Ministry of Education. The chief executive was the dean who, like all other staff members of the college, was appointed by the Ministry of Education and Fine Arts. All matters pertaining to staff, finance, maintenance of equipment and buildings, and serious student problems had to be brought to the attention of the Director of

Higher Education or to the Director General of the Ministry of Education. As a result:

> A large amount of time and efficiency was wasted in meetings with all officials of the Ministry of Education, in endless trips to the Ministry for college equipment and stationery, for monthly allowances, for staff salaries and for many day-to-day administrative affairs. Except for some independence in the programmes and in academic affairs, the College was administered very much like a secondary school with full control from the Ministry of Education.[63]

The fact that the College of Engineering shared the same premises as the Technical School did not help. A different arrangement had to be worked out, but that had to wait for an opportune time.

The Institute of Building Technology, established by a bilateral agreement between Ethiopia and Sweden, was governed by a joint board of one representative from each of the two governments: the Ethiopian Vice-Minister of Education and the Swedish ambassador. The director of the institute was also dean of the college. The two representatives and the director considered and decided "all important matters."

In 1959, after the institute had been operational for about five years, a charter similar to that of UCAA was drafted. However, in view of the institute's eventual incorporation into the plan for Haile Selassie I University, the idea of implementing a separate charter was dropped.[64]

Academic Programs

The various Ethiopian colleges necessarily had different objectives. The objective of UCAA was, in the words of President Matte, "to give an education on broad lines, that is to say a curriculum providing both cultural and specialized subjects, aiming to give the students not only knowledge but also to develop their intellect."[65] Even more explicitly, it said: "The University College aims at providing Ethiopian youth with a sound academic background in Arts as well as in the fields of science. Its curricula lead to professional studies abroad and eventually at the Haile Selassie I University now in the course of construction and organization."[66] In other words, although specialization was provided after the first two years of college work, UCAA was essentially a liberal arts college designed to prepare young people for graduate studies. The other colleges saw their missions as equipping young people with technical knowledge and skills for development.

Throughout the 1950s it was difficult to find enough qualified secondary school graduates for the various colleges, and the policymakers were severely criticized for trying to establish a top-heavy system of national education. In 1953 a national study identified one of the nation's major needs as accelerated expansion of secondary-level education. The report noted: "The task confronting the academic secondary schools, therefore, is to expand and to make other adjustments as soon as possible so as to produce 525 graduates annually [during 1955–1964]."[67] The colleges, which had been established at great cost, had to operate at full capacity in order to produce the high-level work force that was so urgently needed.

The various academic programs of the colleges are summarized in Table 1. UCAA, assuming that its students should have a complete basic general education course before specializing in a major subject abroad, offered a core curriculum consisting of courses in English, Ethiopian languages, sociology, philosophy, and world history, as well as surveys of Ethiopian and African history. The other colleges, reflecting the urgent need to produce people with professional and technical skills, emphasized the training of specialists. However, there were conflicting opinions regarding the quality of programs in these new institutions. One of their critics accentuated his disgust at their lack of liberal education when he characterized the program of the professional colleges as follows: "Liberal education had no place in any of these colleges. They were purely applied technical institutes without any general education equipment, without any course in the humanities, sociology, philosophy or the social sciences."[68] These were valid criticisms, but UCAA went to the extreme in the other direction.

Admission standards also differed among the colleges. While UCAA still required at least an Ethiopian School Leaving Certificate, some of the other colleges accepted students without it. Finally, course requirements were also different, as were standard examinations and promotion.[69] These discrepancies in quality of programs, standards of admission, and quality of instruction among the colleges created apprehension among the college communities.

In library facilities, equipment, and instructional materials, UCAA and the Building College were well-off. The College of Agriculture was later provided with some funds to establish a good library. Many other issues regarding the quality of training on the part of the various colleges, however, remained unresolved.

Teacher Training

UCAA continued to expand and diversify its programs. In 1955 an agreement was signed between the Ethiopian government and

TABLE 1
Development of College Academic Programs,
1950–1951 to 1960–1961

Year	UCAA	Other Colleges
1951–52	Faculty of Arts Faculty of Science a) Mathematics—Physics b) Biology and Chemistry	
1951–52	A Two-year Course in post Administration. Law School (non-degree even- ing or part-time programme).	
1952–53	Arts: Major in Education as of third year. Major in Administration.	College of Engineering a Two- year Diploma Programme.
1953–54	School of Law Extension Department Imperial Charter Granted Degrees granted for first time.	College of Agriculture begins at Jimma (1953).
1954–55	—	Public Health College, Four- year programme begins.
1955–56	Secondary School Teacher Training. Pre-Law major offered in Faculty of Arts.	College of Public Health Four- year programme (B.Sc.) ap- proved. Building College Four- year diploma programme set.
1956–57	Advanced course in Law in the School of Law.	College of Agriculture gradu- ates its first degree students (B.Sc. in Agriculture).
1957–58	Commerce Section opens A Major in Economics and Public Administration offered. Geophysical Observatory begins operation. Department of Engineering in Faculty of Science.	College of Engineering gradu- ates its first degree students (B.Sc. Engineering).
1958–59	First summer session for teachers in-service. Department of Education is set up.	

Source: Adapted from Trudeau, "Higher Education in Ethiopia" (1964), p. 63.

the United States Operations Mission in Ethiopia to start a secondary school teacher training program as a section of the Faculty of Arts. Initially, most of the students for this department were graduates of the Teacher Training Institute (Harar TTI) who, in addition to completing the equivalent of grade 12 education, had taught for at least two years and had passed the special College Entrance Examination set by the Ministry of Education and the United States Mission. In 1959 the section was reorganized to become a separate department. In 1962 the department was once again restructured to become the Faculty of Education, still under the Ethio-United States agreement. The first department head, and later the dean of the college, was Dr. Aklilu Habte, one of the first graduates of UCAA (later in 1969, president of Haile Selassie I University). The Faculty of Education is still the only institution in Ethiopia that prepares senior teachers for government secondary schools.[70] During its formative years, American teachers under the University of Utah contract with USAID provided valuable services in several areas of teacher education.

Adult Education

The university's role in adult education is discussed in chapter 6. Suffice it to say here that adult education was organized at UCAA for the first time in October 1953 when the Law School was opened to give nondegree instruction to Ethiopian lawyers and others who might benefit from courses in basic law. In January 1954 an extension division was opened in the Faculty of Arts which offered evening courses in the arts, business and public administration, and social and political science to part-time adult students who had the equivalent of a high school education. Applicants who were unable to present formal school-leaving certificates were required to pass an English proficiency examination administered by the college. At first, the department offered courses that led to certificates or diplomas, but later it developed a full degree program. It was a wise and timely venture. Adults who otherwise would not have had a second educational opportunity applied in increasing numbers.

The College of Agriculture, in cooperation with the Ministry of Agriculture, developed its own Agricultural Extension Program which was designed to improve agricultural education and Ethiopian farming practices. The Agricultural Extension Program rendered invaluable service to the Ethiopian people at the grassroots level. The Colleges of Engineering and Building Technology also initiated nondegree extension programs to improve the skills of the adult population.

These various extension programs demonstrated an interest in promoting education among all strata of people, regardless of age. The colleges considered these programs as their service arm to Ethiopian society. As rightly noted by one educator who was intimately involved in some of these programs: "Higher education in Ethiopia has not only been oriented toward the education of an elite among the youth of the country, but also toward furthering the education of adults."[71] Although the extension programs were geographically limited to the immediate neighborhoods in which the colleges were located, their success was encouraging.

The Students

As shown in Figure 3, except for the Public Health College, growth in annual enrollment from 1950–51 to 1961–62 steadily increased despite the very limited number of qualified secondary school graduates. The slower growth of the Public Health College might be explained by the fact that it granted diplomas and certificates only to those who completed a three- or four-year program of studies, and that it was very particular regarding the attitude, aptitude, and interests of students who wished to prepare for careers of service as public health officers in the provinces. The College of Agriculture, on the other hand, though located some five hundred kilometers east of Addis Ababa, had the advantage of recruiting its candidates from the two agricultural high schools. It offered a B.Sc. degree at the end of a four-year program.

On the whole, between 1950–51 and 1961–62, enrollment in all colleges grew more than ten times—a startling rate, especially when compared to the enrollment growth rate of the total education system. Figure 4 depicts comparative growth in enrollment at all levels. From 1952–53 to 1961–62 enrollment in the government elementary schools nearly tripled; enrollment in all elementary schools quadrupled. During the same period, the secondary sector grew at twice the rate of the elementary; enrollment in government secondary schools increased seven and a half times; and in all secondary schools it increased nine times. Without including enrollment in the extension departments of the various colleges, enrollment in higher education showed the largest and fastest growth of all sectors of the education system.

"Programming students" according to the priorities of national high-level work force needs was the subject of considerable debate during the 1950s. In practice, however, even in the absence of any deliberate effort on the part of the authorities, the distribution of students between the arts and the science-technology areas was by

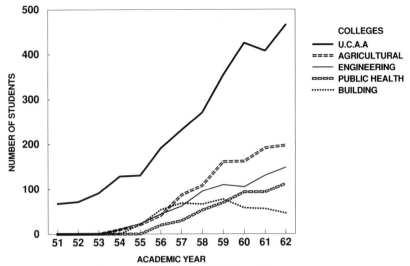

Source: Trudeau, "Higher Education in Ethiopia" (1964), p. 69.

FIGURE 3
Enrollment by Colleges, 1950–1951 to 1961–1962

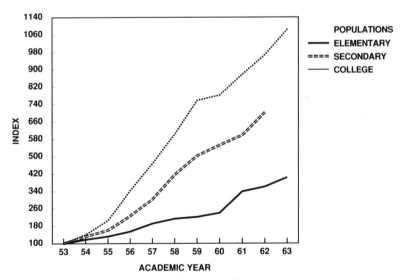

Source: Trudeau, "Higher Education in Ethiopia" (1964), p. 72.

FIGURE 4
Index of Growth of Student Population, 1952–1953 to 1961–1962
at Elementary, Secondary, and College Levels

TABLE 2
Distribution of College Students between
Arts and Science Streams, 1950–1951 to 1961–1962

Year	Arts			Sciences		
	No.	Index	% of Total	No.	Index	% of Total
1950–51	33	100.0	46.5	38	100.0	53.5
1951–52	42	127.3	56.0	33	86.8	44.0
1952–53	52	157.6	55.3	42	110.5	44.7
1953–54	77	233.3	50.0	77	202.6	50.0
1954–55	89	269.7	44.7	110	289.5	55.3
1955–56	146	442.4	40.9	211	555.3	59.1
1956–57	173	524.2	36.0	307	807.9	64.0
1957–58	211	639.4	35.7	380	1000.0	64.3
1958–59	269	815.2	34.9	501	1318.4	65.1
1959–60	322	975.8	40.9	462	1215.8	59.1
1960–61	311	942.4	35.6	562	1478.9	64.4
1961–62	374	1133.3	38.2	604	1589.5	61.8
	2099		38.7	3327		61.3

Source: Adapted from Trudeau, "Higher Education in Ethiopia" (1964), p. 73.

then in favor of the latter, as is shown in Table 2. On the average, 39 percent of the students were enrolled in the arts and 61 percent in the science-technology fields. Hindsight indicates that this was what the UNESCO Conference on the Development of Higher Education in Africa recommended as a goal for African states.[72]

Table 3 shows the index of enrollment growth in grade 12 for all types of secondary schools. Some of these students, perhaps as many as half, were registered in technical, commercial, agricultural, and other terminal programs, upon completion of which they can work. The students of the academic secondary schools were the main source from which the colleges drew their applicants. Column (c) of Table 3 indicates the number of high school graduates who succeeded in passing the ESLCE which qualified them to register in the arts or science streams of the colleges.

On the other hand, Table 4 depicts the number of students who registered as freshmen compared to the number of academic secondary school graduates who registered for and/or passed the ESLCE, and the number of grade 12 students in all types of secondary schools. The admission requirements of the Ethiopian colleges were not always identical. Beginning in 1953–54, the number of students entering colleges exceeded the number of ESLCE holders. Column

TABLE 3
Students Registered in Grade 12,
1951–1952 to 1960–1961

Year	Registered in Grade 12 (Academic & Vocational) (a)		Registered Gr. 12 School Students Who Sat for ESLCE (b)		Those Who Sat The ESLCE* (c)	
	No.	Index	No.	Index	No.	Index
1951–52	83(1)	100.0	83	100.0	63	100.0
1952–53	176	212.0	86	103.6	64	101.6
1953–54	313	377.1	105	126.5	73	115.9
1954–55	278	334.9	159	191.6	88	139.7
1955–56	310	373.5	163	196.4	103	163.5
1956–57	468	563.9	153	184.3	111	176.2
1957–58	606	730.1	317	381.9	197	312.7
1958–59	673	810.8	441	531.3	180	285.7
1959–60	917	1104.8	412	496.4	168	266.7
1960–61	792	954.2	532	641.0	192	304.8
Total	4616		2451		1239	

*Ethiopian School Leaving Certificate Examination
Source: Adapted from Trudeau, "Higher Education in Ethiopia" (1964), p. 74.

(b) shows that an average of 86.9 percent of the academic secondary school population entered college. This percentage does not account for the fact that the College of Agriculture took many of its students from the two agricultural high schools. Nevertheless, it is probably accurate since an equal number of academic secondary school students entered the military academies after grade 12. At any rate, between 80 and 90 percent of academic secondary school graduates went on to college. Noting this phenomenon, Trudeau commented: "In any country, this would be considered quite a miraculous achievement! In a country where 90% of the elementary school age children could not go to school, could not this be considered as over-achievement in higher education? Was this educational policy implemented at the cost of elementary and secondary school education? Should this policy be continued?"[73] The answer to each of these questions is affirmative. People with technical and professional skills were urgently needed. Since the colleges already existed, it was logical to utilize them to the fullest possible extent.

TABLE 4
Freshman Registration, 1951–1952 to 1961–1962

Years	No. of Freshmen	(a) %	(b) %	(c) %
1951–52	39	83.2	73.6	—
1952–53	57	81.0	61.4	—
1953–54	76	118.8	88.4	43.2
1954–55	96	131.5	91.4	30.7
1955–56	187	212.5	117.6	67.3
1956–57	179	173.8	109.8	57.7
1957–58	254	228.8	166.0	54.3
1958–59	318	161.4	100.3	52.5
1959–60	316	175.6	71.7	47.2
1960–61	325	193.5	78.9	35.4
1961–62	336	175.0	63.2	42.4
Total	2183	169.3	86.9	46.0

(a) The percentage of successful academic secondary school graduates of the previous year, who entered college in the year indicated.
(b) The percentage of the total of academic secondary school leavers of the previous year, who entered college in the year indicated.
(c) The percentage of the total of secondary (academic and vocational) school leavers of the previous year, who entered college in the year indicated.

Source: Trudeau, "Higher Education in Ethiopia" (1964), p. 75.

Students were not always successful in gaining admission to the college of their choice. Yet, because college education was free and provided a ticket for admission to the "good life" upon graduation, many young people took advantage of the open-door policy of most colleges.

A number of criteria might be used to evaluate the quality of the Ethiopian colleges: the quality of the programs, the quality of the students, the quality of the staff, and the quality of the graduates as compared to graduates of other colleges of international repute. Two of these criteria are examined here: the quality of the colleges as measured by their holding power, and the quality of the Ethiopian graduates who went abroad to study further.

Holding Power

Table 5 shows the percentage of students left from the previous year (column a); the percentage left from the entering freshman class (column b); student attrition by year (column c); and the percentage of attrition since the first year of college (column d).

TABLE 5
Student Dropouts during College Years for All Colleges, 1950–1951 to 1961–1962

	First Year	Second Year				Third Year					Fourth Year				
	Number	N	a	b	Drop. c	N	a	b	Dropout c	d	N	a	b	Dropout c	d
1950–51	71	36	50.7	50.7	49.3	—	—	—	—	—	—	—	—	—	—
1951–52	39	21	53.8	53.8	46.2	—	—	—	—	—	—	—	—	—	—
1952–53	51	35	68.6	68.6	31.4	22	61.1	31.0	38.9	69.0	—	—	—	—	—
1953–54	76	55	72.4	72.4	27.6	18	85.7	46.2	14.3	53.8	13	59.0	18.3	41.0	81.7
1954–55	96	91	94.8	94.8	5.2	39	111.4	76.5	—	23.5	11	61.1	28.2	38.9	71.8
1955–56	187	167	89.3	89.3	10.7	49	89.0	64.5	11.0	35.5	18	46.2	35.3	53.8	64.7
1956–57	179	161	89.9	89.9	10.1	79	86.8	82.5	13.2	17.7	41	83.7	53.9	16.3	46.1
1957–58	254	172	67.7	67.7	32.3	139	83.2	74.3	16.8	25.7	51	64.6	53.1	35.4	46.9
1958–59	318	236	74.2	74.2	25.8	143	88.8	79.9	11.2	20.1	127	91.4	67.9	8.6	32.1
1959–60	316	238	75.3	75.3	24.7	137	79.7	53.9	20.3	46.1	115	80.4	64.2	11.6	35.8
1960–61	325	266	81.8	81.8	18.2	183	77.5	57.5	22.5	42.5	137	100.0	53.9	—	46.1
1961–62	—	—	—	—	—	202	84.9	63.9	15.1	16.1	170	92.9	53.5	7.1	46.5
Total	1912	1478	77.3	77.3	22.7	1011	83.4	63.7	16.6	36.6	683	82.5	53.7	17.5	46.3
												93.7*	58.3*	6.3*	41.7*

Explanations: N) Number of students.
a) % left from previous year.
b) % left from the entering freshmen class.
c) % of wastage year by year.
d) % of wastage since first year of college.

*After correction, taking into account about one hundred students who left for studies abroad, or who completed a diploma course.

Source: Trudeau, "Higher Education in Ethiopia" (1964), p. 77.

101

The dropout rate between the first and second years of college for the eleven years shown was very high—23 percent. In part this can be explained by the lack of appropriate orientation and counseling programs during the freshman year (though this is not a valid excuse in itself), and the departure of some students for nonacademic, noncollege-related reasons, such as the need to support their families. Between the second and third years, an additional 17 percent left college. This is also a very high attrition rate, especially since it is known that very few of those students went abroad, left with a certificate or diploma, or entered other Ethiopian institutions of higher learning. It seems valid to conclude that a lack of sound academic preparation at the secondary school level and a lack of guidance and orientation during the first year of college were the main reasons that students left higher education in such large numbers.

It is more surprising to see that some 18 percent of the third-year students did not reach the fourth year. This is tempered by the fact that about one hundred students left after completing a three-year diploma program in either the Public Health College, the Faculty of Science, or the Engineering College. Total attrition from entrance to the end of the fourth year was 42 percent. Out of the 683 students who had registered in the fourth year, 380 graduated with degrees and the rest with diplomas.

A comparative study of dropouts from the arts and science faculties is presented in Table 6. Even after allowing for science students who left after completing a three-year program, i.e., 50.5 percent as opposed to 40 percent, more science students dropped out than did arts students. The rate of attrition in the College of Agriculture was quite low compared to the other colleges, perhaps because its academic standards were lower than the others, or most likely, because the students came from agricultural backgrounds and were trained by better-qualified teachers who were supported with outstanding facilities and equipment.

Table 7 lists graduates by institution and by major field of study for all colleges over a period of ten years. During these years a total of 220 B.A. and 200 B.Sc. degrees were granted. In addition, about one hundred science students were sent abroad for further studies—mostly in biology, medicine, and engineering—after completing two- or three-year programs. If these students are included, it is evident that more science than arts graduates were produced during the first ten years of higher education.

Liberal arts graduates, as such, were few. Out of 220 B.A. degrees granted, only 73 were in liberal arts. The others were distributed as follows: 74 in education, mostly for the secondary schools;

TABLE 6
Comparative Study of College Dropouts by Field: Arts, Science, Technology, 1950–1951 to 1961–1962.

Year	College	First Year N	Second Year N	a%	b%	Third Year N	a%	b%	Fourth Year N	a%	b%
1950–51	A	33									
	Sc	38									
1951–52	A	17	25	24.2	24.2						
	Sc	22	11	71.1	71.1						
1952–53	A	28	11	35.3	35.3	13	48.0	60.6			
	Sc	23	10	54.5	54.5	9	18.2	76.3			
1953–54	A	36	17	39.3	39.3	11	—	35.3	13		60.6
	Sc	40	18	21.7	21.7	7	30.0	68.2	(1)		
1954–55	A	33	27	25.0	25.0	18	—	35.7	11		35.3
	Sc	63	28	30.0	30.0	21	—	47.5	(1)		
1955–56	A	78	25	24.2	24.2	25	7.4	24.2	18		35.7
	Sc	109	66	—	—	24	24.3	61.9	(1)		
1956–57	A	65	60	23.2	23.2	24	4.0	69.2	24	4.0	33.3
	Sc	104	107	1.8	1.8	55	16.7	49.5	17	29.2	57.5
1957–58	A	88	40	38.5	38.5	58	3.3	10.8	25	52.7	24.2
	Sc	166	121	34.1	31.3	81	24.3	25.7	26	20.7	58.7
1958–59	A	120	58	31.3	30.8	45	—	48.9	46		41.0
	Sc	198	114	30.8	28.8	98	19.0	41.0	81		25.7
1959–60	A	131	95	28.8	28.8	45	22.4	62.5	47		27.7
	Sc	181	141	37.4	32.7	92	19.3	53.5	68	30.6	34.6
1960–61	A	104	98	22.7	22.7	77	18.9	43.0	42	6.9	52.3
	Sc	221	140	9.6	9.6	106	24.8	41.4	95		42.8
1961–62	A		94	22.2	22.2	76	24.0	26.9	73	5.4	39.2
	Sc		172	22.2	22.2	126	10.0	43.0	97	8.5	51.0
Total	A	733	550	25.4	25.4	392	14.0	28.0	299	5.4	40.0
	Sc	1165	928	21.1	21.1	619	18.0	35.1	384	22.1	50.5

Explanations: N) Number of students registered.
a) % of dropouts for previous year.
b) % of dropouts since first year.
1) During 1953–54 to 1955–56 inclusive many third year science students went abroad for studies. This is why no percent of dropout has been calculated for the years indicated.

Source: Adapted from Trudeau, "Higher Education in Ethiopia" (1964), p. 79.

TABLE 7
Graduates of the Colleges, 1952–1961

University College of A.A.	1952	1953	1954	1955	1956	1957	1958	1959	1960	1961	Total
B.A.—General	—	—	10	7	13	16	—	12	9	6	73
—Education	—	—	3	2	3	7	6	20	16	17	74
—Administration	—	—	—	—	—	—	10	—	3	7	20
—Pre-Law	—	—	—	—	—	—	6	—	8	—	14
—Economics	—	—	—	—	—	—	—	13	10	4	27
—Extension	—	—	—	—	—	—	—	—	2	4	6
—Commerce	—	—	—	—	—	—	—	—	—	6	6
Diplomas in Administration	11	—	—	2	1	1	—	—	—	—	15
Diplomas in Law	—	—	—	40	—	—	12	8	—	—	60
Certificates—Extension	—	—	—	—	—	12	9	5	4	16	46
Total B.A.	—	—	13	9	16	23	22	45	48	44	220
Total Diplomas & Cert.	11	—	—	42	1	13	21	13	4	16	121
Science											
Cert. and Diplomas—Biology	—	3	3	9	—	—	3	6	—	—	24
Certificates & Diplomas	—	6	2	4	7	3	6	13	—	—	41
B.Sc.—Biology	—	—	—	—	—	6	2	1	1	5	15
Total B.Sc.	—	—	—	—	—	6	2	1	1	5	15
Total Diplomas and Cert.	—	9	5	13	7	3	9	19	—	—	65
UCAA Grand Total											
—Degrees	—	—	13	9	16	29	24	46	49	49	235
—Dip. & Cert.	11	9	5	55	8	16	30	32	4	16	186
Total No. of Graduates	11	9	18	64	24	45	54	78	53	65	421

(continued . . .)

TABLE 7 (continued)

University College of A.A.	1952	1953	1954	1955	1956	1957	1958	1959	1960	1961	Total
College of Engineering											
B.Sc.	—	—	—	—	—	—	7	12	19	19	57
Public Health College											
Diplomas	—	—	—	—	—	20	—	29	17	18	84
Building College											
B.Sc.	—	—	—	—	—	—	—	—	—	4	4
Diplomas	—	—	—	—	—	—	—	11	7	12	30
College of Agriculture											
B.Sc.	—	—	—	—	—	11	17	28	24	44	124
GRAND TOTAL FOR ALL											
Degrees	—	—	13	9	16	40	48	86	96	116	420
Diplomas and Certificates	11	9	5	55	8	36	30	72	28	46	300

Source: Trudeau, "Higher Education in Ethiopia" (1964), p. 81.

20 in public administration; 27 in economics; 6 in commerce; 14 in prelaw; and 6 in the extension department.

Studies Abroad

Most of the graduates of the engineering, public health, and agriculture colleges, in contrast to graduates from UCAA, went directly to work after graduation. Their programs were geared to meet immediate high-level work force needs for the country, and these young people began to fill the void by serving as skilled engineers or technicians in the various departments of the Ethiopian government. For several years, all but six of the arts graduates of UCAA were sent overseas for further studies, as were ten students from the Faculty of Science who had obtained their B.Sc. degree in Ethiopia.[74] Then the Ethiopian government decided upon a policy that required graduates to serve at least one year in the country before going abroad for more studies; nonetheless, in the intervening years between 1952 and 1960 many young graduates left to pursue their studies in other countries.

As shown in Table 8, out of a total of 186 arts and science graduates from UCAA during the period 1954–1960, 150 students went abroad. Of these 150, 138 obtained at least one higher degree, reflecting an impressive academic success rate of 92 percent. Among those 138 successful graduate students, 12 obtained a doctoral degree (Ph.D., M.D., Ed.D., or D.Sc.), and 15 to 20 were continuing work with a doctoral degree in mind. This record speaks well for the quality of programs offered by UCAA.

Of the 138 who obtained a second degree, 44 were in business and economics. The next largest group, 30 degrees, was in education; 6 of the 12 doctoral degree holders were in education. On the whole, the distribution of qualifications was good, although at this level the nontechnological fields predominated.

Student Selection

What were the criteria that guided the selection and admission of Ethiopian youth for higher education? Despite the fact that birth and family connections were traditionally determining factors for promotion and reward, in most instances these factors did not operate in education in general and in higher education in particular. Certainly, educational opportunities were not open to all Ethiopians. Selection was based primarily on geographical location; a majority of the first university graduates, many of whom were subsequently to hold key positions in government, were drawn from Addis Ababa, Shoa, and Harar. Aside from this, *de jure* the selection of a "meritocracy" was the guiding policy for university

TABLE 8
Record of Graduate Studies Overseas of UCAA Graduates, 1954–1960

1 Graduation Year	2 No. of Graduates Arts	Science	3 No. Who Went Abroad	4 No. Who Obtained Higher Degree*	5 Earned Ph.D. or Equivalent	6 Failed to Get Higher Degree
1954	13	—	13	12	2	1
1955	9	—	9	9	2	—
1956	16	—	15	15	2	—
1957	23	6	28	26	2	2
1958	22	2	22	21	3	1
1959	45	1	43	39	1	4
1960	48	1	20**	16	—	4
Total	176	10	150	138 (or 92% of 3)	12	12

			% of Col. 2	% of Col. 2		
Grand Total	186		80.6%	74.2%		

*Approximately fifteen to twenty of these students are still working toward a doctorate degree.
**Not including those who might have gone abroad in 1964, or who might go abroad this summer.
Source: Adapted from Trudeau, "Higher Education in Ethiopia" (1964), p. 82.

admission. As one educator who held important academic positions for eight out of the ten years of UCAA's history pointed out:

At the foundation of higher education, a national policy of "equal opportunity for all high school graduates" determined all other policies on admission and standards. To implement such a policy, students were selected according to merit and were all given a full college scholarship that included tuition, board, room and additional fringe benefits, such as some clothing, free textbooks, free extra-curricular activities. The socioeconomic status of the students and of their parents was not considered: *de facto*, if it had been considered, less than 20% of the students who went to college would have been able to get a college education. It was seemingly an expensive affair; actually it was a real investment, which already has been repaid. It is the generation of students of 1950–1960 who, with a few who studied abroad between 1940 and 1950, are at present the backbone of the civil service of the country.

The same policy was in effect for graduate studies. All those who went abroad during those years were sent on full scholarship, either by the Imperial Ethiopian Government or by foreign governments and agencies.[75]

Whether providing all higher education free of charge to a few privileged individuals was a wise policy or not is obviously debatable.

Student Life and Organizations

In the 1950s, UCAA campus life was genteel and sedate. Student life and activities were regulated by the dean of students, the president's deputy in these matters, whose functions were defined by the college charter:

> There shall be a prefect of discipline who shall be called the "Dean of Students." His functions include:
>
> (a) the regulation and coordination of all extra-curricular activities, after the agreement with the Dean of each Faculty and school;
> (b) the drawing up and enforcement of particular regulations involving the conduct and behaviour of students;
> (c) the supervision of discipline, on and off the campus;
> (d) the ordinary exemption of students from disciplinary rules, and the punishment of minor infractions of the same.[75]

In the Ethiopian setting where parental control is emphasized in the proper upbringing of youth, the dean of students was considered an important administrative officer on the same level as the academic dean of each faculty on the council. His duties were clearly outlined as follows:

> He supervises *in loco parentis* and is given full authority and responsibility over all the non-academic activities of the students on and off campus, when they are acting as students of the University. His task is to supervise the discipline and behavior of the students, the administration of the dormitories and dining-halls, the health services necessary to protect and take care of the students' health problems, the occasional financial needs of the students, and finally the athletic, cultural and social extra-curricular activities of the students.[77]

There was also an assistant dean of women who resided in the female dormitory. A housemaster, usually a lecturer, lived in each men's dormitory and was responsible for order and discipline. If qualified and interested, he served as a counselor as well.

Regulations, especially during the early years, were very specific
and detailed, governing almost every aspect of the students' life.
For many, they were an extension of their home life.[78] Occasionally they were challenged by students, especially by the non-
Ethiopian African scholarship students who were accepted for admission to UCAA beginning in 1958. They felt that they were "han-
dling their own problems and affairs outside of the classroom."[79]
Early in the college's history, students formed their own student
government, at first under the guidance of the dean of students.
Gradually, however, it established its own identity and a strong
student union developed which, for all intents and purposes, was
independent of the dean's office. During its first year of existence,
the student union established its own council. This council was
charged with the organization of sports, social activities and clubs:
the drama club, the glee club, and the debating society. The students also published their own newspaper. It originated as a
newsletter and then became a weekly paper which was published
by an editorial board that was appointed or approved by the Press
and Information Office of the Student Council. Although a faculty
adviser was included on the board of editors, the college paper oper-
ated independently of the college administration. As Trudeau observed:

> The college paper has been, as was expected, the most revolu-
> tionary paper in the whole country.
> The mark of transition seems to have been the arrival at the
> University College of a group of students from other African
> countries. These students have been more involved in the poli-
> cies of their countries which were then gaining their political
> independence than the Ethiopian students; another transitional
> impetus was the contact with the international world of
> students.[80]

The political storm that overran the campuses in the mid-1960s
and 1970s had begun. The Student Council, elected by the students,
not only took charge of extracurricular activities, but also expressed
its nonalignment policy in international affairs by keeping in touch
with both communist and noncommunist international student organizations. Trudeau noted:

> A "wind of change," similar to the one felt in the interna-
> tional and national politics of African countries, swept the stu-
> dents' campus. Internally, this brought some temporary clashes
> and misunderstandings. Students became very sensitive to staff
> interference and even staff cooperation with students in the
> students' affairs. Advisers, even coaches for sports, were put

aside by many clubs and committees, and replaced by self-management. The Dean could no longer appoint coaches for students' teams, or select advisers for clubs and committees. Students would call for and select their own coach, if they wished to! For some time the college teams fell apart, the dramatic club lost its reputation, the glee club its audience. It was a necessary crisis, that of the phase of adolescence in student government. The staff understood this attitude and worked with the students, at their request, in a less paternalistic spirit.[81]

As the students became more politicized and open political discussions began to include criticism of long-established institutions such as the church, government authorities, and the emperor, the college staff wondered how to respond. Should they join the students or remain within the established order of Ethiopian society? There were many agonizing debates among the staff and in the minds of individual staff members.

The UCAA students joined with students of other colleges to form several community service clubs. These clubs were established for the express purpose of bridging the gap between academic ideals and the real world—to offer students an opportunity to observe life as the people lived it. They carried out literacy campaigns in the neighborhoods for scores of children and adults. There was no doubt that these student activities grew from a sincere desire to be involved, to help out, and, if possible, to bring about a lasting change for the better. The following is an interesting contemporary opinion:

> Are the teachers, administrators, economists, agricultural technicians, engineers and doctors that came from this 1950–1960 generation real assets to their country, new pioneers in a newly-developing country? Or are they a new "bourgeoisie," a needy establishment? Have the speeches and articles and strong debates of yesterday on "serving the nation" been transferred into action? Does Ethiopia have a new "autocracy" or a real meritocracy of service? The years 1960–1975 will give the answers and will provide the best evaluation of the type of citizens the institutions of higher education in Ethiopia have produced.[82]

The Staff

From 1951 through 1962 the Ethiopian colleges were, for the most part, staffed by foreign personnel. There were no qualified Ethiopians available for teaching. The few well-educated Ethiopians who survived the Fascist liquidation or returned from studies abroad before 1955 were absorbed by the civil service and held senior positions in various government departments. By 1955, however, Ethiopians began to join the colleges as lecturers or administrators; their number increased more rapidly than expected, reaching 25 percent of all full-time teaching staff by 1961–62.[83] In the meantime, the colleges were fortunate to attract and retain the services of many international faculty and staff.

At UCAA, foreign staff members were initially Canadian Jesuits, but gradually educators from many other countries were recruited by the college administration and appointed by the Board of Governors. At the College of Engineering, the Ministry of Education selected and appointed the staff on the dean's recommendation. At the Public Health College in Gondar the staff were primarily appointed by the international organizations that sponsored the college—WHO, UNICEF, and USAID. At the College of Agriculture the staff were recruited by Oklahoma State University and were primarily American. For a similar reason, the staff of the Building College were almost all Swedish. This faculty mixture—from North America, Europe, and Ethiopia—constituted an international amalgam of languages, cultural backgrounds, and educational experiences. As long as they worked together, the host benefited; when conflicts arose, they bordered on catastrophe. As a whole, the colleges were well staffed by qualified people. Even in the College of Public Health, for which statistics are not available, it was known that the college was staffed mostly by people with at least M.D. degrees or the equivalent who were selected and hired by United Nations organizations or USAID.

During the initial years, the student-staff ratio was uneconomically low, ranging from between four and seven students per teacher. As the years went by, some improvement in the student-staff ratio was realized, though, as in all teaching establishments, it was never possible to distribute the teaching load equitably.

Apparently there was no uniform set of policies governing the recruitment, appointment, promotion, or demotion of college personnel that applied to all the colleges, although UCAA had such a policy. However, Ethiopian personnel were paid in accordance with the civil service regulations of Ethiopia, which was less than that paid to foreigners. Staff members employed by international organizations were paid a salary and special allowances fixed by the United Nations; those hired by the U.S. Technical Assistance followed the scale set by the U.S. government; and those hired by the Swedish Technical Assistance followed their own policies. Salaries, allowances, and other privileges differed among the colleges for the same reasons.

At UCAA efforts were made to get the Ethiopian personnel salary scale revised upwards, but without success. Promotion and academic rank, on the other hand, were granted on common criteria, regardless of nationality. As far as the workload was concerned, UCAA staff members taught between ten and twelve hours weekly. In some rare instances the load increased to fifteen hours. "Very few staff members were hired as research scholars, and consequently very few did real research."[84] At this stage in Ethiopia's development, the colleges were teaching colleges, building on what the students had gained from their secondary education. "Academic freedom was not an issue in those first years of higher education. Professors were asked to abstain from religious propaganda and from political activities. Clauses to this effect were actually included in their contracts of engagement, and since teachers acted in accordance with these clauses, no issue was raised in this connection."[85]

Finance

Unfortunately, full financial records for all the colleges are not available but, from the meager information recorded, the following picture emerges: UCAA and the College of Engineering were financed, both for capital and operations, by the Ethiopian government. These expenditures were considered part of the Ministry of Education and Fine Arts budget. Total capital and recurrent expenditures of UCAA for the period 1950–51 to 1960–61 were Birr 12,290,000. About a third of this sum was allocated to capital expenditure. This left approximately Birr 8 million to be spent in eleven years to educate 2,378 fulltime students, at the rate of Birr 3,364 per student per year. Comparing these figures with those of other African countries, Trudeau observed that capital expenditures in Ethiopia were minimal and that by comparison the universities of Ghana and Nigeria were lavishly endowed with beautiful buildings equipped with modern library facilities and laboratory equipment. Yet, he also observed that current expenditures on higher education in Ethiopia could have been lower had there been closer cooperation and sharing of facilities among the various Ethiopian colleges.[86]

On the other hand, expenditures for the College of Engineering during 1959–60, for example, came to Birr 430,000, or about Birr 4,300 per student. Although higher than the per student annual expenditure at UCAA, this figure was low considering the technical nature of the college. The three other colleges—agriculture, public health, and building technology—were financed from joint funds through bilateral or international agreements between the Ethiopian government, foreign governments, and international organizations. Funds from these external sources provided significant assistance in meeting recurrent and capital costs. Detailed summaries of the financial outlays of the respective governments and international organizations are lacking. It was reported that between the years 1952 and 1962 the U.S. government, through the Oklahoma State University contract, contributed a total sum of Birr 18,418,410 to agricultural education in Ethiopia. This was, of course, in addition to the contribution made by the Ethiopian government, which in 1959–60 contributed an additional $1,859,745 to the Agricultural College.

The Public Health College received funds from U.N. organizations and from the U.S. government. Exact totals of expenditures are not available, but it is known that the U.S. government contributed $2,152,000 to the college's joint fund. In 1959–60, the budget of the Public Health College was $1,068,000 from all sources. In general, the three colleges financed by foreign aid were better off than the Engineering College or UCAA.[87]

Notes

1. Edouard Trudeau, *Higher Education in Ethiopia* (Montreal, 1964), 47. Trudeau completed his doctoral program at Teachers College, Columbia University, in 1968. The title of his dissertation is "Survey of Higher Education in Ethiopia with Implications for Future Planning and Development." Four years earlier he had brought out, in limited edition, the same work with the title *Higher Education in Ethiopia*, published in Montreal. The references cited in the present chapter refer to the 1964 edition.
2. Ethiopian Ministry of Education and Fine Arts, "Education in Ethiopia: A Survey" (Addis Ababa, 1961), 25.
3. Jean-D'Auteuil Richards, J.S., "Lucien Matte, 1907–1973" (Montreal, 1973), 1–23.
4. University of Utah Survey Team, *Higher Education in Ethiopia: Survey Report and Recommendations* (Provo: University of Utah, 1959–60), 1–2. See also Lucien Matte, "History of UCAA: An Outline Submitted to the Board of Governors," Addis Ababa, 21 January 1955, 1.
5. Trudeau, *Higher Education in Ethiopia*, 32–34.
6. Aklilu Habte, "A Brief Review of the History of the University College," *University College Review* (Spring 1961): 25.
7. Trudeau, *Higher Education in Ethiopia*, 35.
8. University College of Addis Ababa, memorandum from the President's Office, 18 November 1950 (AAU Registrar's Office), 1.
9. Sylvia Pankhurst, *Ethiopia: A Cultural History* (Woodford Green: Lalibela House, 1955), 655.

10. Trudeau, *Higher Education in Ethiopia*, 35–40.
11. UCAA, "Some Notes on the Development of the University College of Addis Ababa" (unpublished paper in the AAU Registrar's Office), 1–2.
12. Trudeau, *Higher Education in Ethiopia*, 36–40.
13. Ibid.
14. UCAA, "Some Notes on the Development of the University College of Addis Ababa," 1–2.
15. UCAA, "Memorandum from the President's Office to the Students," 6 July 1954 (in the files of AAU Registrar's Office), 1.
16. Ibid.
17. Ministry of Pen, *Negarit Gazeta*, General Notice No. 185 of 1954, "Charter of the University College of Addis Ababa," 28 July 1954.
18. Trudeau, *Higher Education in Ethiopia*, 42.
19. Ibid.
20. Speech delivered by the president of the University College at the first graduation on 26 August 1954 (unpublished three-page paper in the files of AAU Registrar's Office).
21. Trudeau, *Higher Education in Ethiopia*, 41–42.
22. Ibid., 42.
23. Ibid.
24. Ibid.
25. Ibid.
26. Ibid, 43.
27. Ibid., 44–45.
28. University of Utah, *Higher Education in Ethiopia: Survey Report and Recommendations*, 3.
29. Trudeau, *Higher Education in Ethiopia*, 44–45.
30. Ibid., 45.
31. Ibid.
32. "Agreement for a Cooperative Education Program between the Government of the United States of America and the Imperial Ethiopian Government," Article II (15 May 1952), 1.
33. Ibid.
34. Ibid.
35. Ibid.
36. Trudeau, *Higher Education in Ethiopia*, 46.
37. Ibid.
38. Ethiopian College of Agriculture, *Bulletin for the Academic Year 1961–62,* 12.
39. Ibid.
40. Ibid.
41. Ministry of Education, *Education in Ethiopia* (Addis Ababa, 1961), 27.
42. HSIU, *General Catalogue 1973–75* (Addis Ababa, Spring 1973), 172.
43. Ibid.; Trudeau, *Higher Education in Ethiopia*, 172.
44. University of Utah Survey Team, 11.
45. Building College, *Building College Bulletin*, no. 1 (Addis Ababa, 1959): 19.
46. Trudeau, *Higher Education in Ethiopia*, 47.

47. University of Utah Survey Team, 2, 7.
48. HSIU, *General Catalogue 1963-65*, 266.
49. Trudeau, *Higher Education in Ethiopia*, 52.
50. University of Utah Survey Team, 10.
51. Trudeau, *Higher Education in Ethiopia*, 54.
52. USA Operations Mission to Ethiopia, *Report on the Organization and Administration of the Ministry of Education and Fine Arts* (Addis Ababa: Cooperative Education Program Press, 1954), 35-36.
53. Lucien Matte, "History of UCAA," submitted to the Board of Governors, 24 January 1955.
54. Ministry of Pen, *Negarit Gazeta*, General Notice No. 185 of 1954, Article 37.
55. Akalework Habte Wold's letter of 11 December 1954 (Ret. No. 600/10454-66) on file in Addis Ababa University Public Relations Office.
56. Trudeau, "Higher Education in Ethiopia," 1964, p. 35.
57. Ibid., p. 56.
58. Board of Governor's Meeting Minutes of 21 December 1954.
59. Board of Governor's Minutes of 3 February 1955.
60. Trudeau, "Higher Education in Ethiopia," 1964, p. 57.
61. Ministry of Pen, *Negarit Gazeta,* General Notice No. 185 of 1954, Article 37.
62. Trudeau, *Higher Education in Ethiopia*, 58-59.
63. Ibid., 59.
64. Ibid., 60-61.
65. UCAA, *UCAA Bulletin, 1954-55 to 1955-56*, 25.
66. Ibid.
67. Ministry of Education and Fine Arts, *Controlled Expansion of Ethiopian Education* (Addis Ababa: Ethiopian-U.S.A. Cooperative Education Press, 1955), 37.
68. Trudeau, *Higher Education in Ethiopia*, 64-65.
69. Ibid., 65.
70. Aklilu Habte, "Brief Remarks on the Historic Development of the Department of Education . . . ," *Final Report*, Conference on Secondary Education in Ethiopia, HSIU (1-3 May 1962), 27-34.
71. Trudeau, *Higher Education in Ethiopia*, 65-67
72. UNESCO, *The Development of Higher Education in Africa* (Paris: UNESCO, 1963), 71.
73. Trudeau, *Higher Education in Ethiopia*, 75-76.
74. Ibid., 80.
75. Ibid., 83.
76. Ministry of Pen, *Negarit Gazeta*, General Notice No. 185 of 1954, Article 28. See also *Students Handbook* (Addis Ababa: UCAA Dean of Students Office, 1961-62), 2.
77. Trudeau, *Higher Education in Ethiopia*, 84.
78. UCAA, *Bulletin 1951-52 to 1952-53*, 40.
79. Trudeau, *Higher Education in Ethiopia*, 85.
80. Ibid.

81. Ibid., 86.
82. Ibid., 88.
83. Ministry of Education and Fine Arts, *School Census, 1961–62*, 18. See also Trudeau, *Higher Education in Ethiopia*, 92–93.
84. Trudeau, *Higher Education in Ethiopia*, 92–93.
85. Ibid., 93.
86. Ibid., 94–95.
87. Ibid., 95.

4

THE EMERGENCE OF A CONSOLIDATED SYSTEM

The establishment of the six Ethiopian colleges during the 1950s eventually led to the creation of a national university system. The idea of such a system was conceived in 1928 and renewed in 1949 with the appointment of a university committee. A site was selected in the southeastern part of Addis Ababa. The initial funding for the venture was to be drawn from taxes levied on civil servants and business people for the establishment of a monument to the emperor. The national university was to bear the name of the reigning monarch, Haile Selassie I, and was to symbolize the spirit and vigor of the new Ethiopia that was reestablished after five years of devastating war and destruction. At the groundbreaking ceremony on 7 November 1949, Haile Selassie I reiterated that: "The salvation of our country, Ethiopia, as We have repeatedly stated to you, lies primarily in education. As Ethiopia is one, all Ethiopians are also one, and education is the only way to maintain this condition."[1]

While UCAA was taking form in June 1951, the Vice-Minister of Education appointed yet another committee and asked it to consider certain propositions for the establishment of the Haile Selassie I University in Addis Ababa. The committee was asked to advise the Board of Education on the following: (a) general principles involved in the development of a university education in Ethiopia; (b) the courses considered desirable as plans for the first stage of construction of HSIU; and (c) questions of accommodation arising therefrom.

The committee developed plans that provided for an initial enrollment of one thousand Ethiopian and foreign students, both male and female, in the arts, teacher training, law, medicine, dentistry, and pharmacy. The committee also recommended a scholarship scheme, for both national and foreign students, which would be funded by the Ethiopian government and interested outsiders.

In the course of its deliberations, the committee tried to relate the new university to the entire educational system. This was a courageous exercise, but it was not based on statistical data. At that early stage, it should have been apparent that such a large enrollment in the anticipated university was impossible. Collectively, existing secondary schools were producing only a small fraction of one thousand graduates.

The committee opened an office on the site designated for the university campus. Plans, designs, and estimates were prepared by a group of Yugoslav architects. In 1954, when the UCAA Charter was being discussed, some members of the Board of Governors were undecided "whether it was really desirable that degrees should be conferred by a University College rather than by a University, and it was suggested that it might be better to start with a charter for the University itself."[2]

The Board of Governors of UCAA and the Board of Education raised the subject of HSIU during their several meetings. At the 38th meeting it was asked "whether there is not any possibility for the University College to become a full-fledged University." Dr. Matte, then president of UCAA, was asked to investigate this possibility.

In a memorandum dated 18 July 1957, Dr. Matte informed the board that, indeed, UCAA already consisted of the faculties of arts and science, a school of law and an extension department, and that there was a plan to open a faculty of commerce and a "proper Faculty of Law" within a year or two. He proposed, therefore, that the University College "become in September 1959 or 1960, the Haile Selassie I University." The president also suggested that a graduate school be organized in September 1959 consisting of three departments: education, administration, and Semitic languages (a scheme that was not realized until two years later). At the same time, he said, a school of medicine with four departments should be organized and agreements worked out whereby the other colleges could become affiliated with the university. Dr. Matte estimated that these plans would require a budget of $4 million which, he said, could be drawn from the existing HSIU fund.[3]

At this juncture, a struggle arose for control of the development of the university between Ministry of Education and UCAA officials. Both sides sought to gain the ear of the emperor who, after all, was the final arbiter in the matter. In an attempt to resolve the dilemma, it was referred to yet another committee.

At their forty-third meeting, the Board of Governors of UCAA decided that "the matter of unification of the existing colleges should be referred to the Board of Education,"[4] and in the spring of 1958 the emperor appointed a special committee of four to prepare a plan for "immediate action." On 14 May 1958 the members of this committee sent a memorandum to the emperor consisting of the following recommendations:

> Immediate action on the foundation of Haile Selassie I
> University, granting of a university charter, appointment of a

university president; Construction, on the proposed university campus, of an administration building, a medical school, a faculty of engineering, a faculty of law, a university library, an auditorium, residence for students and staff, a cafeteria, etc.; Affiliation of the existing colleges to the university.[5]

Apparently the emperor approved in principle the general provisions of the committee's memorandum. He ordered the secretary of the commission to ask Dr. Matte, then on leave of absence in Canada for health reasons, to come to Addis Ababa. Upon his return, Dr. Matte met with the emperor on 7 and 15 November 1958. During these two interviews, the president of UCAA was apprised of the committee's report and of the emperor's desires regarding the project. On 19 November, Dr. Matte sent a personal memorandum to the palace which set forth his ideas and plans for the project, including step-by-step suggestions to enable the university to open in September 1961. This was the last official contact Dr. Matte had with the palace on this topic.

The break in communications between Dr. Matte and Ethiopian government officials, including the palace, could have occurred for one of many possible reasons. Although the emperor had always shown full confidence in the loyalty and competence of the Jesuit leadership, it may be that he was persuaded that new approaches, philosophies, and personnel were needed to expand the state system of higher education. Furthermore, beginning in the early 1950s the Ethiopian government had entered into formal agreements with the United States government in the areas of culture, education, and defense. This new relationship allowed little room for a third party—especially one that was sectarian in nature.

In the latter part of 1958, Endalkachew Makonnen, a graduate of Oxford University, was appointed vice-minister of education and fine arts. The education portfolio was held by Haile Selassie himself. Endalkachew Makonnen was the first university graduate to occupy that post. He and the Board of Education took the planning for the new university into their own hands. He made tentative inquiries of London as to whether some kind of affiliation could be arranged between a British university and the projected HSIU. Shortly thereafter, the USAID Mission to Ethiopia and the new vice-minister of education agreed to submit a request for a survey of Ethiopian higher education to the U.S. government. In August 1959 the University of Utah agreed to supply a survey team charged with investigating the following topics and other matters inseparable from them:

The present status of higher education in this Empire and the situation with respect to secondary education; the needs to be met through a programme of higher education; define a step-by-step development programme to meet those needs and establish cost estimates for each step; define an organizational structure for higher education development; suggest plans for financing programmes; identify first steps to be taken; and prepare a report of the survey, preliminary and final.[6]

The survey team included the dean of extension (who was chairman), the dean of the medical college, the dean of students, the heads of the departments of chemistry, civil engineering, and educational administration, and a professor of business administration. While in Ethiopia, the group consulted reports and college bulletins and interviewed educational administrators and students in Addis Ababa and elsewhere. Most of the team stayed in Ethiopia for two months. In the introduction of their report, they noted that as a result of the very high demand for a skilled work force for the growing administrative structure of the public service, several colleges and faculties had been founded during the 1950s. In addition to the creation of several unrelated colleges, "a large and expensive programme of sending students abroad had developed."

As anticipated, the team provided a comprehensive report and recommendations favoring the creation of a new national university with strong centralized control that would incorporate all existing units and forms of higher education and teacher training in Ethiopia. To facilitate establishment of this university, they urged that the emperor appoint a Board of Trustees and other officers who would assume responsibility for the budget, personnel, and administration of scholarships no later than the 1961–62 academic year. The report suggested that a College of Education should be organized and teacher training and education should be a priority. They stressed the need to enroll more females in the schools as well as in the universities. Other major recommendations included establishment of a Center for African Studies; transfer of the College of Engineering to the main campus in Addis Ababa; reconstitution of the College of Agriculture; establishment of a Medical Division which would include a Medical College, a teaching hospital, and a clinic; organization of a Bureau of Counseling that would provide guidance and maximize returns on student investment; that English be emphasized as Ethiopia's language of learning; that as Ethiopians become qualified, they replace foreign personnel; and finally, "that a competent Evaluation Team' be brought in at least every three years to study and make sure that needs and interests of the country are being realized and met by the various departments of the university, that the objectives of the collaboration between the United States and other countries and Ethiopia are being attained, and to offer other useful suggestions.''[7]

The rest of the document contained detailed recommendations for a library system, finances, the development schedule, an organization chart, a specimen charter, and reports of the specialists for arts and science, business and public administration, engineering education, medical training, and teacher education.

The report was submitted to both the Ethiopian and the United States governments. Soon afterward, there emerged an agreement regarding the establishment of the Haile Selassie I University. However, an attempted coup d'etat in December 1960 delayed its implementation. On 28 February 1961 the charter of the Haile Selassie I University was published in the *Negarit Gazeta*.[8] In May the emperor appointed the first Board of Governors and by June agreements between the Ethiopian and United States governments were concluded. The U.S. government agreed to provide high administrative officials and make some capital available for construction of new buildings, equipment, additional personnel, and the like. An American academic vice-president, Dr. Harold Bently, was appointed to serve as acting-president until an Ethiopian president was recruited.

The convocation marking the founding of Haile Selassie I University took place on 18 December 1961 on the grounds of the Genete Leul Palace in Addis Ababa. Haile Selassie I was installed as Chancellor of the University and he addressed a huge audience of diplomats, cabinet ministers, faculty, students, and other citizens. Some excerpts from that lengthy address follow:

> A fundamental objective of this University must be the safeguarding and the developing of the culture of the people which it serves. This University is a product of that culture; it is the grouping together of those capable of understanding and using the accumulated heritage of the Ethiopian people. In this University men and women will, working in association with one another, study the well-being of our culture, trace its development, and mold its future. That which enables us today to open a university of such a standard is the wealth of literature and learning now extinct elsewhere in the world which through hard work and perseverance our forefathers have preserved for us. . . .
>
> Music, drama and other forms of arts are rooted in the ancient history of our Empire, and their development to an even higher peak of perfection will be possible in the atmosphere of a University. Ethiopia is possessed of an ancient literature, and its study can be fostered here so that the Ethiopian youth, inspired by this national example, may raise it to yet higher

levels of excellence. The study of the heroic history of Our Empire will stimulate the imagination of budding authors and teachers. The understanding of the philosophy of life which is the basis of our traditional customs will lead us all to a better understanding of our nation and our nation's expression through the arts. . . .

Time was when strength and endurance, courage and faith, were sufficient to make leadership equal to the task. But times have changed and these spiritual qualities are no longer enough. Today, knowledge and training, as provided largely in the universities of the world, have become essential, and today leadership and advancement, both national and international, rely heavily upon accelerated agricultural development, upon mineral exploitation and upon industrial expansion. Here survival depends on these, but they, in turn, depend upon the competence of those who have received and who will receive the essential education and training. It is Our confident hope that this institution, which has been planned for many years, will provide here, in our own land, for our own youth, the higher education and the specialized training required for such development. . . . From the universities . . . must come the ability which is the most valuable attribute of civilized men everywhere: the ability to transcend narrow passions and to engage in honest conversation; for civilization is by nature the victory of persuasion over force. Unity is strength. No nation can divide within itself and remain powerful. It is this strong conviction that underlies the decision to plan for the well-organized and co-ordinated system of education, training, and research which a university represents. . . . A university is the fountain of learning; seek knowledge, and there you shall find it.

Nor can we ignore the importance of the spiritual in the academic life. Learning and technical training must be nurtured by faith in God, reverence for the human soul, and respect for the reasoning mind. There is no safer anchorage for our learning, our lives, and our public actions than that provided by Divine teachings coupled with the best in human understanding. Leadership developed here should be guided by the fundamental values and the moral power which have for centuries constituted the essence of our religious teachings. . . . We charge all of you, the members of this University, that these special values remain foremost, as a foundation for your knowledge and thought, so that the fundamental moral truths will buttress and support the whole structure of University life.

Discipline of the mind is a basic ingredient of genuine morality and, therefore, of spiritual strength. Indeed, a university, taken in all its aspects, is essentially a spiritual enterprise which, along with the knowledge and training it imparts, leads students into more wise living and a greater sensitivity to life's responsibilities. . . .

Education is costly, and higher education is the most costly of all. But it is also an investment, a very profitable investment, and the money spent in coordinating, strengthening, and expanding higher education in Ethiopia is well invested. . . . We are proud of Our people's recognition of the value of education. Their concerted effort in the building of schools and other social activities is most gratifying. Educational institutions, unlike business enterprises, do not exist and operate for profits in dollars and cents. They exist to perform public services. . . .

The study of the humanities must not be neglected, and the college of Arts and Science must be strengthened and encouraged to develop its studies. These are the subjects which contribute most to the understanding and growth of our cultural heritage, and so assist in fulfilling one of the university's primary aims. These studies, which are concerned with human freedoms, will enable youth to develop the understanding and judgement necessary to the formulation of a sound philosophy of life, to the making of wise choices, and to understanding what is involved in these choices.

While laying great stress on education for our younger citizens, we should not forget the obligation and the opportunity which the University will have with respect to the older citizens. . . . Haile Selassie I University should attempt, either at this main site or at a branch, to serve every qualified citizen who wishes and is able to avail himself of the resources of the University if he is willing to do the required work.[9]

The objectives and ideals that inspired the creation of a national university were thus outlined. This was to be an Ethiopian university based on remaining true and responsible to, and delineating and expanding her national heritage. The humanities, the arts, the sciences, and technology were to receive their appropriate places and emphases in the scheme of program development and resource allocation.

At the formal opening ceremonies of the university, the emperor presented his main residence, Genete Leul Palace (Paradise of the Prince), to the university. Although the gift was dated long before the unsuccessful coup d'etat in December 1960, many knowledgeable observers felt that this decision was made in the aftermath of the attempted coup. The uprising by the Imperial Body Guard occurred while the emperor was in Brazil on a state visit. After several days of fighting between the coup leaders and loyal members of the armed forces, the fleeing rebels massacred eighteen of the senior government officials whom they had captured when the rebellion began. Several buildings were extensively damaged. The beautiful main palace building was little more than a shell of its previous splendor. It is most likely, therefore, that under such circumstances the emperor thought it proper to donate the palace buildings and grounds to the university as he moved to his newly-built Jubilee Palace some four miles south. Whatever the motivation, the gift was a welcome gesture for the university. Almost immediately it was put to good use as offices for the central administration as well as to house the Ethiopian Studies Institute offices, its library, and the museum.

As might be expected, there was no unanimity regarding the establishment of a university in Ethiopia where over 90 percent of the population was illiterate and where secondary school graduates still numbered fewer than one thousand a year. As Haile Fida, a graduate of UCAA, wrote, "A university in a highly illiterate society is almost certainly a little out of place."[10] Those who opposed establishment of a university argued that spreading fundamental literacy to the majority of the population should be assigned higher priority than investing in higher education for a few people. This argument was not without merit. Given the need for a skilled and semiskilled work force for social development, however, it could not be supported by many. In fact, the Addis Ababa Conference of African Ministers of Education, which took place at about the same time HSIU was founded, supported the principles adopted by Ethiopia, noting: "It is of the highest priority to ensure that an adequate proportion of the population receives secondary, postsecondary and university education; this should be put before the goal of universal primary education if for financial reasons these two are not yet compatible."[11]

The creation of a national university structure in Ethiopia was justified by still other considerations. Since 1949 it had been publicly announced by the emperor that such a university was forthcoming; his prestige and self-interest were at stake. In addition, the need to coordinate the several postsecondary schools that were sprouting up everywhere and competing for the same students and national resources was increasingly urgent. The total cost of operating these institutions in 1960 was about $6 million for fewer than one thousand students. Some departments were operating at a fraction of their full capacity for lack of qualified candidates. At the same time, many young Ethiopians were undertaking undergraduate studies abroad at considerable cost to the country.

Furthermore, a unified national university had a better chance of attracting badly needed external aid than did the separate institutions. In practice, this was true. Private foundations, friendly governments, and international organizations played increasingly significant roles in the realization of university goals once HSIU was established. Considering all of these factors, the establishment of the national university was wise and timely. In retrospect, few regret it, except perhaps the politicians who eventually became its victims.

Organization and Governance

The factors that influenced the establishment of HSIU determined its administrative and organizational structure—especially the need to unify the existing institutions of higher learning. One of the highest priorities was efficiency, including common utilization of available human resources, plant and equipment facilities, and control of expansion of all units of higher education in the country. For the immediate future, at least, HSIU was to be a highly centralized institution.

The HSIU charter, published on 28 February 1961, provided for administrative bodies and organs. At the head of the organizational hierarchy was the "Chancellor appointed by His Imperial Majesty where the Emperor did not assume that office."[12] The emperor was also to appoint a vice-chancellor who would carry out the functions of the chancellor when necessary. The chancellor was to preside over the convocations in which degrees, diplomas, and certificates were awarded.

Article 4 of the charter established a Board of Governors consisting of the president as ex-officio member and eight members to be appointed by the emperor, three of whom would be representatives of the ministries of education, agriculture, and public health, respectively. Once the graduates of HSIU numbered two hundred, they were entitled to elect a representative to the board.

Article 12 provided for the establishment of a Faculty Council of the university, consisting of the president, the vice-president, the deans of each faculty, the dean of students, the directors of departments or institutes where such units were not part of a faculty, and three members of each faculty elected by the full-time teaching staff. Article 13 stipulated that the president should act as chairman of the Faculty Council and the academic vice-president as vice-chairman ex-officio.

Article 15 provided that, subject to any general or special direction of the board, the council was empowered to maintain established faculties, centers, or institutes, to determine the degrees, diplomas, and certificates of proficiency to be granted by the university and the persons to whom they should be granted, and to grant such degrees or diplomas; to determine the general admission examinations and graduation requirements of students; and to settle disciplinary problems short of expulsion from the university.

The president was the chief executive of the university. Article 20(b) specified that each staff member would be "subordinate to him and shall carry out his directions and instructions whether given to him directly by him or through members of the staff to whom he has delegated responsibility." His other duties which required consultation with the council and the approval of the board were: to employ and fix the terms and conditions of employment of "all staff"; to prepare the annual budget for consideration by the board; and to be responsible for the proper expenditure and accounting of university monies.

Articles 25, 26, and 27 provided for the establishment, organization, and responsibility of each college, faculty, or school of the university, as well as procedures for determining the different ranks of the teaching staff. Articles 29 and 30 established academic commissions within each faculty or college and stipulated their duties. Duties included: determining the program of studies for the faculty and making changes in the program, "but not so as to affect the general academic policy of the University"; determining the annual and final examinations to be taken in the faculties; recommending to the council that appropriate diplomas, degrees, or certificates be granted; and resolving academic problems which concerned the respective faculties. With the dean as chairman, the membership was to consist of five persons elected by the fulltime teaching staff.

These provisions were similar to those recommended by the University of Utah Survey Team and to those of the UCAA Charter. There were, however, some important modifications to the structure recommended by the survey team. For instance, the recommended African Study Center never did materialize; instead, an Institute of Ethiopian Studies was established. The Asmara University Center was omitted (except for some extension programs), perhaps because of the establishment of the private University of Asmara. The proposal for "General Studies" was not incorporated, and Arts and Sciences emerged as separate colleges.

Centralization was facilitated by two important factors. First, the university was fortunate in attracting two dedicated Ethiopian university graduates. *Lij* Kassa Wolde-Mariam (later called *Dejazmach*) served as president of HSIU during one of its most crucial periods, from 1962 to February 1969. From February 1969 to 1974 Dr. Aklilu Habte, one of the first graduates of UCAA (1954) and one of the first two or three Ethiopians of the postwar generation to earn his doctorate (from Ohio State University), was president. Dr. Habte brought to the presidency a useful combination of academic qualifications, knowledge of Ethiopian society, and academic and administrative experience. These two young men provided competent, dedicated leadership in the face of overwhelming

126

problems. Ethiopian higher education owes them a debt of gratitude for their service in an atmosphere of political and economic upheaval.

The other important factor in HSIU's centralization was the relatively efficient operation of its Faculty Council. The Faculty Council functioned through an executive committee and standing committees; ad hoc committees were created from time to time to carry out specific tasks for the council. As of 1973–74 there were thirteen standing committees of the council: academic standards; board of admissions; curriculum, development, and finance; HSIU Editorial Board, Ethiopian University Service; extension; staff development and promotions; library; scholarship; training; grants; study abroad; and student affairs. All but student affairs were functional. The council expedited much of its business through these committees. The standing committees were responsible to the Faculty Council through the executive committee. All members were elected by the council.

The successful operation of the executive and legislative branches of HSIU facilitated integration of the various colleges and faculties. Once the process of integration had been completed, however, a tendency toward decentralization arose again. It was expressed in the wish to delegate more responsibility for day-to-day activities to the respective colleges and to departments within the colleges, and to establish the regional universities recommended by the survey team.

The university's role in relation to the external environment was more difficult to define. Its responsibility for service to the nation, its relationship with governmental departments and ministries, and questions of autonomy and university governance needed to be clarified and communicated to all segments of the population. These interrelated roles, so vital to university autonomy and academic freedom in relation to teaching, research, and service obligations, were under constant review by the Faculty Council and by the Chancellor's Advisory Committee on Higher Education.

The Search for Autonomy and Academic Freedom

As Sir Eric Ashby points out, the traditions of institutional autonomy and academic freedom in state-supported institutions of higher learning cannot be taken for granted. These concepts, precious and necessary as they are for the discharge of the university's responsibilities in the interest of all concerned, must be cultivated and understood among the general public that provides funding as well as moral support—the politicians, and all members of the university community.[13] If informed support for academic tradition is not forthcoming, the institution will inevitably suffer. When it was established, HSIU was one of the largest universities in sub-Saharan Africa and a new venture for Ethiopia. To survive and flourish as a center of warmth and enlightenment for the whole nation, many new trails had to be blazed and substantial obstacles had to be overcome.

The responsibility for establishing and nurturing autonomy and academic freedom was assumed by the Faculty Council and by the Chancellor's Advisory Committee on Higher Education. The development committee, whose membership was drawn from several internationally known colleges and universities, reported to the Faculty Council:

> All universities worthy of the title university operate under similar conditions; their ultimate responsibilities are their own jurisdiction. If these conditions were otherwise, the university would enjoy little confidence at home, less abroad; it would offer little attraction, little challenge to teachers of competence; it would not enjoy academic powers; it would never be able to serve the very ends for which it was created. . . .
>
> Obviously, a national university in a developing country must lay peculiar stress on its public service role; its relationship to government must reflect the fact that a national university in a country lacking expansive revenue resources represents a major public investment designed to promote goals of development and change as these goals are articulated through constitutional processes. *The investment must yield rewards measured in terms of our graduates' ability to contribute effectively to national progress. . . .*

On the issue of the mutual need for confidence between the university and the government, the committee continued:

> [the] university must enjoy the confidence of government, just as government reposes confidence in it through its Charter. Our budget, under the Constitution, is submitted through the Council Ministers; Parliament notes the taxes which provide our revenue. The public pays. To exercise the powers reposed in us, we must enjoy a confidence based on an appreciation of the precise natural role of the university. The university must demonstrate that within the limit of our resources and subject to our integrity as a university, and obedience to our Charter and other limits of the Empire we are committed to public service and goals of national development. Cultivation of this reciprocal confidence between the university and government

requires continuous interchange, co-operation and good will
in all essentials. We believe that this confidence exists and hope
it will continue to exist.[14]

These salient analyses were directed primarily to the government
which was still ambivalent about the role of the university in the
cultural, intellectual, and spiritual development of the society.
However, the university community—faculty, staff, and students—
needed reminders as well. By this time, there was increasingly clear
evidence that student leaders as well as certain faculty thought they
could use the university as a fortress from which they could mount
attacks on the government. This attitude, as we shall see later,
created a heavy burden for the infant institution as it struggled to
find its way into the hearts and minds of the Ethiopian public.

The president of the university at that time, Aklilu Habte, decided
to go further than the committee in challenging the university community. The reciprocal relationship could only be built, he said,
if the university was able to "use [its] autonomy to generate a commitment, a set of values . . . which will command respect for their
relevance."[15] Another committee of the Faculty Council added its
plea: "Having a diversity in our teachers and teaching programs,
tied to no particular foreign blueprint, enjoying a location at the
international capital of Africa, this university is in a position to
achieve a unique position among its peers. And it will, if pressure
for progress is maintained. With our administration, the Council
must maintain and direct that pressure."[16]

Vigilance was the order of the day. Academic freedom, like any
other freedom, is a perishable commodity. The Ethiopian academic
community was to learn this truth first hand in the coming years.
Pressures were brought on the university to coordinate its admission and graduation policies with the work force needs of the country. The UNESCO-sponsored Tananarive Conference of 1962
recommended that African college enrollment patterns establish a
goal of 60 percent in the science-technology areas, and 40 percent
in the humanities and social sciences. In addition, Ethiopia's shortage
of teachers was so acute that the government applied tremendous
pressure on the university to meet this critical national need.

The university's official position was that although it recognized
an overwhelming need for highly trained citizens in almost all areas
of the nation's economy and understood its responsibilities in meeting those needs, government work force planning was narrowly
conceived, inexact, and provided no opportunity for university personnel to provide assistance. The university asserted that it was dan-
gerous to think of high-level work force training as a mechanical
process whereby a given number of students trained in a given field

would automatically emerge as specialists capable of immediately relieving specific work force shortages. Motivation, academic standards, the relevance of what is taught to current professional requirements, and postacademic training are more decisive factors than are the size of the department or the number of students in a given production line. It was the university's position that the interests of the university and the nation would be better served by (1) involving qualified university personnel in work force planning, and (2) assuring the university a measure of latitude and freedom to pursue its academic goals without government pressure to meet arbitrary targets. To a degree, the university was successful in standing its own ground on this issue.

Equally difficult were issues surrounding the freedom to conduct research and to publish. A government regime that had absolute control over the media and all other forms of communication was apprehensive about allowing young academicians free rein. At the same time, the regime must have understood that the university, to remain worthy of its name, must be granted access to these commodities. At any rate, faculty were concerned about censorship and there were reports that government spies were planted in some classes. However, there were no major crises over these particular issues, probably because the largely foreign faculty practiced a degree of self-censorship, and most of their publications were in English and appeared in overseas journals. They were, therefore, of no immediate threat to the Ethiopian regime. In some instances, however, the government transferred university personnel to other nonuniversity positions.

The major crises for freedom were initiated by the student unions. Their radical political activism eventually led to police and later military intervention in campus life. Beginning in 1967, some students and faculty were humiliated and/or imprisoned; in 1969 some students were shot and killed. In the hope of staving off intervention by the armed forces, university authorities struggled to control these internal political elements, to contain campus political activism, and keep the police from the campus.

Nevertheless, the university's original desires, plans, and demands to be allowed to pursue its mandates unhampered by internal strife or outside intervention persisted. In the words of the Faculty Council's committees:

> The university, subject to the laws of the Empire which govern all persons generally and pursuant to its own, established internal law, is responsible for the recruitment, ranking, salaries, promotion and discharge of its staff. While presumably all university staff stand ready to give public service

when requested, the removal of university personnel or appointment to the university by outside bodies is inconsistent
with our Charter and inconsistent with recognized principles
of academic freedom. . . .

Subject . . . to the laws of the Empire governing all of us,
the university is responsible for student-university relationships
and student discipline.

Subject to the laws of the Empire, the university is free to
publish, without interference, materials which it believes are
of sufficient scholarly merit and utility to warrant its im-
primatur (italics omitted).[17]

These statements were directed primarily to the politicians of
the time but also to members of the university community. Nevertheless, university traditions such as autonomy and freedom must
be grounded in the minds and hearts of the national community
which, in the final analysis, determines the parameters of the institution. In other words, it is not enough for the university to dedi-
cate itself to the public good in a detached way by simply pursuing
the advancement and dissemination of knowledge. It must also in-
form and persuade the public that this detached dedication is a national necessity, or as Eric Ashby puts it, the university "must
educate the public into what a university is for."[18] HSIU, like many
other African universities, was unwilling or unable to do that effectively. The result was chronic misunderstanding. Years later, at
the height of the revolution, the university was without many
friends and extremely vulnerable to propagandistic attacks from
all corners.

Academic Personnel

The essence of any academic program is the quality and composition of the faculty. The Ethiopian national university was no exception. However, certain historical factors and conditions
complicated staffing considerations at HSIU. For one thing, the 1935
Italo-Ethiopian war and the subsequent five years of Italian occupation left the country bereft of an educated work force. As a result
of the destruction or exile of most young professional people, and
the total absence of any training during the occupation, a fresh start
had to be made. In 1941, then, the restored government began to
recruit foreign personnel to fill teaching positions in the grade
schools. This policy was still active in the 1960s. Therefore, when
HSIU was established, international faculty and staff were recruited
for all units. The results were mixed. On the one hand, the university was fortunate enough to attract some outstanding, well-
seasoned, and dedicated academicians. These people, whether in

administrative or teaching capacities, rendered wise and competent leadership to the young institution. On the other hand, many others were young (immature) and, though most meant well, lacked sensibility, understanding, tact, and competence in their dealings with young minds in the Ethiopian milieu.

On balance, reliance on expatriate staff brought with it some problems as well as advantages. On the positive side, expatriates contributed valuable international teaching and research perspectives and experiences as well as fresh insight into the problems and concerns of Ethiopia. On the negative side, the stiff competition in the international market for quality faculty; the high turnover; and the high salary, maintenance, and transportation expenses involved in hiring expatriate staff posed problems. The only sensible long-range solution to these problems was to recruit, develop, and employ competent Ethiopians to assume teaching, research, and administrative positions. A comprehensive policy covering the orderly "Ethiopianization" of university faculty and staff was needed.

The first documented proposal on this subject was drawn up by Dr. Aklilu Habte—then dean of the education faculty. The proposal, dated 27 October 1962 and addressed to President Kassa Wolde-Mariam, argued the imperative of "staffing . . . our university with qualified and competent Ethiopians at all levels and in all sectors."[19] The university, he said, could not continue to rely on expatriate faculty due to the great expense involved and the high rate of turnover. However, he also cautioned:

> we should not staff the university with Ethiopians who are not qualified merely for national prestige. Such a move would be destructive to the university, to the nation, and could indeed be labelled as being characteristic of young, inexperienced and immature policy. The only sound policy is therefore to prepare Ethiopians systematically . . . (while retaining) present and future staff by providing satisfactory (working) conditions.[20]

The document suggested specific plans for recruiting and sending promising young Ethiopian scholars to overseas universities. The funding for this venture would be obtained from the Ethiopian government, international agencies, and private foundations, as well as from bilateral arrangements with foreign governments. Recalling the fact that many Ethiopians were already studying in foreign countries, the document also provided plans to recruit some of these young people upon completion of their studies. In all cases, argued Aklilu Habte, "The principle to bear in mind should be to give the right person the right job at the right time. But," he added, "the absolute amount of salary paid to the young Ethiopian faculty of the time (24 percent of the entire faculty) as well as the discrepancies between what Ethiopians were paid compared to non-Ethiopians, was shocking and unsatisfactory. This," he said, "ought to be rectified."[21]

These recommendations seem to have been accepted in principle, but implementation was slow. For a long time afterwards, faculty positions at HSIU were filled by non-Ethiopians. Table 9 shows that the approximately 212 expatriates employed in 1973 represented fifteen different nationalities. At that time, 76 came from the United Kingdom, 70 from the United States, 16 from West Germany, 13 from India, and 12 from Sweden. Most occupied senior positions. The problems which arose from this diversity of languages, cultures, and philosophies were counterbalanced by the wealth of experience represented in the faculty, which enriched the educational and cultural experience of their students.

During the first decade of HSIU's existence, however, progress was made in the process of indigenization. Except for a few months in 1961 when the American Dr. Harold Bently served as acting-president, the position of president has been filled by highly qualified, competent Ethiopians. In 1961 almost all of the eight colleges and schools and most of the research institutes were headed by expatriates. By 1973–74 all of these posts were filled by Ethiopians. Moreover, at the instructional level, progress was also impressive. Table 10 shows that in 1973, 314 of the 446 academic administrative staff (or just over 70 percent) were Ethiopian. This is a remarkable achievement. However, a closer look at the figures reveals that most of the Ethiopians were below the professional rank and in the lower echelons of the academic hierarchy. There was not a single Ethiopian full professor until 1980 when two in the medical faculty achieved that position. This phenomenon may be attributed to the age and inexperience of the Ethiopian faculty, and the deliberate, sometimes unrealistically cautious, attitudes of the university regarding promotion.

The Ethiopian faculty and staff were all young. From the university president down to the level of research assistant, they were products of the post-World War II period. Most had received their credentials from foreign universities, and in the 1970s all were in their twenties or thirties. Most—perhaps all—were the very first university graduates in their family traditions.[22] Academic tradition, which is usually taken for granted in developed communities and other countries, was not a part of the cultural heritage of these Ethiopian intellectuals. This phenomenon was exacerbated by a lack of communication between the more mature but less educated senior officials in government and the university staff. As a result of this generation and education gap, there was increasing distrust, and

TABLE 9
HSIU, Expatriate Staff by Faculty and Nationality, July 1973

	American	British	Nigerian	Indian	Dutch	Swedish	Indonesian	Canadian	Egyptian	French	W. German	Italian	Polish	Sudanese	Belgian
Agriculture	12	—	—	1	1	—	—	—	—	—	—	—	—	—	—
Arts	15	20	—	—	—	3	1	4	1	2	1	1	—	—	—
Business Adm.	4	—	—	—	—	—	—	—	—	—	—	—	—	—	—
Education	10	13	—	3	—	—	—	—	—	—	—	—	1	—	1
Law	5	—	—	—	—	—	—	—	—	2	—	—	—	—	—
Medicine	—	10	—	4	—	4	—	—	—	—	3	—	—	1	—
Public Health	3	1	—	1	—	—	—	—	—	—	—	—	—	2	—
Science	8	11	—	2	—	4	—	2	—	—	2	—	—	—	—
Social Work	1	—	—	—	1	—	—	—	1	1	—	—	—	—	—
Technology	—	4	—	1	—	1	—	—	—	—	10	—	—	—	—
Theology	—	—	—	1	—	—	—	—	—	—	—	—	—	—	—
Inst. of Devel. Research	—	3	—	—	—	—	—	—	—	—	—	—	—	—	—
Inst. of Ethiopian Studies	—	1	—	—	—	—	—	—	—	—	—	—	1	—	—
Pathobiology	5	8	—	—	1	—	—	—	—	—	—	—	—	—	—
Freshman Program	—	1	1	—	—	—	—	—	—	—	—	—	—	—	—
Library	4	2	—	—	—	—	—	—	—	—	—	—	—	—	—
HSIU Press	—	1	—	—	—	—	—	—	—	—	—	—	—	—	—

(continued . . .)

TABLE 9 *(continued)*

	American	British	Nigerian	Indian	Dutch	Swedish	Indonesian	Canadian	Egyptian	French	W. German	Italian	Polish	Sudanese	Belgian
Registrar's Office	1	—	—	—	—	—	—	—	—	—	—	—	—	—	1
Testing Centre	1	—	—	—	—	—	—	—	—	—	—	—	—	—	—
Central Administration	1	1	—	—	—	—	—	—	—	—	—	—	—	—	—
Total	70	76	1	13	3	12	1	6	2	5	16	1	2	3	1
Percentage	30.2	32.8	0.4	5.6	1.3	5.2	0.4	2.6	0.9	2.2	7.3	0.4	0.9	1.3	0.4

Source: Computed from data obtained from HSIU, Office of the Associate Academic Vice-President for Staff.

The Guest Models

TABLE 10
Total HSIU Academic Staff, 1973–1974*

Faculty	Professor		Assoc. Prof.		Asst. Prof.		Lecturer		Asst. Lect.		Grad. Asst.		Tech. Asst.		Instructors	
	Eth.	Exp.	Eth.	Exp.	Eth.	Exp.	Eth.	Exp.	Eth.	Exp.	Eth.	Exp.	Eth.	Exp.	Eth.	Exp.
College of Agriculture	—	2	2	3	14	2	15	6	2	—	8	—	14	—	1	—
Faculty of Arts	—	3	5	—	14	12	11	20	3	8	5	—	—	—	—	—
College of Business	—	2	2	—	4	—	8	1	1	—	—	—	—	—	—	—
Education	—	2	3	1	12	4	4	1	6	—	2	—	4	—	14	13
Freshman Program	—	—	—	—	1	—	—	—	—	—	—	—	—	—	—	—
Law	—	3	1	1	2	1	6	—	2	—	1	—	—	—	—	—
Medicine	—	8	4	2	8	3	5	—	2	—	1	—	—	—	—	1
Public Health	—	1	—	—	2	1	9	—	9	—	2	—	—	—	2	—
Science	—	5	3	6	5	13	14	3	5	—	11	—	4	—	—	—
School of Social Work	—	—	—	—	3	—	2	1	—	—	1	—	—	—	—	—
Technology	—	3	3	5	11	1	16	4	3	—	2	—	—	—	2	—
Theological College	—	1	—	—	1	—	3	—	—	—	—	—	—	—	—	—
Inst. of Dev. Research	—	—	—	1	—	—	1	—	—	—	—	—	—	—	—	—
Inst. of Eth. Studies	—	1	—	1	1	—	1	—	—	—	—	—	—	—	—	—
Pathobiology	—	—	—	—	1	—	—	—	—	—	—	—	—	—	—	—
Dean of Students	—	—	—	—	—	—	—	—	—	—	—	—	—	—	7	—
Academic Administration	—	—	3	—	2	—	—	—	—	—	—	—	—	—	—	—
University Library	—	—	—	—	—	—	—	—	—	—	—	—	—	—	—	—
Total	—	31	23	20	82	37	95	36	33	8	33	—	22	—	26	14
%	—	100	55	45	69	31	73	27	80	20	100	—	100	—	65	35

*Includes those with no academic rank and excludes staff on study leave.
Source: HSIU Office of Associate Academic Vice-President for Staff.

eventually mutual contempt, between the two generations of intellectuals.[23]

There were, of course, more seasoned foreign faculty members who could have provided reasoned guidance. However, because of the nationalistic feelings held by the Ethiopians and the reluctance of foreigners to be drawn into the ferment of national politics, they seldom came forward. The result was increased polarization between administration and faculty, between the older and younger generations of the faculty, and between the teaching and nonteaching staff. The campuses at Addis Ababa, Gondar, and Alemaya were all negatively affected by the push and pull of these growth pains. Students were also drawn into these conflicts, seizing the opportunity to make indirect attacks on the government, and to criticize the faculty, whom they labeled "stone-age" (politically inactive) graduates.

As a state-supported institution, HSIU was very much in the government and the public eye. In a society where the concept and culture of a national university were unfamiliar, the internal issues that gave rise to open conflicts were perceived as an inability of the younger generation of highly educated, highly paid, privileged people to govern themselves. The traditional political regime, which began to feel that its values and institutions were under attack, seized opportunities such as campus turmoil to pontificate on the virtues of traditional Ethiopian values such as civility, obedience, and timidity toward one's elders, political leaders, or parents as anchors and beacons in the building of a stable society. For their part, many university staff members, particularly the younger faculty, perceived the university as a citadel or fortress from which the regime could be attacked—at least until 1974 when political events overshadowed everything else and all voices were silenced.

Despite these serious difficulties, the university struggled on. Fortunately, the two presidents who led it during the 1961–1974 period were outstanding. The first president, *Lij* (later *Dejazmach*) Kassa Wolde-Mariam, was a graduate of an American university and married to Princess Sebil Desta—one of the emperor's granddaughters. In 1962, after working for some time at the palace, he was appointed to lead the university during its formative years. He was viciously attacked by student leaders and some faculty because of his relationship to the royal family. Nevertheless, he brought to the office, on balance, unexcelled competence, civility, insight, and integrity. As president, he was articulate and generous. For those who worked closely with him he inspired confidence and loyalty. Eventually, however, long hours of work—year in and year out—took their toll and he asked to be relieved. In the winter of 1969 he was given the title *Dejazmach* (leader of the right flank, the third highest rank in the realm) and appointed governor of the Wollega region.

Unexpectedly, the emperor called upon Dr. Aklilu Habte to assume the presidency. This young man, following his return to Ethiopia, had served in various teaching and administrative capacities at UCAA and later at HSIU. He had a reputation for being radical, hard-working, and uncompromising on principles. At any rate, despite his considerable experience in senior, subpresidential positions, Aklilu Habte was not even in the position of academic vice-president when, surprisingly, he was suddenly appointed president in 1969.

A number of factors undoubtedly influenced Haile Selassie's appointment of Aklilu. By 1969 the student movement had been radicalized to the point that it was directly challenging the claim, position, and person of Haile Selassie himself. It may be, then, that the emperor thought that Aklilu, a man who had established himself as professional and progressive, would be able to quiet the agitation. He may also have been impressed with Aklilu's reputation for hard work and unassailable loyalty to his society. Aklilu served as president from 1969–1974. His term of office coincided with the onslaught of the revolution that eventually engulfed Ethiopia. As president, he provided strong leadership despite the fact that this was a most difficult period for both the university and the nation.[24]

At the lower levels of the administrative apparatus there were vigorous, competent leaders who, to their credit, contributed greatly to the development of the university. Along with a number of others were Aklilu Lemma, Mulugeta Wodajo, Fasil G. Kiros, Asefa Mehretu, Akalu Wolde-Michael, Germa Amare, and Mesfin Wolde-Mariam, and the American Jim N. Paul.

A presidential commission appointed to evaluate and plan the university's progress best summed up the situation prevailing in the second part of the 1960s. They noted:

> It must be remembered that the leadership of the university, the administration, the staff and most deans and department heads were, on the whole, new to their jobs and certainly inexperienced in developing a university in the context of a developing country. Some were foreigners who had to adjust to Ethiopia; all had to adjust to each other and to the totally novel circumstances of this university. At the highest level of the university, the administration has become increasingly over centralized, overworked, desperately pressed for time simply to think.[25]

Shortages of qualified staff at all levels, financial shortages, the increasingly volatile national political atmosphere, and the novelty of the institution in the Ethiopian milieu which made it a focus of suspicious attention, all threatened the development and growth of the institution. Despite these, the university continued to prevail.

Finance

An attempt to analyze the finances of HSIU is hampered by the lack of organized data. Nevertheless, a brief analysis of the sources and the means of financing the university's operations follows:

The university drew its financial support from external and internal sources. External assistance can be divided into seven broad categories: (1) program development, (2) capital grants, (3) loans for capital purposes, (4) cultural representation, (5) technical assistance, (6) faculty development, and (7) student scholarships.[26]

Though external assistance played a significant role, the largest financial burden was borne by the Ethiopian taxpayers. Ethiopian students received free tuition, board and lodging. Some paid a small health fee and some deposit against loss of university property. Otherwise, virtually everything was provided free to the student. This generous program of student support was financed by the central government treasury.

Recurrent Expenditures: Tables 11 and 12 show the composition of the recurrent budget, and a comparison between government appropriations for education in general, and the university's share of the total appropriation. In 1965-66, from the Birr 397 million appropriated for the total government budget (which represented a growth of 12 percent over the previous year), the education sector received Birr 52 million; from this, HSIU received Birr 10 million, or 20 percent of the total operating budget allocated for education. Over the years, while there was a noticeable decline in the rate of growth of the total government operating budget, HSIU's share remained more or less constant.

Table 13 shows the total government operating budget and the government appropriation for HSIU, as well as the rate of increase over a ten-year period. Throughout the period, the operating budgets of the government and HSIU remained constant or decreased. For instance, HSIU's share of the government operating budget in 1964–65 was just over 2 percent, and ten years later, in 1973–74, it was only 3 percent. However, a comparison of the rate of increase of the national operating budget and that of HSIU shows that the university improved its position.

From the total operating budget received, allocations were as follows: Over two thirds of the money went to instructional activities. The remainder was spent on educational services. Within the faculties and colleges, over 40 percent of the money was allocated to the science-technology areas, about 13 percent to the social

TABLE 11

Estimates of Actual Revenue and Recurrent Expenditure by HSIU, (Birr million)

1964–1965 to 1971–1972

	1964–65	1965–66	1966–67[a]	1967–68	1968–69	1969–70	1970–71	1971–72
Eth. Gov. Appropriation	8.55	10.25	10.25	10.85	12.15	12.54	13.15	14.15
HSIU Internal Revenue	–	–	–	0.58	0.61	0.55	0.62	0.71
External Assistance	7.70	7.70	10.71	10.21	9.00	13.23	8.60	8.60[b]
Total Operating Budget	16.25	17.95	20.96	21.64	21.76	26.32	22.37	23.46

(a) Opening year of Medical Facility
(b) Estimate

Note: There appear to be slight discrepancies between this table and the others in this category due to the sources, but they are not significant enough to change the meaning.

Source: Fassil G. Kiros, *et al., Education Sector Review Final Report: Financing Education* (Addis Ababa: Ministry of Education, 8 July, 1972), Annex III-L.

TABLE 12
**HSIU's Share of the Total Government Operating Budget Appropriation
for Education (Birr million), 1964–1965 to 1973–1974**

Fiscal Year	Total Govt. Operating Budget	Growth Rate in %	Government Appropriation For Education	HSIU's Share of Gov. Education Appropriation	HSIU's Share in % of Gov. Education Appropriation
1964–65	330.4	—	48,143	8,454	17.6
1965–66	397.4	20.3	51,616	10,247	19.9
1966–67	425.8	7.1	62,560	10,247	16.4
1967–68	453.2	6.4	50,269	10,847	21.6
1968–69	497.1	9.7	60,400	12,148	20.0
1969–70	501.4	0.9	70,462	12,539	17.8
1970–71	516.2	3.0	75,383	13,150	17.0
1971–72	538.3	4.3	85,519	14,150	16.6
1972–73	583.2	8.3	99,056	15,150	15.3
1973–74	—	—	113,694	16,901	14.9

Source: 1. HSIU, Office of the Vice President for Business and Development, 22 Dec 1973.
2. HSIU, Planning Office, "Haile Selassie I University Assessment of Accomplishments 1961–1965 E.C.," p. 23.

TABLE 13

Relation of Government Operating Budget Appropriation for HSIU to Total Government Operating Budget (million current Birr), 1964–1965 to 1973–1974

Fiscal Year	Total Govt. Operating Budget	Govt. Appropriation For HSIU	% of Govt. Operating Budget	Percent of Increase	
				Government Operating Budget	HSIU Appropriation
1964–65	356.4	8.5	2.38	—	—
1965–66	397.7	10.2	2.56	11.59	19.90
1966–67	425.8	10.2	2.39	7.06	—
1967–68	453.2	10.8	2.38	6.43	5.90
1968–69	497.1	12.1	2.43	6.69	12.00
1969–70	501.4	12.6	2.39	0.87	3.20
1970–71	516.2	13.2	2.56	2.95	4.90
1971–72	538.3	14.2	2.64	4.28	7.60
1972–73	584.2	15.2	2.60	8.53	7.07
1973–74	620.9	16.9	2.72	6.28	11.50

Note: Differences between this Table and the previous one were in the sources.
Source: HSIU, Office of the Vice-President for Business and Development, 22 December 1973.

sciences, and the rest was divided among the other academic programs. This pattern of expenditure, perhaps with the exception of the teacher training program, was in accordance with major university policies. Considering the critical need for school teachers, allocations to teacher training programs were impressive.

The percentages paid out in salaries and in nonsalary costs over a three-year period are summarized in Table 14. In 1971–72, 70 percent of the operating budget went to salaries and only 30 percent to nonsalary costs. For the last two years shown, however, salary costs were decreasing while nonsalary expenses were increasing. Assuming that the savings in salary costs were not realized at the expense of a sound personnel policy, this trend was healthy.

Capital Investment: Most of the funds for capital development were obtained from external sources. Table 15 indicates the proportion of capital funds allocated from Ethiopian and external sources. Of the Birr 15 million invested between 1965–65 and 1969–70, only one million came from internal sources. The rest was obtained either as loans or grants. Since that time, capital expansion has been hampered by lack of funds. As a result, the university has been unable to accommodate the growing number of qualified candidates for admission.

Table 16 and the accompanying Figure 5 illustrate the discrepancies between HSIU's capital needs and the government's ability to meet them. In 1971–72 the university requested about 9 million dollars. The actual appropriation was half the amount requested. During the subsequent three years, HSIU managed to get an average of 55 percent of what it requested. This was unsatisfactory but, for reasons which will be discussed later, there was not much that could be done to alter the situation. The availability of capital investment funds for construction, equipment, library, and textbooks was a serious problem then and continues to be one today. One solution is to transfer part of the cost of student maintenance to the students themselves, thereby releasing funds for capital development.

Financial Constraints: HSIU's lack of adequate financial support has always been a major problem. This has been reflected in the backlog of physical plant and equipment maintenance, delays in building programs, and expenditures for tuition and student support.

Within the university, instructional costs per student varied among the several faculties or colleges. Figure 6 presents the cost differentials among the twelve faculties, the amount of money provided by the Ethiopian government, aid or loans obtained from external sources, and the average instructional cost per student. In 1968–69 the faculty of medicine was the most expensive

143

TABLE 14
Percentage of Financial Resources Allocated for Salaries, (Birr) 1971–1972 to 1973–1974

Programs	1971–72		1972–73		1973–74	
	Salaries	Non-Salary Costs	Salaries	Non-Salary Costs	Salaries	Non-Salary Costs
Faculties & Colleges	87.0	13.0	86.0	14.0	87.0	13.28
Educational Services	65.0	35.0	70.0	30.0	72.0	28.00
Student Services	18.0	82.0	18.0	82.0	16.0	84.00
Administrative Services	57.0	43.0	60.0	40.0	57.0	43.00
Total University	70.19	29.81	69.84	30.16	68.53	31.47

Source: AAU, Office of the Vice-President for Business and Development, 22 December 1973.

TABLE 15
Capital Investment Program,
1965–1966 to 1969–1970 (in Birr)

Year	Project	Source of Money	Amount	Total Investment
1965–66	New Classroom Building	Ethiopia	871,240	
		Loan from Contractor	1,000,000	1,871,240
1968–69	Utilities	Ethiopia	37,000	
		Federal Republic of Germany	8,750,000	8,787,000
1968–69	Law Students' Dormitory	Ethiopia	121,000*	121,000
1969–70	Technical Education Building	Construction Loan From IDA	479,000	
		Equipment Loan from IDA	500,000	
		Small Equipment USAID Grant	125,000	1,104,000
		Kennedy Memorial Library Construction— USAID Grant	2,473,885	
		Furniture— USAID Grant	1,091,950	3,565,835

Total Ethiopian Contribution		1,029,240
Total External Assistance		14,419,835
Grand Total	Birr	15,449,075

*Includes contribution from Ethiopian citizens and foreign residents.
Source: AAU Planning Office.

(Birr 11,300 per student per year), followed by theology, social work, law, building (engineering), public health, education, science, business, and, finally, the arts. The high costs per student in theology and social work may be due to the fact that these colleges were not functioning at full capacity. In subsequent years, when enrollment reached optimum size, instructional costs per student decreased.

Figure 5 dramatically illustrates that as the number of students increased, the amount of the Ethiopian government's appropriation decreased significantly. The reasons for the apparent inability

TABLE 16

HSIU Budgetary Appropriations and Actual Expenditures on Capital Projects (Birr Million), 1971–1972 to 1974–1975

Fiscal Year	University's Proposal			Government Appropriations			Actual Expenditures			Ratio of Approved Budget to Request
	Eth. Govt.	Loan	Total	Eth. Govt.	Loan	Total	Eth. Govt.	Loan	Total	
1971–72	4,211.5	4,609.6	8,821.1	933.5	3,597.4	4,530.9	887.6	4,013.6	4,901.2	0.51
1972–73	5,912.6	5,711.2	11,623.8	2,690.0	3,050.0	5,740.0	2,541.1	3,050.0	5,591.1	0.49
1973–74	4,318.7	3,702.8	8,021.5	1,173.6	3,702.8	4,876.4	—	—	—	0.61
1974–75	5,791.7*	1,455.3	7,247.0	2,093.0	1,805.4	3,898.4	—	—	—	0.54

* The budget for 1974–75 was still in the approval process. The figure indicated under the approved column is, therefore, the figure recommended by the Planning Commission for approval by the Government Budget Committee.

Source: HSIU, Office of the Vice-President for Business & Development.

146

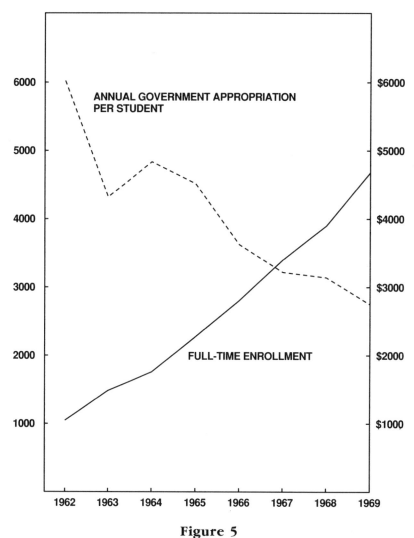

Figure 5

**Enrollment and Annual Government Appropriation
Per Student for Operating Expenses, 1962–1969**

of the government to increase its appropriation may be the slow
growth of national revenue; the lack of growth of land-based taxes
in relation to the actual growth of land income; the fundamental
stagnation in import duties due to the changing composition of imports; and, more generally, the lack of a progressive income tax
to compensate for stagnation in other revenues.[27]

147

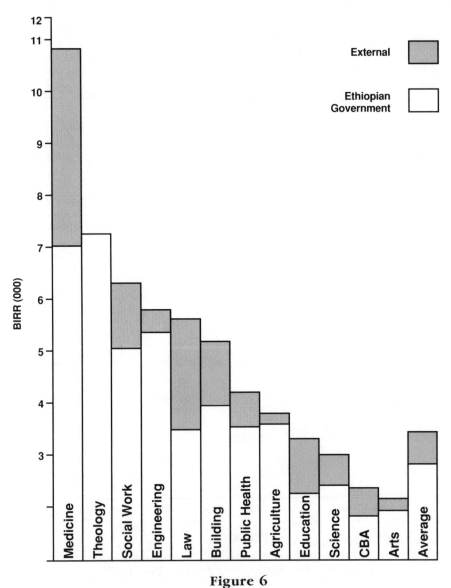

Figure 6

**Per Student Instructional Costs by Faculty and
Source of Funding, (Birr 000) 1968–1969**

The relative decline in government appropriations to HSIU may
be attributed to a shortage of national revenue rather than to
an unwillingness to appropriate adequate funds for university

programs. However, the government was unwilling or unable to devise a loan scheme that would shift some of the cost of student support to the students themselves or their parents. Though such a policy was accepted in principle by the Board of Governors, the Faculty Council, and the university administration, it was never implemented.[28]

The HSIU budget process was the subject of study and comment by a number of individuals and committees representing the university as well as donor agencies. Among the most important studies were the two undertaken by the Chancellor's Advisory Committee on Higher Education—the first in 1966 and the second five years later. In 1966 the committee found that HSIU budgeting and planning left much to be desired:

> A firm base for university planning must be established. This brings us to a comment which is central to our whole report. We were dismayed to find that those who have to determine policy in the University are unable to make forward plans because the University's income is not assured for more than a few months ahead.
>
> A University's commitment is to the future. Every student admitted is a financial obligation for four years to come. Every faculty member engaged . . . involves similar financial obligations. A decision to erect a building commits the University to expenditures five or more years ahead, and to higher operating costs. These decisions must be controlled by plans.
>
> A University's budget is the translation of an academic plan into financial terms. As such it is essential for both planning and operation.[29]

The advisory committee reassessed the situation in 1971. In their second report, the committee commended the government for "its substantial and growing support of the University." They also noted that foreign agencies and foundations were providing significant support to the university. However, they went on to say that as nongovernmental funds and foreign aid recede, the "Government must give high priority to further support for higher education."[30]

The committee identified the following potential sources of additional university income:

(a) payment by parents of all or part of the cost of higher education for their children (with provisions for scholarships for those who were unable to pay)

(b) student employment, so that students could earn part of the cost of their education by working for the university or elsewhere

(c) foundation support for special programs as well as general operating costs

(d) local support where possible

(e) corporate support for scholarships or special programs

(f) student loans or a pay-as-you-earn system "in view of the fact that University graduates owe their higher earning capacity in part to education received through Government support, it is wholly just to expect them to repay at least part of the cost of the education that enabled them to earn more. This appears in Ethiopia to be not only just but necessary"

(g) cooperation with other African universities in the provision of scholarships[31]

It was clear that the traditional sources of support were unable to accommodate the growing demand for expansion. Securing additional sources of revenue and improving the efficiency of available resources were critical challenges. As we shall see, as the consolidation of the various programs took effect, some gains in program efficiency—one of the major goals of the consolidation efforts—were realized.

Notes

1. Ministry of Information, *Selected Speeches of His Imperial Majesty Haile Selassie* (Addis Ababa: Ministry of Information, 1967), 1–3.
2. Edouard Trudeau, "Higher Education in Ethiopia" (Montreal, 1964), 101.
3. Ibid., 101–2.
4. Ibid., 102.
5. Ibid.
6. University of Utah Survey Team, *Higher Education in Ethiopia: Survey Report and Recommendations,* 9–10.
7. Ibid, 25–28.
8. Ministry of Pen, *Negarit Gazeta*, General Notice No. 284 of 1961, Haile Selassie I University Charter, Article 17 (a), (b), (c); Article 18.
9. Ministry of Information, *Selected Speeches of His Imperial Majesty Haile Selassie I*, 19–27. See also *Ethiopian Herald*, 20 December 1961, 3.
10. Haile Fida, "Do We Need a University?" *UCESA Educational Journal* 2 (Addis Ababa: University College Education Students Association, 1963–64): 18; Trudeau, 110.
11. UNESCO-ECA, *Final Report: Conference of African States on the Development of Education in Africa*, Addis Ababa, 15–25 May 1961 (Paris: UNESCO/ED/181, 1961), 10.
12. Ministry of Pen, *Negarit Gazeta*, General Notice No. 284 of 1961, Haile Selassie I University Charter, Article 17 (a), (b), and (c); Article 18.

13. Sir Eric Ashby and Mary Anderson *Universities: British, Indian and African: A Study in the Ecology of Higher Education* (Cambridge: Harvard University Press, 1966).

14. Aklilu Habte, *A Forward Look: A Special Report from the President* (Addis Ababa: Haile Selassie I University, 1969), II-17. Also see "Interim Report of the Development Committee to the Faculty Council," (Addis Ababa, HSIU, December 1965), 1-12 (mimeographed).

15. Aklilu Habte, *A Forward Look*, II-17.

16. "Interim Report of the Development Committee to the Faculty Council," December 1965, 2.

17. Ibid., 7-8.

18. Sir Eric Ashby, *African Universities and Western Tradition* (Cambridge: Harvard University Press, 1964), 28-29.

19. Aklilu Habte, "Plan for the Ethiopianization of Staff at Haile Selassie I University," (Addis Ababa, Haile Selassie I University, 27 October 1962), 2-3.

20. Ibid.

21. Ibid., 5.

22. There were several Ethiopian men and a few women who had graduated from European or American universities before the 1935–1941 war and occupation period. However, none of these people nor their offspring found a way into the university. The few who survived the occupation period were attracted to the civil service where they held prestigious senior positions as cabinet ministers or administrators.

23. One must refer to such intellectual giants in the best of the Ethiopian tradition as the late Merse Hazen Wolde-Kerkos, and the brilliant economist, Yilma Deressa. Although these two men served as chairmen of the Board of Governors for a long time, their impact on the intellectual maturity of the university remained, at best, indirect.

24. It is reported that in the late 1950s, when the emperor learned that a certain student of UCAA had criticized his government, he directed that the student not be awarded a diploma at graduation. On the day of the ceremony, the emperor presiding, Aklilu Habte, as dean, read the student's name. The emperor was obviously embarrassed, but eventually awarded the diploma.

25. Presidential Commission on Planning, Reorganization and Consolidation of Academic Programs of the University, "Final Report," Haile Selassie I University, June 1968, 7 (mimeographed).

26. John Summerskill, *Haile Selassie I University: A Blueprint for Development* (Addis Ababa: Haile Selassie I University, 1970), 137–59.

27. Ibid., 132-33.

28. Ibid.

29. HSIU, *First Report of the Advisory Committee on Higher Education to His Imperial Majesty Haile Selassie I, Chancellor of the University* (Addis Ababa: Commercial Printing Press, 1966), 19-20.

30. Ibid., 20, 24-25.

31. HSIU, *Second Report of the Advisory Committee on Higher Education to His Imperial Majesty Haile Selassie I, Chancellor of the University* (Addis Ababa: Commercial Printing Press, 1971).

5
ACADEMIC PROGRAMS, STUDENTS, AND RESEARCH, 1961–74

At the inception of the Ethiopian national university, the concerns, apprehensions, and uncertainty expressed by members of the national community concentrated on several factors: that it was a secular institution, modeled on foreign ideas and staffed by foreigners, and offered instruction primarily in English. These concerns were expressed both formally and informally. The official speeches emphasized the responsibility of the university to the Ethiopian essence—its economics, culture, and need for renewal and development. The morning after the inauguration of HSIU, the prominent daily newspaper, *The Ethiopian Herald*, summarized these expectations: "It is hoped [that] this University will dig out Ethiopia's glorious past and preserve the best part of her traditions."[1] The national hope was that HSIU would authentically root itself in Ethiopian soil; excel in discovering, reconstructing, improving, and expanding the cumulative heritage of this ancient land; and at the same time address the development questions of the country and share skills and knowledge among all members of the human community.

In 1966 and again in 1971 the Chancellor's Advisory Committee on Higher Education reiterated the paramount nature of the university's responsibility to the local community as the university evolved to conform to standards of international academic excellence. The committee observed that HSIU had a dual responsibility: (1) to the community it served, and (2) to the international fraternity of universities. If it failed in the first, it did not deserve the support of the people. If it was weak in the second, its credentials would not represent a respectable standard of learning and its graduates would not have full access to the other universities in the world and the opportunities they could offer. The way to meet these challenges and responsibilities was to teach and conduct research on subjects relevant to Ethiopian needs, and to perform these teaching and research functions in a manner that conformed to international standards of accuracy and integrity.[2]

Initially, Ethiopian academic policies were based on imported thoughts and experiences. By the late 1960s, however, the disadvantages of relying on borrowed models became increasingly apparent. The need for a thorough rethinking and the possible realignment of academic programs to conform to the realities of Ethiopia became pressing.

It was no doubt understood from the beginning that any first-rate university should consider research to be one of its major functions. However, due to limited resources and the urgent need for trained personnel in almost all areas of national life, in its early years the university regarded its main function as that of providing excellence in teaching at the undergraduate level.[3] Having decided on that, the next step was to design programs that would have primary relevance to the social and cultural development of Ethiopia and other developing countries. However, the goal of establishing a balanced range of such programs continued to be elusive. As a result, in 1967 the university established a presidential commission to streamline program policies. Its recommendations were gradually adopted over several years.[4]

Student Life and Characteristics

HSIU was established in a country with deep-rooted traditions and customs, a country inhabited by groups with different linguistic, religious, and ethnic traditions, and a country in which most citizens made their living by cultivating the land or raising cattle. These various cultural, geographic, and economic backgrounds were reflected in the characteristic composition of the student body.

Few studies on the socioeconomic background and the educational and career aspirations of HSIU students have been undertaken. Considerable research in this area is required if the university is to be effective in educating and leading youth. The educational process in Ethiopia can improve only when the psychology and sociology of the Ethiopian student is better understood.[5]

One study, carried out by R. Giel and J. N. Van Luyk of HSIU, was a longitudinal study of 1,066 freshmen who entered HSIU in 1966. According to their findings, the student body at HSIU was primarily male. Approximately 60 percent of the students entering the university were under twenty years of age and 90 percent were under twenty-five. The largest single group of students (38 percent) came from farms; about 16 percent had fathers who were merchants or clerks; and 10 percent had fathers who held high governmental or judicial positions. As far as ethnic background was concerned, 45 percent were Amharas, 26 percent Tigre, 10 percent Oromo, 4 percent Gurage, and 15 percent from other ethnic groups. Approximately 66 percent said that Amharic was their first language. Regarding religion, 83 percent were Orthodox Christians, 10 percent Protestants or Roman Catholics, and 7 percent Muslim.

Of the freshmen studied, 20 percent came from Addis Ababa, 4 percent from Asmara, 10 percent from provincial capitals; and 66 percent from towns and villages. However, most reported that they had moved to larger cities for their secondary education. Thus, 53 percent attended high school in Addis Ababa, 80 percent in Asmara, and 21 percent in other provincial capitals. A large proportion of the students (72 percent) received no support of any type from home. At the time of the study 63 percent lived in university hostels, 14 percent in rented houses or rooms off-campus, 12 percent lived with their families, and 11 percent lived with relatives or teachers.

One third of the students stated that they considered Addis Ababa their family place of residence, while about 50 percent reported that their family was more than one day's travel from the capital. Two thirds of the students indicated that they were not living with their families prior to entering the university. However, the majority of the students said that, despite the distance involved, they visited their families "often" or "occasionally." Finally, 50 percent of the students said that they came from broken homes and one third said that one of their parents had died.

Regarding medical treatment at HSIU, 60 percent had sought medical treatment in the twelve months prior to entering the university. The most common complaints were diseases of the eye (24 percent), nosebleeds (13 percent), intestinal parasites (11 percent), gastric complaints (8 percent), dysentery (8 percent), and gonorrhea (7 percent). About one third of the students complained of emotional stress.

As far as academic performance was concerned, during the first year 29 percent failed or dropped out. However, whether or not the students entered the university through the ESLCE did not seem to affect their academic performance. "In general, family and ethnic background factors were not related to academic performance in the first year."[6]

In summary, Giel and Van Luyk said that they were "impressed by the endurance of the Ethiopian student and his willingness to pursue his education at all levels without significant material and immediate emotional support from his closest relatives. Under these circumstances, it is not surprising that a third of the freshmen indicated that they had symptoms of psychological distress before entering the University and that more than a third visited the student health clinic with minor complaints during their first semester at the University."[7] The student characteristics delineated by the Giel and Van Luyk study shed some light on student life at HSIU.

In September 1969 the president of HSIU reported: "Student unrest—a worldwide problem—has been of deep concern here. We have had our share of crises over the past five years; and today, with finance and planning, the sector of student affairs presents a most difficult and urgent challenge to our institution."[8] This was an appropriate assessment of the situation and it remained so for some time. Obviously both the problem of student unrest and the measures taken by the police to control it had roots in the tension between the nature of Ethiopian society and the new, secular national university.

To begin with, HSIU students were the first generation to attend a university in Ethiopia. Relatives, most being illiterate, were unable to understand or communicate with their offspring. In turn, since the values and beliefs held by the older generation came into being to meet the prescientific needs of a traditional conservative society, they were rejected by the students. This rejection was then extended to include the values, ideas and beliefs of most authorities, including those in high positions in traditional religious and political institutions. The generation gap, coupled with the tremendous educational gap, fostered feelings of alienation between university students and their elders.

At the same time, the university was a state-supported institution where students were increasingly challenging the social and political status quo. The government under Emperor Haile Selassie, basing its argument on traditional values of obedience to one's elders and willingness to be guided by them, was at times patient but progressively dealt with student demands unyieldingly. There were clashes between the police and students; classes were interrupted and students were suspended from the university. Many hours of instruction and much university property were lost over the course of nine years. As the years went by, the university became a vast, impersonal community. Contact between staff and students was limited and formal. In 1969 Aklilu Habte noted that "it has become harder and harder for students to secure an identity within the institution, and to identify with it."[9]

Attrition was another problem. Its causes were many and varied, but its occurrence influenced the feelings and attitudes of the students.[10] The president summarized the problem and its effects as follows:

> Students in Ethiopia . . . desire to participate in the political process, to articulate their concerns, indeed the "demands" for reform felt by many younger citizens. Student leaders at Haile Selassie I University . . . have become increasingly militant in carrying on this political activity. This year [1969] confrontation with the government produced a temporary disruption of the University, the withdrawal of about two-thirds of the full-time student body, the arrest of some students

and a waste of no less than Eth. $4 million of the taxpayer's money. . . . The additional social and psychological costs of this disruption are immeasurable, but plainly serious.[11]

After 1964, a number of reports on student activities were submitted to the Faculty Council, including the Report of the Special Student-Staff Presidential Commission of 1964; the Awad-Strauss Report of 1967; and the Student Affairs Committee Report of September 1968. These documents covered a wide range of issues, influenced Faculty Council policies, and included a series of reports from the Student Affairs Committee that addressed issues related to housing, nutrition, student health, sports, and discipline. In 1969 the present author, as dean of students, submitted a comprehensive annual report which included a review of the material as well as his own observations and proposals for action. The University Testing Center also conducted a series of studies which were reported to the university community.

The studies and reports indicated the need for dialogue through many channels between the university administration, faculty members, members of Parliament, cabinet ministers, and community leaders. It was important to preserve respect for reason, law, the human person, and property. There was a need for new intellectual challenges. Reservations about most of the university students were revealed in these studies and reports. In summary, it was felt that the students did not read very much and had read very little beyond the required texts during their past educational experience; they had not yet developed skills of individual research and investigation, problem analysis, logical argument, and concise reasoning; they had not received counseling to help them relate their career goals more effectively to their academic study and thus were often poorly motivated to pursue a particular field of study; they had little understanding of what a university is—or should be—and what distinguishes it from other educational institutions; they often felt unchallenged by much of what was presented to them in the classroom, particularly in the lower classes. The better students were seldom stimulated or encouraged to move at a faster, individual pace and to attempt a broader scope of studies—rather, all students were seemingly encouraged to move "lockstep" through a highly structured, sometimes boring curriculum. They were often not given enough opportunity to realistically consider Ethiopian situations and the real problems at issue "here and now" in the classroom. Rather, they were sometimes encouraged to think that "flabby generalizations" and "slogan solutions" are valid answers to hard problems. In many cases, they did not work very hard outside the classroom on projects calling for individual initiative in research, including field work, analysis of data, and responsible and realistic proposals for action.[12]

These appraisals were made before the freshman program was initiated in 1969. Since no comprehensive study on the subject was ever conducted, there is no evidence that these problems were ever effectively addressed. The forces marshalled against the establishment of an effective learning-teaching environment and process remained in place.

Student publications, student unions, and the rules and regulations governing them became increasingly political. As a result, student publications and unions on all campuses were banned by the Board of Governors. The underlying reason for the banning was contained in a 1966-67 report by the dean of students:

> It is my opinion that the problem of student unions in Addis Ababa is directly related to the political awareness of the University students and that the University, as a University, does not have the necessary mechanism to control this force nor should it. *This problem is a problem that will last; the Dean of Students, SAC (Student Affairs Committee) and the University must determine what their attitude should be and what decisions must be taken in view of such a problem* [emphasis added].
>
> The question of student newspapers is closely related to the question of student unions. The newspaper is one way for the union of contacting its members, of communicating its ideas. This question has been studied throughout the year by the SAC and Dean of Students; unfortunately no satisfactory solution has been found.[13]

Wastage and Innovation

One measure of the efficiency of a university is the proportion of entrants who graduate. Since the inception of higher education in Ethiopia, student wastage has been a serious problem. Several surveys and studies pointed out the need to address this important issue. The wastage rate was as high as 40 percent in the mid-1960s. In its 1966 report, the Chancellor's Advisory Committee on Higher Education pressed for a solution. It noted that the cost of putting a student through the university was so great that the nation could not tolerate such a large loss of potential graduates and that, in the long term, the success of the university would be judged more by its output of graduates than by its input of freshmen. According to the committee, "a drop-out is not only an unfinished product: he is also a potentially resentful and uncooperative citizen."[14]

The presidential commission and the advisory committee identified the following problems that contributed to attrition of first-year students: most freshmen arrived at the university with little or no orientation toward university structures, teaching methods, and academic demands; most were forced on entry to make a "career choice" that they were often ill-prepared to make; they were not given adequate aptitude testing and counseling; the orientation system was either nonexistent or, at best, ad hoc and contained little in-depth work and experience. In English language skills, reading speed, vocabulary, comprehension, problem-solving, and analytical ability the freshmen were rated far below the levels required for successful entry to the second year of studies. Deficiency in language skills affected both motivation and academic prowess.[15]

A Freshman Program

In an attempt to confront these serious problems, a freshman program was designed to develop skills in language, conceptualization, and reasoning. Increased motivation was viewed as essential in response to evidence that an alarming number of freshmen were poorly motivated, expected to coast through the year, and were satisfied to enter the second year on probation—resulting in attrition in the upper classes. It was recommended that the freshman program exist as a distinct unit within the university; that to the maximum extent possible all freshmen take a common program of studies in both "science" and "non-science" subjects; and that the freshman year consist of three terms with a defined unit of work that had to be completed at a basic level of competence before students could qualify for enrollment in a faculty and become candidates for a degree. At the end of the year, according to the proposed freshman program, qualified students would apply to the college or faculty of their choice. If the existing quota provisions permitted, they would be allowed to enroll.[16] Obviously, students who had preformed well during the freshman year would have a better chance of being admitted to the college of their choice. It was hoped that this would provide additional incentive for improved academic performance.

A new position, Director of Freshman Programs, was proposed. The director would be assisted by a committee of faculty representatives drawn from the various colleges of the university and the office of the dean of students.

This proposal, which gained favorable support among faculty and students alike, was considered a great step forward in the improvement of performance and efficiency within the university.

159

The proposal was implemented in 1969. Although no formal evaluation of its effectiveness was carried out, the Director of Freshman Programs, and others closely associated with the program up to 1974, expressed satisfaction with its operation.

Upper Class Programs

A frequent criticism of college graduates was that they considered themselves superior to those who did not possess degrees and that they expected special treatment, such as a comfortable office job in Addis Ababa rather than field work in the provinces. It was said that graduates, though they may have been proficient in their specialties, lacked the motivation, responsibility, and broad perspective which should be a part of the makeup of the privileged few who had the opportunity to acquire higher education. This was supposed to reflect a lack of civic education on the great issues facing Ethiopian society.

It was assumed that the university had a dual responsibility to train citizens for the professions and specific occupational tasks, and to prepare students for civic leadership and responsibilities in a changing world. It was also assumed that the handful of Ethiopian citizens who earned academic degrees at HSIU had a profound obligation to understand and participate in a process of rapid change which was the essence of the development process. Whether physician, lawyer, teacher, or artist, it was essential that the graduate develop a realistic perspective of the dramatic contemporary issues confronting his society and an awareness of comparative developments in Africa and elsewhere.

Accordingly, in 1968 a study commission was appointed to develop some general courses which would focus on the nature of Ethiopian society and its problems of change and development as well as other contemporary issues confronting Ethiopia and the developing world. Some of these could be achieved, it was thought, by structuring courses *vertically*, drawing from the resources of disciplines such as Ethiopian history, government, economics, business, sociology, geography, and others. These courses would discuss the culture, traditions, and peoples of Ethiopia; problems of economic and political development; and social change and social tensions in a changing society.[17] Furthermore, it was considered desirable that all students take a wider spread of courses in the sciences and humanities independent of their main course of studies; a goal which could be accomplished by requiring humanities students to elect courses in the sciences and vice versa.

It was recognized that one of the constant problems confronting

universities in developing countries was the importation and reten-
tion, without adequate thought, of disciplines and departmentalized
knowledge and courses conceived in other times and in other places.
It was also necessary to remember that in the real world, especially
in societies such as Ethiopia, engineers became managers and administrators and lawyers became vice-ministers of commerce,
economists had to manage as well as theorize, and public administrators needed substantive knowledge as well as methodological
skills. "The lateral mobility of good students from role to role in
society is obvious, and one function of the University in our setting is to provide some *breadth* of perspective and knowledge *as
well as depth*.[18]

Obviously, there was no simple panacea for balancing the competing demands implicit in the conflict between breadth and specialization. However, once the broad policy questions were recognized
and new course requirements established, it was decided that all
units of the university would be required to constantly review, experiment, and innovate to insure that the educational experience
conformed to the Ethiopian situation. The central need was to increase the interdisciplinary experience of students and to improve
interdisciplinary, interfaculty planning of curricula and educational
experiences.

A year after the final report of the Presidential Commission, the
president of HSIU convened a special committee composed of senior
academic staff, public officials, and businessmen to study the formation of a college of social sciences and development administration. The committee was asked to explore the possibility of
merging the several social science departments with the College
of Business Administration and the School of Social Work to facilitate the study commission's recommendations aimed at producing
graduates who were technically competent and broadly grounded
in the social sciences, the humanities, and the scientific method
of reasoning.

After a lengthy debate involving all members of the university
community, the establishment of the new college was indefinitely
postponed. Instead, the Institute of Development Research was
created. Although the idea of an interdisciplinary approach to instruction and research was accepted in principle, when the time
arrived to make the idea operational, some faculty members revolted
against it. Once again, tradition and the molds of the past imprisoned
imaginative thought. Nevertheless, despite internal resistance to such
bold initiatives, the university made some progress in its efforts to
graduate young people who were well aware of the wider developmental issues of the country.[19]

161

Academic Policies and Programs

In the process of centralizing higher education in Ethiopia, one of the major steps taken by the HSIU Faculty Council was the unification of several academic policies and practices such as standardization of admission policies, introduction of a general education core curriculum, adoption of a unified system of grading, and establishment of a uniform academic calendar.

The Faculty Council had appointed a Board of Admissions for all colleges and faculties of the university. All full-time and part-time degree students and some diploma students were required to apply to the Board through the Office of the Registrar. New standards for all colleges were adopted as early as August 1962. Though at that early stage qualified candidates were at a premium, it was agreed that eventually all students desiring to register for a degree program in any of the colleges would need the Ethiopian School Leaving Certificate (ESLCE) or its equivalent. The new standards were not consistently applied, however. Due to many loopholes in the regulations, and the eagerness of the colleges to fill spaces during the academic years 1962–63, some students with low academic qualifications were admitted. Trudeau reported that this compromise of standards prompted the president to write a strong memorandum to the deans and other officials in the colleges expressing regret that approved admission policies had not been strictly followed.[20]

Although no provision was made for it in the HSIU charter, the Office of the Registrar was established in August 1962. Its functions developed out of current practice and included preparing documents for admission to all colleges, keeping student records, producing the university catalogue, issuing transcripts and grades, programming classroom utilization, and maintaining the secretariat of the Board of Admissions. The task of implementing admission policies was shared between the Office of the Registrar and the Board of Admissions. The Registrar reported directly to the academic vice-president.

After a full year of study, on 17 May 1963, the curriculum committee of the Faculty Council presented an overall curriculum policy. The council approved the policy in short order. All courses were to be offered on a semester basis. The minimum credit requirement for a degree was set at 130 semester hours. The minimum student load per semester was set at fifteen and the maximum at eighteen semester hours. All degrees were to have a major field of specialization in which the student must complete a minimum of forty-two semester hours. All degree students were to take general education courses for a minimum of thirty-one semester hours. A new standardized grading system for all colleges was introduced in 1962–63. It was based on the method of letter grading and grade point averages similar to that used in North America.

In its early years admission to HSIU was based on the successful completion of one of several examinations: the ESLCE or such foreign examinations as the General Certificate (G.C.S.) of the University of London, the Cambridge Overseas Certificate, the West African School Certificate, the Oxford Examination, or other qualifications acceptable to the HSIU Board of Admissions. Most Ethiopian students were admitted to the university through the ESLCE; the admission requirement was a "passing grade" in five subjects, including Amharic (the national language), English, and mathematics, with a grade point average of 2.00 or "C", and acceptable performance on the University Entrance Aptitude Test. Students with grade point averages of 2.4 or above had a better chance of acceptance than those with lower scores. In the foreign entrance examinations, the student needed five passes at the ordinary level, including English language and mathematics. The other three subjects had to be appropriate to the faculty the applicant wished to join. There were some sixteen additional channels that could lead to university admission. As more qualified applicants appeared, however, the importance of these avenues gradually diminished. For diplomas, such as those offered in technical teacher education and land surveying, admission requirements were lower (three passes in the ESLCE instead of five). It was expected that these requirements would be raised later as determined and approved by the respective faculty commission.

The ESLCE rules required that students desiring to enter the' university take the examination during the last half of the final year of secondary education. The examination was administered annually in more than thirty-one different centers across the country under the joint sponsorship of the university and the Ministry of Education.

Table 17 depicts the number of candidates that sat for the ESLCE and the percentage of passes and failures over the twenty-year period from 1950 to 1970. The ESLCE, augmented by the General Certificate Examination of London (ordinary level) became operational in 1950-51. Of the 53 students who took the first examination, 47 passed and only 6 failed. By the end of that decade the number of candidates had increased to 412. However, only 168, or about 41 percent, passed the examination. A decade later, 4,750 sat for the examination and only 856, or about 17 percent, passed; 82 percent failed—the exact reverse of conditions twenty years earlier. The rate of failure in the ESLCE was so alarming that on 6 July 1966 the Council of Ministers appointed a six-member committee "to establish the causes of failure (in the ESLCE) . . . to identify factors resulting in low standards in secondary schools and to give short-term and long-term recommendations for the improvement of secondary education in Ethiopia."[21]

TABLE 17
Ethiopian School Leaving Certificate Examination Results, 1950–1970

Year	Total No. of Students Sat	No. Pass	% of Passes	No. of Failures	% of Failure
1950–51	53	47	88.7	6	11.3
1951–52	83	63	75.9	20	24.1
1952–53	86	64	74.4	22	25.6
1953–54	105	73	69.5	32	30.5
1954–55	159	88	55.3	71	44.7
1955–56	163	103	63.2	60	36.8
1956–57	153	111	72.5	42	27.5
1957–58	317	197	62.1	120	37.8
1958–59	441	180	40.8	261	59.2
1959–60	412	168	40.8	244	59.2
1960–61	481	176	36.6	305	63.4
1961–62	933	220	23.6	713	76.4
1962–63	2045	293	14.3	1752	85.7
1963–64	2649	338	12.8	2311	87.2
1964–65	2793	407	14.6	2386	85.4
1965–66	3821	490	12.8	3331	87.2
1966–67	2294	506	22.1	1788	77.9
1967–68	2702	719	26.6	1983	73.4
1968–69	3852	738	19.2	3114	80.8
1969–70	4750	836	18.0	3914	82.4

Sources: Teshome Wagaw, "Access to Haile Selassie I University," *Ethiopia Observer*, p. 43; E. Trudeau, "Higher Education in Ethiopia," p. 17.

After a full investigation, the committee identified the following factors as major contributors ot the problem: (1) the small size of the elementary school system from which secondary students were drawn; (2) the unsatisfactory quality of the elementary school system in general; (3) the relatively high promotion rate from the elementary to the secondary level; (4) the very inadequate teaching permitted in the secondary schools; (5) the withdrawal of many secondary school students before taking the ESLCE; (6) the general shortage of teaching materials, equipment, and supplies in the secondary schools; and (7) the high rate of staff turnover in the secondary schools. In essence, the committee indicated the entire educational system for the students' dismal performance on the ESLCE. The director of the ESLCE best summed up the problem:

> For in the final analysis, the ESLCE reveals the cumulative results of the candidates' entire secondary school education. . . . A cursory reading of the reports of the chief examiner . . . will reveal what has been obvious to us all along, namely, the quality of secondary education has not kept pace with the very marked increase in secondary school enrollment.[22]

In addition, the ESLCE, as an instrument of candidate selection, was questioned by many thoughtful citizens. Serious questions were raised about whether it was fair, inclusive, or effective in identifying potentially able candidates; whether it was a good predictor of success in the university; and whether it discriminated against candidates from rural areas (where 90 percent of the people lived). As this author observed in 1971: "All in all . . . access to HSIU is limited to young people who come from urban-based high schools. In addition to the concept of fairness, the question that might be raised is, will these be the people that would accelerate the development of Ethiopia in general, and rural Ethiopia in particular?"[23]

In the early 1960s the shortage of qualified secondary graduates for admission to the colleges was a critical problem. The expansion of enrollment in the lower grades from the mid-1960s on, however, did away with most of the numbers problem. Beginning in the late 1960s, the concern focused on the selection of applicants and the quality of candidates for admission.

The Planning of Quotas, Admission, and Enrollment

Traditional responsibilities relative to the number and quality of students admitted to the university and the types of programs they pursued were assumed by the various colleges and the students themselves. Aptitude, qualifications, and interests were among the factors considered in determining the most suitable college or area of studies. However, as a developing country, Ethiopia had a great need for a trained work force in almost all areas. Since there was, for all practical purposes, only one source of trained graduates, the government took steps to influence the university's admission policies based on a series of five-year national development plans.

In 1955 a member of the Board of Governors, no doubt directed by higher authorities, asked whether students should not be trained according to the development needs of the country. The college president replied that college level students should not be

165

"programmed" against their will. According to the Board of Governors' minutes, the matter was dropped then and there.

In 1961, and more significantly in 1963, when African political and educational leaders met under the auspices of UNESCO, first in Addis Ababa and later in Tananarive, they came out in favor of channeling students to enroll in areas that would fulfill national development requirements. They also recommended several guidelines, including a 60:40 enrollment ratio in favor of science and technology over the social sciences and humanities. In Ethiopia this was a welcome step. Without delay, the government proceeded to follow these recommendations. Emphasis was placed on engineering, technology, and the training of science teachers. In the late 1960s, the ratio of science and technology students in Ethiopia to those studying the social sciences and humanities came to about 50:50. Though the recommendations of the Tananarive conference remained official policy, attainment of the 60:40 ratio goal was limited by the realities of student interest and the availability of faculty and facilities.

Table 18 depicts the enrollment figures and patterns of the twelve Ethiopian colleges or faculties and the HSIU freshman program from 1961 to 1974. When HSIU was established, total enrollment stood at 974. Thirteen years later, in 1973–74, total enrollment climbed to 6,474, a 664 percent increase; a growth rate of 51 percent per annum. This phenomenal growth occurred despite the university's efforts to bring enrollment growth in line with its capacity to provide quality education.

The same table also shows the enrollment patterns of the various colleges. In 1961–62, 37 percent of the students were enrolled in the Faculty of Arts and 20 percent in the Agricultural College. Reflecting the national work force requirements in mid-decade (1966–67), over 28 percent were enrolled in the Faculty of Education. In 1973–74, over 16 percent of the total enrollment was in the education faculty, twice that of any other faculty except the Science College (10 percent). Thus, despite the unplanned rate of rapid expansion in total enrollment, HSIU was able to respond to the increasingly insistent demands of national development requirements.

Another problem, less obvious from these statistics, was the underrepresentation of female students in the university. During its earliest years the number of female students at HSIU was practically insignificant. By 1972-73, however, women comprised 9.4 percent of the total enrollment. Most of the female students were enrolled in public health (40 percent), primarily in nondegree programs; social work (30 percent); and business administration (18 percent). Thus, while an average of 9 percent was an improvement

TABLE 18

Full-Time Student Enrollment at HSIU
Classified by Faculty or College and Percentage, 1961–1962 to 1973–1974

College / Faculty	1961-62[1] No.	% of Total[4]	1962-63 No.	% of Total	1963-64[2] No.	% of Total	1964-65 No.	% of Total	1965-66 No.	% of Total	1966-67 No.	% of Total	1967-68 No.	% of Total	1968-69[3] No.	% of Total	1969-70 No.	% of Total	1970-71 No.	% of Total	1971-72 No.	% of Total	1972-73[5] No.	% of Total	1973-74 No.	% of Total
Agriculture	195	20.0	220	20.2	211	14.0	196	11.0	258	11.4	228	8.1	236	7.0	347	9.0	444	9.6	461	10.1	519	10.4	271	6.9	533	8.2
Arts	356	37.0	299	27.4	299	19.8	290	16.3	356	15.8	412	14.6	441	13.1	527	13.6	453	9.3	370	8.1	392	7.9	262	6.7	400	6.2
Building[6]	111	11.4	112	10.2	111	7.4	107	6.0	83	3.7	88	3.1	84	2.5	122	3.2	—	—	—	—	—	—	—	—	—	—
Business (CBA)	—	—	—	—	148	9.8	204	11.5	292	13.0	366	12.9	454	13.5	479	12.4	414	8.9	390	8.6	348	7.0	190	4.8	297	4.6
Education*	—	—	127	11.6	210	13.9	431	24.2	624	27.7	799	28.3	993	29.5	1106	28.6	969	20.9	817	18.0	861	17.3	576	15.1	1063	16.4
Engineering[6] (Technology)	146	15.0	161	14.8	203	13.5	200	11.3	219	9.7	286	10.1	271	8.1	319	8.2	373	8.0	343	7.6	326	6.5	260	6.6	452	7.0
Law	—	—	—	—	60	4.0	68	3.8	94	4.2	110	3.9	189	5.6	177	4.5	276	6.0	259	5.7	340	6.8	168	4.3	334	5.2
Medicine & Ph.	—	—	—	—	16	1.1	25	1.4	41	1.8	60	2.1	79	2.3	109	2.8	119	2.6	130	2.9	153	3.1	135	3.4	190	2.9
Public Health	46	4.7	63	5.8	75	5.0	76	4.3	104	4.6	142	5.0	156	4.6	169	4.4	171	3.7	165	3.6	163	3.3	179	4.5	363	5.6
Science	106	10.9	95	8.7	122	8.2	140	7.9	127	5.6	248	8.8	368	10.9	398	10.3	288	6.2	319	7.0	377	7.6	261	6.6	669	10.3
Social Work	—	—	—	—	26	1.7	22	1.2	37	1.6	61	2.2	63	1.9	83	2.1	68	1.5	83	1.8	93	1.8	74	1.9	82	1.3
Theology	14	1.4	14	1.3	23	1.6	20	1.1	21	0.9	28	0.9	34	1.0	34	0.9	33	0.7	29	0.7	29	0.8	45	1.2	58	0.9
Freshman Prog.[7]	—	—	—	—	—		—		—		—		—		—		1048	22.6	1177	25.9	1367	27.5	1494	38.0	2033	31.4
Total	974	100.0	1091	100.0	1510	100.0	1779	100.0	2255	100.0	2828	100.0	3368	100.0	3870	100.0	4636	100.0	4543	100.0	4978	100.0	3935	100.0	6474	100.0

*Education was under the Faculty of Arts up to 1962.

Sources: 1. The Figures for Arts of 1961–62 include students of Social Work and Education.
2. Data for 1961–64 were obtained from Edouard Trudeau, p. 129 (there were 6 special students in 1963–64 comprising 0.4% of the total).
3. Data for 1964–69 were obtained from the Registrar's Office HSIU (Admitted by data of enrollment between 1961–65 are not consistent since they were taken at different times (e.g. first or second semesters).
4. "Percent of total" is of the total University enrollment.
5. Data for 1969–70—1972–74 were obtained from the Registrar's Office HSIU.
6. Colleges of Building and Engineering were incorporated under the Faculty of Technology in 1969–70.
7. Freshman Program was launched in 1969–70.

Note: Freshman enrollment is for the first semester. Some variations might have occurred during the second semester.

over previous years, the rate of female participation remained discouraging. In part, low female enrollment was due to traditional constraints such as early marriage. It was also true, of course, that not many groups or individuals were advocating greater female participation in higher education.

One interesting dimension of the university's student enrollment pattern was the presence of foreign students in its halls. Beginning in 1958, when the Haile Selassie I Scholarship was inaugurated, and continuing through the 1960s, most foreign students were from other English-speaking African countries. In later years, however, students from Asia and Europe, usually those with parents stationed in Addis Ababa, also attended HSIU. Over a ten-year period beginning in 1958, some 1,080 foreign students were enrolled. The arts, science, technology and agriculture colleges attracted the greatest number of these students.

In recognition of the presence and contribution of the international students, the university set up an office headed by a "mature, sympathetic, and experienced Ethiopian, who was responsible for the administration, supervision, and guidance of Foreign students, and who could help in all ways possible with their personal, financial and other difficulties."[24]

Although the doors of Ethiopian higher education were opened to foreigners in 1958, the sociocultural conditions of the country were not fully prepared to offer them cordial hospitality. Nonetheless, the presence of foreign students proved to be a welcome leaven which, among other things, stimulated Ethiopian students to think about their own political and economic conditions. As will be shown in chapter 8, the decision to admit foreign students may have contributed immeasurably to the drastic radicalization of the student body which culminated in the 1974 revolution.

Despite the many problems it confronted between 1961 and 1974 HSIU produced a total of some 10,000 graduates from the degree and subdegree programs combined. These graduates plus the nearly 2,000 Ethiopians who returned from overseas colleges and universities constituted the backbone of Ethiopia's highly trained and educated work force of this generation.

Research and Graduate Programs

When the University College of Addis Ababa was established in 1950, personnel were recruited primarily for teaching and administrative purposes. Except some student and faculty work related to ethnographic studies, no research was expected and not much was produced. However, with the formation of the consolidated university in 1961, the need for research, particularly for the purpose of developing instructional materials related to development issues, was apparent. In 1966 the Chancellor's Advisory Committee on Higher Education urged the university to excel in both teaching and research on subjects relevant to the country's needs "under world standards of accuracy and integrity, standards which are known and accepted by scholars anywhere and are measured by quality of work and not by amount of knowledge."

A presidential commission appointed to assess the university's needs, mission, and performance reported in 1968 that the question of research was still pending. "In general," it noted, "the productivity of our University staff has been poor." According to the commission, the reasons for this poor productivity included excessive teaching and administrative responsibilities, lack of both human and material support resources, and poor motivation. While it recognized that not every teacher would publish scholarly articles in professional journals or books, the commission noted that research must be considered the lifeblood of intellectual development. Particularly relevant to the university were "The development of materials primarily for instructional purposes, which will focus on the problems of Ethiopia and the problems of developing nations and comparative experience in development and change." It noted that it was unfortunate that students, particularly in the social sciences, lacked basic materials on the economic, social, cultural, and educational development of Ethiopia. The committee concluded: "A University which does not engage in systematic efforts to push forward the frontiers of knowledge of and theories concerning Ethiopia, becomes stagnant."[25]

To facilitate the research process and in response to policies established by the Faculty Council, the university administration established the University Press to publish and make distribution arrangements for books and professional journals produced under university sponsorship. It also established a number of special research institutes and facilities in addition to the previously established Institute of Ethiopian Studies: the Institute of Development Research, the Geophysical Observatory, the Creative Arts Center, the Institute of Science and Technology, and the central and law libraries.

These special research units were designed to address the broad national needs for research. However, research and dissemination of knowledge requires more than material, institutional, and human support. It also requires that other national institutions, such as the political parties, parliament, the religious organizations, and in the case of Ethiopia, the monarchy, be understanding, supportive, or at least tolerant of the fundamental importance of free inquiry, dialogue, and the propagation of information. Unfortunately, these prerequisites were totally absent. Through various means—threat, bribery, persecution, and the like—the political system in Ethiopia inspired fear and timidity in the hearts and minds of people of even the strongest convictions. This kind of atmosphere inspired self-censorship, which is often worse than external censorship. When one dared to challenge the status quo or the accepted wisdom in any area of national life, one was ridiculed, exposed, attacked, and otherwise accused of being the prodigal son of Ethiopia. This is a nerve-wracking predicament that one must experience firsthand to fully appreciate its effects.[26]

In addition, there were many other constraints that inhibited faculty research. One was the lack of readership. It is unlikely that many of the national policymakers referred to any piece of scientific work in attempting to formulate sound policies. Likewise, it was doubtful that many people outside of the university read scholarly works for enjoyment or information. It was no wonder, therefore, that a large proportion of the promising faculty members accepted administrative posts where financial rewards, social prestige, and national visibility were greater. The act of scholarly pursuit was primarily relegated to the few who either had no connection with the political or administrative apparatus or had shunned the expedience of the day for their professional calling. The latter were very few indeed. As Cohen and Seleshi observed, "significant research was not done by those particularly qualified to do it. Subtle but pervasive patterns of censorship and reward helped maintain the low level of Ethiopian research on rural and urban sectors."[27]

Nevertheless, slow progress was made over the years, and a few respectable outlets, such as the *Journal of Ethiopian Studies, Ethiopia Observer*, and the *Journal of Ethiopian Education*, disseminated sound research. The efforts of Richard Pankhurst, head of the Institute of Ethiopian Studies for more than twenty years, were invaluable to the furtherance of Ethiopian scholarly research. Since the 1974 revolution, however, much of Ethiopia's academic research and publication activity has been seriously interrupted. Perhaps this situation will prevail for some time to come—until the scholars are assured that the academic environment is relatively secure.

Since the early 1960s a series of commissions recommended the establishment of graduate programs at HSIU in such areas as economics and public administration; education; health and medical care administration; the sciences, with emphasis on epidemiological, biological, and public health issues; law and legal administration; and Ethiopian studies. Until recent times, however, such steps were not taken, due primarily to lack of sufficient financial support. A modest effort began in the late 1970s. It remains to be seen what impact this initiative will have on scholarly output.

Notes

1. *Ethiopian Herald*, 19 December 1961.
2. HSIU, *Second Report of the Advisory Committee on Higher Education to His Imperial Majesty Emperor Haile Selassie I, Chancellor of the University* (Addis Ababa: Haile Selassie I University, 1971), 3.
3. For proposals along this line see Teshome Wagaw, *Report on Student Support* (Addis Ababa: Office of the Dean of Students, HSIU, 9 May 1969), 30–48; John Summerskill, *Haile Selassie I University: A Blueprint for Development*, 107.
4. Presidential Commission on Planning, Reorganization and Consideration of Academic Programs of the University: "Final Report" (Addis Ababa: Haile Selassie I University, 1968) (mimeographed).
5. See Summerskill, 107.
6. Ibid., 107–10.
7. Ibid., 110.
8. Aklilu Habte, *A Forward Look: A Special Report from the President*, II-18.
9. Ibid.
10. Ibid.
11. Ibid., II-19.
12. Ibid., II-19, II-20.
13. Ciles Pion, *Annual Report, 1966–67* (Addis Ababa: HSIU, Office of the Dean of Students, n.d.), 5.
14. HSIU, *First Report of the Advisory Committee on Higher Education*, 22.
15. Ibid. See also Presidential Commission on Planning and Reorganization, 28; Harold S. Madsen, "Coping with English Language Transition Problems at Secondary and University Levels in Ethiopia" (Addis Ababa: Haile Selassie I University, May 1970), 10–25 (mimeographed).
16. The quota systems provided for channeling students to faculties according to national work force requirements, such as teaching, agriculture, or health education. Refer to Summerskill, 107–11. Also, see Presidential Commission on Planning and Reorganization, Part I, 30; and Aklilu Habte, *A Forward Look*, II-3. The goal of the quota system was to achieve parity with needs which provided for the early 1970s, 31 percent in teacher training, 15 percent in technology, 12 percent in agriculture, 10 percent in public health, 10 percent in science, 12 percent in administration, 5 percent in law, and 5 percent in the humanities and theology.
17. Presidential Commission on Planning and Reorganization, "Final Report" (Addis Ababa: Haile Selassie I University, 1968), 11–13, 27–32. Analysis for this section of the chapter was drawn primarily from this document unless indicated otherwise.
18. Ibid., 31.
19. It is interesting to note that it took the 1974 revolution to bring about a merger of the various units of the social and behavioral sciences with the business college. For a summary of the controversy see Aklilu Habte, *A Forward Look*, III-13–36.

20. Trudeau, 118.
21. For a more complete analysis of the admission problems refer to Teshome Wagaw, "Access to Haile Selassie I University," *Ethiopia Observer* 14, no. 1 (1971): 31–46.
22. Million Neqniq, et al., "The Current Operation of the Education System in Ethiopia" (Addis Ababa, November 1966); and "Ethiopian School Leaving Examination Report" (Addis Ababa, 1966), 23 (mimeographed).
23. Wagaw, "Access to Haile Selassie I University," 38.
24. HSIU, *First Report of the Advisory Committee*, 5; and Summerskill, 110.
25. Presidential Commission on Planning and Reorganization, 21.
26. This author presented a research paper to an interdisciplinary seminar at Haile Selassie I University in 1971. The subject had to do with the effect of the multiplicity of holidays, both for religious and secular reasons, on farming productivity. It opened a floodgate; even the *Abun*, head of the Ethiopian Church, gave an interview to denounce my position, which was based on field research. The effect was a question to myself: "Is it worth it?" In time, these research results were used by the new government to promulgate a law curtailing the number of holidays to be observed.
27. John M. Cohen and Seleshi Sisaye, "Research On Socioeconomic Development in Ethiopia: Past Problems and Future Issues in Rural-Urban Studies," Bulletin no. 84 (Ithaca: Cornell University, June 1977), 34.

6

OUTREACH PROGRAMS

In 1971 the Chancellor's Advisory Committee on Higher Education reiterated the university's responsibilities:

> A strong university must be relevant to the society it serves. It can grow and become more effective only when the economy and society in which it functions, grows and prospers. It can achieve popular support only when the people who nurture it believe that what it is doing is essential to the well-being of the nation. Haile Selassie I University is no exception. Its strength derives from its service to the *real* and *urgent* needs of Ethiopia [emphasis added].[1]

These needs, according to the committee, included the exploration, identification, development, and utilization of the full resources of the country. Fulfillment of these urgent needs would lend essential support to a successful program of national development.

The general thrust of the university's mandates, opportunities, and responsibilities was supported by the university community, though serious questions arose as to how to maximize the limited human and material resources at the university's disposal to insure that it would have the greatest impact within a reasonable time. Basic research, regular classroom instruction, and the dissemination of research and scholarly products are all part of the normal functions of a university. However, a university trying to establish a niche for itself in a traditional and developing society cannot afford to limit its activities to the confines of university campuses. It must reach out and let the people see, hear, and feel that it is working to identify, research, and provide solutions to pressing problems in agriculture, education, transportation, communications, health, and the like. Tangible evidence is needed to help people of all positions to understand the role, the mission, and the purposes of a national university. To the extent that they understand and share its mission, they may be willing to provide material and political support. As the president of HSIU once stated, faculty and students must recognize that the burden on the tax-payer of higher education, is, in relative terms, exceedingly heavy. *The University must be seen as an investment in their behalf for the future. . . .* We must continuously make clear the University's commitment to the values of sacrifice, service, work, and greater social justice. We must avoid the danger of fostering the wrong kind of essentially selfish, individualist, elite attitudes which may have begun to characterize some other universities in the developing world.[2]

The national university was surrounded by the stark realities of Ethiopia—mass illiteracy, undeveloped human and material resources, political oppression, and the urgent need to overcome centuries of conservatism and stagnation. It was clear that different approaches had to be proposed and implemented if, in addition to its traditional responsibilities, the university was to have some dramatic and positive impact to the national scene. Hence, a number of unorthodox programs were initiated: the Ethiopian University Service, the Summer Teacher In-service Program, faculty and staff involvement in consultation activities with government departments, and formal and nonformal extension programs for adults who for one reason or another could not enroll as full-time students. Some of these programs are considered in this chapter.

Education Sector Review

The 1971–72 Education Sector Review was organized to thoroughly overhaul the education system in order to make it more efficient and responsive to the Ethiopian scene, and at the same time make basic and functional education available to the majority of Ethiopian children and youth by the end of the twentieth century.[3] The *Review* was a collaborative effort of the Ethiopian Ministry of education and the World Bank. However, the major brain power was provided by the university. Out of 87 participants in the exercise, 33 were university faculty and another 33 were graduates of the university.[4] The scale of university involvement provided unusual insight and relevance to the quality of the final product.

There were, of course, complaints to the effect that in its preoccupation with political and social control, the government was not fully utilizing the rich, extensive, and readily available human resources represented in the university, and was instead relying too much on foreign expertise or less-skilled civil servants.[5] In many respects these were valid criticisms. The regime was preoccupied with prolonging its power, and many of its programs could not withstand rigorous analysis and criticism by Ethiopian academicians without exposing its many weaknesses. It was apparently spending too much effort in censoring ideas and controlling their dissemination, rather than challenging or encouraging intellectuals to come forth with solutions to the many political, cultural, and social ills of the country. Despite these impediments, the university provided its expertise to the government by way of consultations.

Summer Teacher In-service Program

The supply and quality of teachers in Ethiopia has always been a limiting factor in the development and expansion of education. Beginning as early as 1958, the national university, in cooperation with the Ministry of Education, tried to improve the quality of teachers. Since most of the teachers were available during summer vacation, the university organized a series of summer in-service programs for primary school teachers—many of whom had a limited amount of formal education. As Table 19 indicates, over the years the number of participants in the in-service programs increased. The number of participants in 1961-62 was 192; thirteen years later, in 1973-74, that number had increased by 847 percent to 1,819. Albeit dramatic, this increase was not nearly sufficient to meet the need to upgrade the teaching force. It was nevertheless significant. Though most of the participants were primary school teachers, many school administrators, supervisors, and junior and secondary school teachers also took advantage of the in-service programs. Graduates of these programs could be found in schools throughout the country. Upon returning to their classrooms, or as they participated in the Ethiopian Teachers Association (the largest professional association in Ethiopia), they had considerable impact on their students and colleagues alike.[6]

Though the in-service program was originally supported by general university and Ministry of Education funds, it gradually became self-sustaining. Eventually, its entire budget was provided by fees paid by the participants. Its financial success was augmented by its clear benefits to the national education system. It facilitated improved communications between teachers and Ministry of Education officials, and between teachers and university faculty. It also provided the university with valuable feedback from the field for curricula development and improved teacher recruitment procedures and training.

University Extension

The creation of an Ethiopian national university emerged primarily in response to the critical need for a trained work force at all levels of society. Accordingly, higher education in Ethiopia was multifaceted, rather than homogeneous or monolithic. From the outset the various units of the university emphasized development of

TABLE 19
Summer School In-Service Enrollment

Summer of Academic Year	Number of Teachers
1961–62	192
1962–63	233
1963–64	351
1964–65	527
1965–66	512
1966–67	887
1967–68	833
1968–69	948
1969–70	1073
1970–71	1100
1971–72	1220
1972–73	1908
1973–74	1819

Source: Aklilu Habte, "The Public Service Role of the University," p. 78.

a broad range of postsecondary programs. Subdegree and part-time programs were developed to train rural sanitarians and community nurses, school teachers, land surveyors, secretaries, community development officers, police officers, business people, and civil servants. In fact, more than 50 percent of the students were enrolled in such nontraditional courses.[7]

For some time the university was the only state-supported institution that assumed responsibility for providing the skills required for development of the nation. In order to carry out its role as the center from which enlightenment, joy, and skill development radiated to the outer reaches of the empire, the university instituted an extension division.

There were some who insisted that the role of a national university was to serve as a center of excellence in teaching, creative research, and innovation—not to become involved in service activities better left to other government departments and postsecondary institutions. Others thought that a national university supported by the state should try to justify its expensive existence by creatively combining its regular teaching and research activities with an extensive national outreach program. Gradually, the position of the latter group prevailed.

The University Extension Division at HSIU was established in 1962. As part of the newly reorganized national university, the division was to supplant extension activities previously carried out by UCAA and the engineering college, where evening classes had been offered since 1952. Under the new scheme the extension division expanded its activities beyond the confines of Addis Ababa. Beginning in September 1963, extension centers were established in Harar, Asmara, Debre Zeit, Gondar, Nazreth, and Massawa. In September 1964 additional centers were established in Jimma and Dire Dawa. At the same time, the mission and objectives of the extension division were reformulated and solidified as follows:

1. To offer educational opportunities to adults unable to attend regular university classes in Addis Ababa and in some other important centers in the provinces.
2. To provide various specialized diploma and certificate programs to enable individuals working for the government or private organizations to be competent and efficient in their respective professions.
3. To provide lectures and seminars that are of interest to the public.
4. To organize discussion groups on an informal and noncredit basis for the continuing education of adults.
5. To stimulate and encourage lifelong learning at all levels.

The mandate of the extension division was as broad and as vast as the country's needs for a skilled work force and enlightenment. It was to organize formal and informal, degree and subdegree programs in as many centers as possible. The number and types of programs were limited only by human and material resources, and the imagination and energy of those charged with its administration.

The headquarters of the extension division were located at the main campus in Addis Ababa; branch headquarters were located at the eight centers listed above. Each center was headed by a director of extension who reported directly to the extension dean in Addis Ababa.

Degree, diploma, and certificate programs were offered in the extension division. Most of the programs were offered in cooperation with other HSIU colleges or faculties. In most cases, the academic commissions of the respective colleges decided on the degrees and requirements for graduation of extension students. Admission requirements were generally similar to those of other HSIU colleges (a successful pass in the ESLCE or its equivalent), but provisions for special admissions were established for graduates of the Military Academy and members of the Ethiopian Air Force. A "mature age" admission regulation was also instituted, providing a second chance for older students who had not taken the ESLCE. This group still had to complete secondary school and pass the University Entrance Aptitude Test. On the whole, the HSIU extension program contributed to the development of a skilled work force by providing a second chance to adults who would otherwise have been unable to gain access to the opportunities provided by higher learning.

The extent of student participation in the extension division over a period of eleven years is depicted in Table 20. The first three centers located in Addis Ababa attracted the largest numbers. Some of the other centers were eventually disbanded, due primarily to a lack of sufficient "qualified" participants.

The instructional programs offered by the extension division were extensive in number and wide-ranging in quality and coverage. For the 1973–74 period, for instance, some 140 courses were offered in the areas of law, economics, business and public administration, accounting, political science and government, education, secretarial sciences, agriculture, highway technology, civil, electrical and mechanical engineering, statistics, and library science. Typically, it took about eight years to complete the requirements of first degree programs. Completion of subdegree programs took two to five years, depending on the amount of work students were able to carry in addition to their full-time employment. Most of the instructional staff were drawn from the regular university faculty, though some were recruited from government, business, and industry. In all instances, faculty recruitment was carried out in full consultation with a regular unit of the university. The extension division had no power to recruit instructional staff directly.[8]

In a university chronically short of sufficient funds to operate its many activities and in which university education was free to all regular full-time students, the extension division was nearly financially self-sufficient. Since its students were mature individuals who were gainfully employed, they were able to pay their own educational expenses. While tuition fees imposed an additional burden on some extension students, and might even have excluded others, the division's independent source of income was nonetheless instrumental to its rapid expansion.

The quality and number of its graduates are reliable measures of the effectiveness of a department's programs. While it is not easy to ascertain the qualitative impact of the extension division's graduates, Table 21 indicates the number of graduates over a period of twelve years. Graduates of the B.A. degree, diploma, and certificate programs totaled, respectively, 252, 1,962, and 617—a total of 2,831. This was no small accomplishment for a society that was starved for an educated high-level work force.

However, the approaches and programs of the extension division were criticized for a number of reasons, including that the curricula duplicated full-time university programs instead of experimenting and innovating with new programs suited to mature, adult, fee-paying students; the broad vision, philosophies, and mission of the university were not carried out; the regular instructional staff continued to insist on applying strict admission requirements; the kind of

TABLE 20
University Extension Enrollment, 1961–1962 to 1971–1972

Centers	1961-62	1962-63	1963-64	1964-65	1965-66	1966-67	1967-68	1968-69	1969-70	1970-71	1971-72
Main Campus*	980	1212	1029	1120	1242	1164	1029	1272	1368	2912	3024
Engineering*	46	64	50	112	169	220	115	291	247	847	705
Main Campus Law*	—	—	—	—	—	—	—	672	401	823	516
Asmara	—	127	129	125	278	170	120	166	125	309	392
Debre Zeit	—	54	50	40	40	61	434**	59	27	53	107
Dire Dawa	—	—	—	15	35	60	—	—	—	—	—
Harar	—	—	206	111	71	75	102	102	93	102	170
Jimma Ext. Law Centers	—	—	—	—	—	—	—	—	43***	—	—
Total	1026	1457	1464	1523	1835	1750	1800	2562	2304	4546	4914

*Addis Ababa
**Including some high school students.
***For second semester only. All other enrollment figures are for the first semester.

Source: Addis Ababa University, Office of the University Extension.

TABLE 21
Number of Graduates by Year and Type of Credential

| Year | Type of Credential | | | Total |
	Degree	Diploma	Certificate	
1962–63	12	—	10	22
1963–64	22	—	26	48
1964–65	6	34	21	61
1965–66	13	72	55	140
1966–67	9	99	—	108
1967–68	24	226	—	250
1968–69	40	286	111	437
1969–70	28	181	230	439
1970–71	23	192	148	363
1971–72	34	105	6	145
1972–73	26	470	6	502
1973–74	15	297	4	316
Total	252	1962	617	2831

Source: Adapted from: Aklilu Habte, "The Public Service Role of the University," p. 76.

courses offered and the methods of instruction followed were more suited to guiding young, inexperienced, and not always highly motivated full-time students.[9]

Other problems emerged. Abebe Ghedai pointed out that, as far as participants in Addis Ababa were concerned, continuing university education was provided primarily to a group that was predominantly male, unmarried, and under thirty years of age. Two thirds of these students were graduates of general secondary schools, and many were full-time employees in the civil service or in private organizations. About 50 percent had incomes twenty times greater than the average Ethiopian citizen. When asked why they participated in continuing education, the reasons given, in order of importance, were: the desire for professional advancement, association with other people of similar interests, and a desire to be of social service.[10]

These phenomena are, of course, worldwide. The more education one has, the more education one wants. This tendency influences, in turn, the shape of curricula, the methodologies, and the perceptions of adult education at the expense of the *larger, undefined numbers of potential students* waiting to be served. Those directly involved in the administration of the division complained in 1969:

the program is not fully assimilated into the academic structure of the University, but on the other hand, does not have the autonomy to set its own standards. Present administrative arrangements are felt to be too restrictive, since they do not lend themselves to the courses which cut across faculty lines, do not allow innovations in the curriculum, and require rigid interpretation of standards and regulations which apply to regular day students.[11]

A long-range goal of the program was to become financially self-sufficient, but the dean of extension recommended that a subsidy be continued to support courses offered in smaller provincial capitals and to develop library facilities and teaching materials.

Though the extension program offered higher education to adults who otherwise would not have had such opportunities, and the country benefited from the services of extension-trained citizens, the extension division was unable to achieve equity by crossing geographic, age, sex, ethnic, and linguistic lines. The instructional staff were also constantly concerned about offering courses through the extension division that might be construed as being less rigorous and less demanding than other university programs. In the early 1970s, therefore, the university approached UNESCO about the possibility of organizing a mission of consultants to study and evaluate the work of the extension division and to formulate recommendations regarding its relevance and expansion.

The mission was organized in 1972. It was composed of Professor Charles A. Wedemeyer of the United States, team leader; Professor Rupert D. Goodman of Australia; and, as secretary, Dr. Jagbans K. Balbir of India, a UNESCO employee.[12] Field work began that summer. They interviewed a large number of people inside and outside the university and government before returning to Paris to draft their findings and recommendations. The report was divided into seven broad sections—introduction, historical framework of HSIU extension, evaluation of present extension programs and services, the need for new extension concepts, recommendations, further problems for research, and conclusion. Generally, though the work was competent as far as it went, it was clear that the mission did not comprehend the almost insurmountable financial and human resource limitations that confronted the university and Ethiopia. Aside from this the report was farsighted and thorough. Since the import of this mission's report was so significant, some of the more salient aspects of their evaluation follow.

Evaluation

The mission learned that, administratively, the Dean of Extension was responsible to the academic vice-president. This arrangement was quite unlike that of the other HSIU deans, who reported to the faculty council through an academic commission that was composed of the dean and three elected faculty members. The extension division itself had no power to offer programs leading to a degree or a diploma. That responsibility was reserved for the colleges or faculties. Approved extension courses were taught by members of the department in which the courses were offered. At times, faculty members who did not carry full daytime teaching loads would be assigned extension teaching as part of their regular workload. Since the extension division was only an administrative unit with no faculty nor academic commission of its own, the dean of extension had to seek approval of the division's programs from the other deans. The faculty council had a standing extension committee, but it did not have the same representation from the extension division that other faculties had on their academic commissions.

While the success or failure of extension programs was the responsibility of the extension division, responsibility for its offerings was diffused throughout the faculty and administrative structure. This arrangement placed the dean of extension in a difficult situation as he attempted to develop and expand appropriate programs. The mission therefore concluded:

> the present administrative machinery by which matters affecting extension are decided within the University without adequate voice by extension, is in urgent need to reform. The diffusion of authority has led to confusion, the multiplicity of operations involved has led to frustration, and the inevitable delays in decision-making on important matters have been detrimental to the best interests of students who, wrongly, but understandably, blame extension.[13]

The mission noted the rate of increase in student enrollment of over 460 percent between 1961 and 1971–72 with great satisfaction. It added that this remarkable achievement was a reflection of the department's initiative and efficiency in spite of difficulties, and a measure of "the hunger for learning on the part of those adults who are unable to attend full-time courses at the University." However, it regretted the fact that the extension service had reached only those in the few big cities, and that counseling services were not provided for the 2,500 students then enrolled.

As far as extension degree programs were concerned, the mission found that the Faculty Council's legislation requiring students to complete work within a prescribed time (about seven years) was too rigid and that the range of degree programs did not appear to be broad enough to accommodate the wide range of extension students' needs. The mission report noted that of the forty courses offered in 1971–72, none were in science, public health, technology, or agriculture areas, even though earlier studies had listed these as areas of acute work force shortage. It added:

> No attempt appears to have been made to establish degree courses different in content from those offered to regular students, to meet the different needs of adults who are already involved in the practical problems of business and the professions. Courses in computer science, urban studies, adult education, medical care, administration, Ethiopian studies, literature, the fine arts and creative arts—would be extremely relevant to the needs of Ethiopian society and the interests of adults.[14]

The report added that there was no need to wait until such courses were offered to regular students in residence programs as a condition for their presentation to the adult clientele for whom the extension division was created in the first place.

Other criticisms included the failure of extension to offer courses in areas of expertise that were currently filled by expensive expatriates, and the absence of consultation with government and private organizations in assessments of the extension program's needs and relevance. As a result, the extension courses were viewed as "too general and theoretical, and not closely enough related to the practical needs of the adult student who is already working in the profession."[15] This state of affairs was, of course, a consequence of faculty insistence that extension courses be similar in content to those offered to regular students. Among the faculty it was felt that if extension was to be responsible for providing courses relevant to the adult citizen, radical administrative and faculty policy changes were imperative. Similar observations were made regarding courses offered at the diploma and certificate levels, with the additional suggestion that entry requirements be relaxed and that instruction be provided in Amharic to minimize the language difficulties of adult students.

The extension division was also faulted for not providing formal and informal programs of interest and value to the adult population. According to the UNESCO mission, extension could have been a direct service to the larger community had it offered seminars or discussion groups for the general public; coordinated its programs with other authorities in the areas of public health, community development, and agricultural extension; and devoted attention to the betterment of women through appropriate courses. Noting the great opportunities existing in the country, the mission reiterated:

> [it] was struck by the repeated reference, in various Government agencies, to Ethiopia's urgent need for development and coordination of strong adult education programs at the community

level. In the face of such widespread evidence of need recognition and apparent willingness to cooperate and coordinate in adult program efforts, extension has an unusual opportunity to initiate significant adult education activities through the media.[16]

As far as course completion and attrition rates were concerned, the mission found that while up to 100 percent completed courses in practical and "relevant" areas, the completion rate for most courses in mathematics and physics was between 40 and 60 percent. Possible reasons for this unsatisfactory record were that the students were poorly prepared at the lower levels, poorly taught in extension, or badly examined. In any case, the failure rate was too high, especially in areas of acute human resource shortages, and the mission recommended that the specific causes be identified and remedial steps be taken. It was also suggested that, in order to shorten the average of seven to eight years required to complete the degree program, some scholarships be offered to selected students so that they could finish relatively early and present themselves for further service. The mission suggested that charging extension students for tuition, fees, and books was discriminatory and should be abandoned if the same practice was not applied to full-time regular students. Finally, it found the practice of specifying that a degree had been awarded through extension to be repugnant.

The mission concluded that in spite of the frustrations, bottlenecks, and lack of human and material resources, the growth and influence of the extension program was significant. Had the faculty and administration viewed it as a worthy activity on a par with other university programs, its impact might have been greater.[17]

Summary

A national institution of higher learning such as HSIU, which is trying to find its way into the hearts and minds of the people who gave it birth in the first place, has the moral and intellectual obligation to reach out and search for solutions to the many daily problems of mostly rural, poverty-stricken people. In doing so, it not only cultivates understanding and support for itself but also contributes in a tangible way to the development of the artistic, economic, and social life of those who live beyond the confines of the regular university premises.

Toward this end, and despite many cultural, political, and economic constraints, the Ethiopian university conducted summer teacher in-service programs, became involved in the government's socioeconomic planning activities, and initiated extension centers where civil servants, business people, and farmers were able to obtain education at the degree or subdegree levels without disrupting their ongoing occupational activities.

Although the outreach programs, particularly extension, were criticized by an external team for weaknesses in conception and methods of delivery, these apparent deficiencies on the part of the university were measures of success insofar as they indicated a genuine concern for and a desire to be involved in the immediate pressing problems of the majority of the people that lived outside the parameters of the colleges. It is hoped that, given a favorable national climate for these kinds of activities and the increase of professional personnel in its ranks, the embrace of the university's extension activities might be extended to include an ever-increasing number of people.

Notes

1. Haile Selassie I University, *Second Report of the Advisory Committee on Higher Education,* 6–7.
2. Aklilu Habte, *A Forward Look,* II-13.
3. See Ethiopian Ministry of Education, *Education: Challenge to the Nation.* For an analysis including problems of implementation, refer to Teshome Wagaw, *Education in Ethiopia,* 183–97.
4. Aklilu Habte, "The Public Service Role of the University," in *Higher Education and Social Change: Promising Experiments in Developing Countries,* vol. 2, eds. Kenneth W. Thompson, Barbara R. Fogel, and H. E. Danner (New York: Frederick A. Praeger, 1977), 80–81.
5. Solomon Inquai, who served as dean of extension in Addis Ababa for several years, was one of those who felt the government was not availing itself of faculty services. See "The University and the Public" in *Haile Selassie I University: The Last Decade* (Addis Ababa: Artistic Printers, 1972), 34. For a contrasting view, see Mulugeta Wodajo, "Haile Selassie I University: A Glimpse Over Its Past Record," in *Haile Selassie I University: The Last Decade,* 14–17.
6. Later in chapters 8 and 9 I will show the political impact of the teachers association on the national scene.
7. See, for instance, Aklilu Habte, "Higher Education in Ethiopia in the 1970's and Beyond," in *Education and Development Reconsidered,* ed. F. Champion Ward (New York: Frederick A. Praeger, 1974), 215.
8. HSIU, *General Catalogue 1973–75* (Addis Ababa: Office of the Registrar, Spring 1973), 276. See also Aklilu Habte, "The Public Service Role of the University," 75–76; and Teshome Wagaw, *Configuration of Education and Culture: An African Experience* (Ann Arbor: The University of Michigan Program of Adult and Continuing Education, 1984).
9. HSIU, Advisory Committee on Higher Education, "Second Report of the Advisory Committee on Higher Education to His Imperial Majesty Haile Selassie I, Chancellor of the University," 18; Aklilu Habte, "Public Service Role of the University," 77.

10. Abebe Ghedai, "Some Characteristics and Motivational Patterns of University Continuing Education" (Ed.D. dissertation, Syracuse University, 1977), ii.
11. Summerskill, *Haile Selassie I University*, 179.
12. The report of the mission is contained in C. A. Wedemeyer, R. D. Goodman, and J. K. Balbir, *Evaluation of Extension at the Haile Selassie I University, Addis Ababa* (Paris: UNESCO, 1973), 1–86.
13. Ibid., 11.
14. Ibid., 13.
15. Ibid., 14.
16. Ibid., 16.
17. Ibid., 30.

7

THE ETHIOPIAN
UNIVERSITY SERVICE

The Chancellor's Advisory Committee on Higher Education referred to the Ethiopian University Service (EUS) as "an inspiration of genius for its creative approach of continuing education experiences with service to the nation."[1]

The original idea of university students rendering community service was initiated by the students themselves when they began to undertake such work during summer, Christmas, and Easter vacations. As the idea expanded there were many discussions on how to organize student community service in such a way as to maximize benefits for the students, the university, and the national community. At the opening meeting of the National Union of Ethiopian University Students in 1961, the students asked themselves, "What can we, as students, do for our country?" Subsequently, this question was further explored by student groups, faculties, and the university administration. Unfortunately, most of these discussions were not properly recorded; those that were lack dates, citations of authorship, and details of their specific circumstances. At any rate, a thorough review of the oral and documentary information that does exist has generated this summary of the development of the Ethiopian University Service.

Even in its earliest years the university was concerned that, given the highly politicized nature of university students, the political authorities and the general rural community might not be receptive to the idea of student service. To forestall possible problems arising from these concerns, the university took time to thoroughly weigh the pros and cons of the service concept before any plans were made public.[2] Fortunately, senior Ethiopian faculty members were involved and able to provide leadership from the beginning. One of them, Professor Mesfin Wolde Mariam, articulated the fundamental needs for such a concept and its possible benefits.

> After spending one year's service in the rural areas, the students will become more conscious of their problems and their education will be more meaningful to them. Mastering a book written either by an American or a European will have no real

meaning unless we can determine the points which will be applicable to our own country. This can only be done when we know the ins and outs of our own country. Education then becomes a highway to service and does not merely remain a ladder for personal promotion and accumulation of wealth. Thus, education can be diffused and promoted and not confined to only those who acquire it.[3]

By early 1963 the executive committee of the Faculty Council had set up a study committee which eventually led to the formal establishment of the Ethiopian University Service (EUS) on 17 April 1964. The statute was ratified and implementation of the program began in September of the same year.

The Philosophy

The original philosophy of the EUS was to provide educational experiences for students in rural settings and, at the same time, provide services to the community under the joint guidance and supervision of the university and the employing agency without compensation. The Faculty Council specified:

The program wherein university students spend one academic year using their university training to provide services to local communities will be beneficial, not only to the national welfare but to the students in an educational sense. The program will enable students to understand, in a much more significant way, the problems and the needs of their country, particularly its less developed areas.[4]

The statute provided that the several faculties of the university would be called upon to participate in planning specific programs, in the placement and supervision of their respective students, and in evaluation. These tasks were to be undertaken in cooperation with the EUS administration and the committee established for this purpose. To the greatest extent possible, the statute permitted diversification of the ways in which university students might employ their special skills to discharge their service obligations in accordance with the standards set forth by the Faculty Council.

Service programs were to be carried out in collaboration with government and other agencies; while on service, students would be expected to abide by the rules and regulations of these agencies. The general administrative responsibilities, including planning, orientation, assignment, and logistical arrangements, were to remain in the hands of the university, since the basic premise was that EUS was a part of the university's educational program.

Requirements Defined

The Faculty Council defined service to include work:

(i)   for the purpose of establishing contact and rendering service to essentially rural communities;
(ii) in any capacity entailing the use of special skills developed by University training;
(iii) with an adequate living allowance provided;
(iv) for a period of one academic year while the University is in session;
(v)   for the purpose of improving student understanding of local community needs, problems and development.[5]

As defined above, service was to be rendered by university students who were Ethiopian citizens and enrolled full-time in a regular university program. The service obligation was to be fulfilled before completion of the fourth academic year of studies. Other arrangements for university service could be authorized by the EUS standing committee when warranted by sound educational policy and other considerations. Exemption from the service requirements could be granted by the committee to students who were currently employed by an appropriate government department or agency or who were, for medical or other reasons, unable to function effectively in a rural setting.

Responsibility for Planning and Administration

The Faculty Council established a special EUS standing committee composed of seven members appointed by the council at the beginning of each year. The dean of students and the EUS director were permanent members, and the committee was empowered to recruit representatives of officially recognized student groups and other organizations.

The secretary of the standing committee was an EUS administrator who, according to the advisory committee, "should be a person with experience both in education and administration." The secretary was accountable to the committee, the president, and the vice-president. The committee, together with the administrator, was charged with the placement, administration, and evaluation of the EUS program and was to make periodic reports to the council and the university executive committee. The committee, the administrator, and various subcommittees were responsible for the effective orientation of students entering the program, maintenance of liaison between students in the field and personnel from the students' faculties, evaluation of the program and its participants, determination of disciplinary cases, provision of an adequate living allowance, regular consultation with the university student body and the several faculties, and provision of a clear statement of the standards of conduct expected of students during the period of service.

Through their academic commissions, the several faculties were expected to participate fully in the assignment, supervision, and evaluation of their respective students. In other words, EUS was conceived as part and parcel of the university's academic programs and, as such, its success was the responsibility of all units whose students were carrying out assignments under the provisions set out by the statute.

Student Reaction

The proposal of a compulsory year of national service was, as expected, controversial both before and after the establishment of EUS. Since students were to go out for a year of service in remote rural areas with little faculty supervision, their enthusiasm and full cooperation were very important. Their initial reaction was for the most part negative. They felt that the university had no right to impose a year of compulsory service. They felt that despite the fact that all education, including college education, was provided free to all Ethiopian citizens, the interruption of their education for one year of service would delay their availability for full-time employment. They also felt that their services in a rural area would be of minimal benefit to all concerned.

Accordingly, students attempted to revoke at least the compulsory nature of the national service. Led by the law students, they challenged the university service statute in the courts. The lower court ruled in favor of the students, whereupon the university appealed to the high court. While this litigation proceeded, the first EUS students were already assigned and working in the field. Eventually, the case was dropped altogether. Some students claimed that the government had interfered with the judicial process by removing some judges from the case, but it is likely that by this time the students themselves found the experience of serving in the rural areas of their country rewarding and they were generally in support of the program. The EUS was saved.

The single piece of controlled research on the EUS was carried out during the first year of the program. Korten and Korten studied student attitudes toward the program before and after their field experience.[6] A summary of their findings shows that the initial resentment of the compulsory nature of the program began to diminish once the students experienced how critical the needs of the rural people were and how much they enjoyed their service experiences. At the end of their national service, most thought the experiences were very useful for both participants and the rural communities, and that the service should continue to be compulsory for all students. Students assigned to teaching (practically all of them) were more critical of the program before they entered it than were students assigned to nonteaching responsibilities relevant to their field of specialization. However, primarily due to the clear need for teachers, teaching participants changed their attitudes more significantly than did those assigned to nonteaching jobs. The researchers concluded that initial student resentment would have been minimized had the students been consulted in the development of EUS, and had they been given more time to consider its importance to the nation. The study also indicated that initial resentment was largely confined to the first group of participants, that subsequent groups had a more positive attitude, and that relatively few students remained resentful to the end. The researchers concluded:

> Although, to our knowledge, the Ethiopian program is the only service program of its type which is compulsory, the outcome indicates that a compulsory program can result in the same good work and enthusiastic dedication usually associated with voluntary service programs. Prerequisite to achieving such results, however, are competent and respected administrators for the program and *the feeling among the participants that they are providing needed and worthwhile service* [emphasis added].[7]

Orientation and Assignment

As provided by the statute, prospective EUS participants were required to complete a rigorous orientation program before beginning their service assignments. In earlier years, orientation lasted for about two weeks. However, as additional experience was gained, it became obvious that the students needed to more adequately prepare and fortify themselves for the challenges and hardships they might encounter in rural and often very isolated areas. Therefore, the orientation programs were incorporated into the structure of the general university curricula for the third year of academic training. It was felt that these changes in structure and substance would provide ample time for reflection, interaction, and mental adaptation before the students left for their service assignments.

A prospectus described the orientation course as one that:

> Seeks to identify some of the major problems which work against change for the better in the Ethiopian society in general and in rural communities in particular. The course will give

the student an opportunity to examine the social, economic, legal, cultural, and political factors which must be taken into consideration when efforts are made to introduce planned change. It also seeks to give the student the opportunity to identify those positive elements in local customs, or any practices in rural communities, which may be used as points of departure when introducing innovations. Finally, the course seeks to give the prospective EUS participant a better insight into the nature of the problems he/she is likely to face when he goes to work in a small community.[8]

The orientation course, which carried one credit hour, was led by faculty members from various disciplines. It emphasized the dynamics of change and development; the structure and policy of local and national governments; the social and cultural values of the different ethnic, religious, and linguistic groups; health and education problems and practices as well as community development needs; cultural and social barriers to change; and methods of motivating attitudinal change and establishing rapport with the local people and government agency representatives.

In general, field placements were based on three fundamental objectives: (1) the assignment should be educationally relevant to the participant; (2) it should be relevant to the community; and (3) without jeopardizing objectives 1 and 2, participants should be placed where work force needs were greatest.

Ideally, to promote the educational-career development of the EUS participants and to maximize their contributions to the rural communities, participants should have been placed according to their field of specializations. To some extent, these dual objectives were realized; but most of the students (over two thirds) ended up as classroom teachers in the junior and senior high schools. Since EUS participants were to work in conjunction with already established government or nongovernment agencies, placement was largely dependent on the extent to which these agencies were ready or able to receive them. As it happened, the Ministry of Education was one of the agencies most in need of the students, for until that time it had been forced to rely on the services of unqualified Ethiopian teachers or expensive expatriates.

Table 22 shows the pattern of EUS participation by college or faculty, as well as by teaching or nonteaching assignments, for a period of one decade (1964–65 to 1973–74). As might be expected, almost all students from the education faculty were placed in teaching positions; most of the students from the schools or colleges of agriculture, arts, business administration, and social work were also assigned to teaching positions. Some students from the other colleges were teaching, but most were in nonteaching positions. Those in nonteaching positions, however, were not necessarily in positions directly related to their disciplines. Overall, some 70 percent of the participants worked as classroom teachers. Therefore, any assessment of the impact of EUS on Ethiopia's rural transformation must focus on the schools and their students.

TABLE 22
EUS Assignments by Faculty/College, 1964–1974

Faculty/ College	Teaching	Non- Teaching	Total	Percent Teaching
Agriculture	317	158	475	66.7
Arts	378	60	438	86.3
Business	452	88	540	83.7
Education	1136*	19	1155	98.4
Law	12	169	181	6.6
Pharmacy**	1	82	83	1.2
Science	233	62	295	71.0
Social Work	7	72	79	8.9
Technology***	188	292	480	39.2
Total	2724	1002	3726	73.1

*Includes 6 Home Economics students.
**Pharmacy was in the Department of Medicine. After five years of pre-clinical and clinical training, medical students serve an internship. They did not generally participate in EUS.
***In 1969–1970 the Building and Engineering Colleges have been amalgamated to form the faculty of Technology.

Sources: 1) HSIU, *The Ethiopian University Service* (Addis Ababa, March 1973), pp. 25–27.
2) EUS Office, 28 December 1973 (for 1973–1974 data).

Students who were assigned to work in their own fields or related areas took positions in the various specialized agencies as assistant engineers in municipalities, social workers and pharmacists in rural hospitals, as agriculturalists, and in varying roles with the Election Board, the Prison Department, the Ministries of Mines, Land Reform, Justice, Interior, Public Health, and Community Development, as well as with some nongovernment agencies. Over a period of ten years, 967 students served in these nonteaching, profession-related areas. It was observed that EUS participants assigned to areas directly related to their fields of specialization tended to maintain clearer perceptions of their roles in the program, and made every effort to link themselves with agencies which could provide maximum exposure to their future professions.

During this period, nearly 4,000 young people participated in the EUS program. This figure is impressive for a country that was starving for educated minds and hearts to aid in its transformation. The political and cultural impact of the EUS venture is dealt with in chapter 8. Suffice it to say here that placing EUS participants in rural Ethiopia had a leavening effect which over time contributed to the eruption of the sociopolitical volcano in 1974.

To make the program as flexible and unburdensome as possible, the Faculty Council statute empowered the EUS standing committee to waive requirements regarding the definition of ruralness. Thus, students in the following categories were exempted from national service: extension and part-time students, members of the armed forces, and other students such as those who had worked in rural areas for at least six years prior to being admitted to the university—that is, school teachers, supervisors, and administrators or civil servants who were temporarily released from their normal duties. Later, for practical reasons, students of the School of Medicine and the Public Health College, whose regular program of studies required prolonged field experience, were also exempted.[9]

The committee was also empowered to consider applications for special placement for family (defined as consisting of husband or wife and children), medical, and research reasons. The rules provided that special placement based on the requirements of research projects could only be granted with the approval of the appropriate academic commission which would judge the relevance of the research project to the participant, the university, and the nation in general. As for special assignments for health reasons, the assignment committee relied on the evaluation of the university medical staff. The number of students that fell under any of these categories was very small and created very few problems, if any, as far as placement was concerned.

Related to assignment was the question of workload during national service. Initially, this was not considered a problem. While in the field, participants were expected to work as much (or as little) as any other employee of a given agency. By and large, EUS participants were meticulous in carrying out their responsibilities. However, some reports from students in the field and supervising faculty and staff indicated that (1) participants were exploited by being required to carry more than normal workloads, (2) there was a need for more involvement by participants in community programs beyond their normal work requirements, and (3) there were sound educational reasons for participants to engage in research or data-collection activities as part of their national service.

Eventually, the Faculty Council reformulated student workload requirements during national service. The council provided that participants would be required to devote a maximum of twenty-five and a minimum of eighteen hours per week. The deans of the various faculties would assign faculty advisors to participants to ensure that effective liaisons were maintained. The advisor would: (1) advise each participant on the selection of a suitable study or research project for the EUS year, (2) provide guidance and assistance during the execution of the project, and (3) at the end of the service year evaluate the participant's work and project. "This report and evaluation together with other reports would in turn be used by the EUS office in determining whether or not the service academic requirements had been satisfactorily discharged while at the same time contributing to a fuller appreciation and understanding of the problems of rural development in Ethiopia."[10] In this way, the university improved its supervision of EUS to insure that the understandable need for more involvement of EUS participants in providing service did not outweigh the other spheres of their responsibility, i.e., research, systematic observation, and informational interaction with members of the local communities.

Sources of Finance and Logistics

Whether or not it was an intentional part of the design, the EUS was part of a general social revolution. It was the creation of the "elite and a daughter of national pride; they couldn't stand to see the Peace Corps and other programs working in rural areas—and Ethiopians not there, too," said a foreign observer.

The EUS program was conceived and administered primarily through the efforts of the national university. Initially, the university had to do some hard selling to convince the conservative government that the EUS served the national interest. The EUS statute provided a monthly allowance of U.S. $75 per participant (to be paid by the employing agencies); married students and students assigned to hardship areas were paid 10 to 15 percent more. The university provided each participant with a canvas bed, a folding table, chair, kitchen and first-aid kits, and, in some instances, water filters and lamps. A plan to provide teaching-aid kits was postponed for lack of funds. Equipment costs per student, per academic year, came to U.S. $50. The total annual cost of equipment, supplies, EUS staff salaries, and medical care for participants was U.S. $40,000. The employing agencies paid transportation costs and the subsistence allowance mentioned above.

As the program expanded and the number of participants increased, and as participants aroused the misgivings of the government with their political activity, the financial picture became more burdensome. As a last resort, the university appealed to the employment agencies for a direct contribution of Birr 50 (U.S. $25) per participant to offset the administrative expenses of the program.[11]

The university also explored the possibility of attracting funds from foreign philanthropic organizations, and received some limited help from the Ford Foundation. However, financial problems were never satisfactorily resolved and they continued to handicap the progress of the program.

Feedback from the Field

Despite their initial resistance when the EUS was instituted as a requirement for graduation, once in the field, students responded with valor to the challenges they found in rural Ethiopia. Going beyond the call of duty wherever they went, most students organized literacy campaigns for adults and children; conducted evening classes for adult school teachers, civil servants, military, and police personnel; organized welfare programs and engaged in fund-raising activities to help needy students who had come from remote areas in search of education; and organized scouting troops, photography, drama, language, and debating clubs, etc. In cooperation with students from the local high schools, they initiated agricultural clubs for the exhibition and sale of farm produce, staged demonstrations of gardening and poultry raising for local farmers, and built simple houses, erected fences, and worked in the yards of infirm and elderly people. Some studied local crop diseases; others experimented with the development of disease-resistant strains of the staple crop, *teff.* They organized communities to build sports fields and helped schoolchildren cultivate aptitudes and skills in carpentry as well as in simple but scientific gardening and farming. Faculty field supervisors' notes are replete with heartwarming and valorous reports of EUS students as initiators, teachers, and participants.[12]

Even on an unscheduled visit to an assignment area, one was likely to find EUS participants tutoring children after class in the classrooms, on the sports fields, or in their own homes. During lunch hours the school surroundings were busy with groups of students working on their projects in gardening or experimenting with other similar projects. One cannot do adequate justice to what was witnessed in the field. Simply stated, experiencing these events firsthand was a momentous phenomenon that one could never forget. I am tempted to say that rural Ethiopia, where 90 percent of the 25 million people lived, was in the process of profound social transformation.[13]

On the academic side, the EUS students gathered data in the field which served as material for the senior essays they were expected to produce in order to satisfy degree requirements. University faculty members also reported that EUS returnees exhibited mature and realistic assessments of the Ethiopian situation as a result of their field experience. Employers' representatives from the field, in most cases, assessed EUS participants as qualified, hard working, and enthusiastic. There were other employer representatives who maintained suspicions regarding the participants' political activism. Few, if any, faulted EUS students for lacking zeal and commitment in their willingness to go beyond the call of duty. The contribution so far was excellent, but more effort was needed to push it even further. As was stated, "The EUS has contributed a great deal of the nation-building effort, but much more is expected from the Ethiopian educated community."[14]

Major problems arose in two major categories as byproducts of the success of the EUS program: (1) the interaction between educated youth and the sociopolitical conditions prevailing in Ethiopia, and (2) an acute awareness of the undeveloped administrative, political, and economic infrastructure of the country.

One of the major headaches of the EUS program was communication with the students in the field. Although attempts were made to place groups of students into relatively accessible areas, it was often difficult for representatives of the EUS office and the respective faculty representatives to maintain frequent contact with them due primarily to poor roads, lack of adequate transportation, and the inordinate amount of time required to travel to the field. It was estimated that, on the average, a faculty member spent upwards of 65 percent of his time traveling. This proved to be very expensive for the faculty and the university alike.

Another problem was the difficulty some students encountered in receiving their allowances on time. In some areas students, as well as government employees, were not paid for four to five weeks or more, due to the lack of local banking facilities as well as to bureaucratic inefficiency. Mail service was very irregular (at best) or nonexistent, preventing students from maintaining regular contact with other students in the field, as well as with faculty and students on campus. There were also reports that some local officials suspected that the students were investigators sent out by the central authorities, and that the students' reports were reports on the local bureaucracies.[15]

The most difficult problems, however, arose from the political activism of EUS students in the field. Students as individuals and members of the two main university student unions had adopted radical ideas regarding the political and social order of the country under the *ancien regime*. Once in the field, the EUS students addressed the central issues as they perceived them and shared their views openly in and out of class with the students as well as with the larger community. They tried to articulate the sharp contrasts they perceived between the existing conditions of poverty, ignorance, apathy, and fatalism among the peasants, and the intolerable greed, corruption, and pure incompetence of the ruling oligarchy who were supported by the relatively small land-owning classes. In their attempts to expose the status quo, the targets for attacks included everyone from the emperor to the lowliest police officer and local governor.

This inevitably led to serious conflicts with local governors, police officers, traditional village leaders, and citizens. As a result, a number of EUS participants were imprisoned, expelled, transferred from their assignments, or punished in other ways. Most often, the university was held responsible for producing such a rebellious, antiestablishment breed of young people. The state-supported university no doubt paid dearly for this in one way or another, but EUS continued.

In the earlier days of the EUS, the zeal, activism, and increasingly political actions of participants won converts, primarily among the upper elementary and secondary school children and youth. Most of the peasants and townspeople were suspicious of and, at times, openly antagonistic toward the revolutionary doctrines propagated by these audacious youngsters. They gradually became convinced that what the EUS students stood for was, for the most part, intended to benefit the poor, the disowned, and the disenfranchised—the abolition of unjust taxation systems, the equitable distribution of land, in short, the abolition of the exploitation of the many for the benefit of the few, as well as the extension of health care services and educational opportunities.

This gradual shift in the attitude of the rural people spurred the EUS students to yet more intensive attacks on government policies. The students began to take bolder political action and through sophisticated political maneuvering and elaborate communication networks, organized most of the university and high school students across the country for confrontation with the government. In the process, the university was drawn into the conflict between the students and the political leadership. The students claimed university protection based on the abstract principle of academic freedom. The government saw, in the university and its students, a concentration of hotheaded rebels and unruly people who defied the traditional Ethiopian values of obedience and civility. The university, as a state-supported institution, paid for this situation by having to endure budgetary cuts and other forms of political pressure which severely restricted continued program expansion and development.[16]

As with education in general, we shall never be able to fully assess the attitudinal and behavioral changes that occurred among the peasantry and their tragically conservative communities as a result of EUS. It is safe to conclude that, without the daringly unprecedented vocal and physical activism of the EUS students, the dramatic changes that began in the winter of 1974 could never have come about.

Achievements

Assessment of the EUS must be based on three of its original goals: (1) the extent to which it contributed to the education of the university student, (2) the extent to which it helped meet the critical work force needs of the country, and (3) the impact it left on the communities it served.

University students, according to Korten and Korten, moved rather quickly from staunch opposition to EUS to stalwart support for its goals and the educational experiences it offered. After a year of service, however, their attitudes toward dogmatism and the benefits and drawbacks of technological development, and their perceptions of the assumed characteristics and values of the peasantry had not changed. Participants claimed to have developed a better understanding of the problems of rural Ethiopia and to have learned the satisfaction derived from helping others. Many of them also indicated that they would be willing to serve in rural areas after graduation, or that they had changed their career plans as a result of rural service. "The vast majority . . . considered the service experience intrinsically rewarding, feeling both that they had benefited from it and had contributed to the welfare of their countrymen."[17]

In their attempt to reconcile the seemingly conflicting attitudes that students maintained in relation to the peasantry and their contributions to rural welfare, the Kortens quote one student who said that the broader, generalized attitudes had been learned in the abstract and remained intact, while the direct contact with conditions of the rural poor had influenced specific attitudes. The Kortens concluded:

> certain kinds of significant changes occur in the participants of a national service program. These changes revolve very closely around the participant's particular service activity and his perceptions of himself in relation to that activity. The fact that so many of the participants felt the experience was intrinsically rewarding may be the most significant result because they probably will be more receptive to future opportunities for similar experiences. This in itself will be a positive outcome of the program for both the individual and his country.[18]

The attitude changes identified in the Kortens' study were apparent through the history of the EUS. However, whether the general student attitudes regarding peasant conservatism and inertia continued to prevail was not ascertained. The Quarmbys, who visited

Ethiopia in the late 1960s to examine the operation of the EUS program, categorically stated that "Undoubtedly the EUS's major immediate achievement is the contribution it is making to the education of Ethiopian university students."[19] This contribution arose from the experience of living and working with people whose language, culture, religion, and ethnic backgrounds were very different from those of the student; the experience of working at a full-time job with its responsibilities, restrictions, discipline, frustrations, and satisfactions; the experience of feeding and clothing themselves and otherwise budgeting their incomes, energy, and time; seeing the usefulness or irrelevance of their education; and the experience of living and working with foreign teachers and volunteers.

It was observed that EUS returnees exhibited keener and more mature attitudes toward their university studies. They also tended to be more sober in their categorical criticism of Ethiopian socioeconomic and political conditions. Their reactions to questions about what they had gained from the experience included: "Now I understand how to live with people, what life looks like outside the area where I was brought up and outside the place [where] I was studying. . . . I have also discovered that living in a small town for a long stretch of time is not, after all, a difficult thing. . . . I have now realized how much responsibility means."[20]

Regarding the second important criterion of evaluation, the role of EUS in alleviating critical work force shortages, the program made a vital contribution. Ethiopia had always had a teacher shortage. Classrooms were crowded; the qualifications of most of the local teachers were minimal; foreign teachers were expensive, unfamiliar with Ethiopian conditions and of short-term benefit; foreign volunteers were available as teachers, but important as they were, they too were limited by language and cultural factors. With few exceptions, and despite the fact that some of them had no teaching experience or training, the EUS teachers were enthusiastically received by the schoolchildren and, in addition to their technical knowledge and skills, served as wonderful role models for Ethiopian youngsters. The EUS program provided 2,742 classroom teachers and another 1,000 in nonteaching, developmental activities—the vast majority worked in rural, hardship areas. In the nonteaching areas, participants made significant contributions to Ethiopia's development. Agriculture, engineering, social work, geology, and pharmacy students assigned to rural areas clearly enhanced the development efforts of their country.

As this author has noted elsewhere, despite the errors in judgment, misutilization, administrative inefficiency, lack of cooperation from professional workers, financial problems, irrelevant field placements, political and economic hardships, community resistance,

200

and occasional mistakes in the art of teaching and human relations, there was no doubt that the year the students spent away from the university was, in many ways, the most educational aspect of their entire university experience. In the students, towns, and villages, the presence of the EUS students injected a novel approach to tackling community problems and a refreshing, contagious curiosity that frequently spread among the students and townspeople alike.[21]

The third fundamental objective of the program, the identification of EUS participants with the local community and their willingness to be fully involved in their development, anticipated the fact that Ethiopia's population was comprised of several ethnic groups with distinct dialects and cultural traits which might not lend themselves to national unity and integration. The fact that students went to regions other than their places of origin enhanced understanding, tolerance, and cohesion among people of different ethnic groups and, in turn, facilitated national unification and integration policies.

The EUS venture is well summed up by the first report of the Chancellor's Advisory Committee on Higher Education which stated, in part: "We have no hesitation in saying that [the EUS] is . . . an inspiration of genius.' So far as we know, Ethiopia is leading Africa, and indeed most of the world, in this enterprise."[22]

Notes

1. Quoted in HSIU Office of Public Relations, "The Ethiopian University Service: An Inspiration of Genius," 1966 (mimeographed).
2. There are a number of interesting working papers in the author's files that show the extent and quality of discussions among the faculty and university administration. Most are undated and without attribution to an author, signifying the kind of precaution deemed necessary at that time. From the progression of the concepts of service, dates can be roughly estimated.
3. Translation from the Amharic text in Andrew and Diana Quarmby, "The Ethiopian University Service" (Geneva: International Secretariat for Volunteer Service, 1970), 2.
4. HSIU, "University Statute of the Faculty Council Establishing a Program of Ethiopian University Service" (1966), 1 (mimeographed).
5. Ibid., 2.
6. David C. Korten and Frances F. Korten, "Ethiopia's Use of National University Students in a Year of Rural Service," *Comparative Education Review* 10, no. 3 (October 1966): 482–92.
7. Ibid., 492. See also Quarmby and Quarmby, 14–15; and Teshome Wagaw, "The Participation of Youth in Ethiopia's Rural Development," *Rural Africana*, no. 30 (Spring 1976): 80. The author is grateful to

the publisher of *Rural Africana* for permission to use passages from this article.

8. HSIU, Office of Public Relations, "An Inspiration of Genius," 76–77; see also Wagaw, "Ethiopia's Rural Development," 76–77.
9. See Wagaw, "Ethiopia's Rural Development," 75–86.
10. Ibid., 79.
11. A letter to this effect from the university president, Kassa Wolde Mariam, in Amharic and English is in the author's file.
12. See HSIU, "Ethiopian University Service" (1968), 1–10 (copy in author's file).
13. I had the opportunity of being the field supervisor during the crucial period of 1966–67. This responsibility took me to the remotest parts of Ethiopia and gave me the unique chance to observe the real Ethiopia at close range.
14. HSIU, "Ethiopian University Service" (1968), 11.
15. Quarmby and Quarmby, "The Ethiopian University Service," 25.
16. For further elaboration, see Wagaw, "Ethiopia's Rural Development," 80–83.
17. David C. Korten and Frances F. Korten, "The Impact of a National Service Experience upon Its Participants: Evidence from Ethiopia," *Comparative Education Review* 13, no. 3 (October 1969): 323. The Kortens were on the faculty of HSIU in the 1960s.
18. Ibid.
19. Quarmby and Quarmby, "The Ethiopian University Service," 25.
20. Ibid., 27.
21. Wagaw, "Ethiopia's Rural Development," 83.
22. Quoted in the "Draft Report of the Ethiopian University Service Standing Committee to the Faculty Council, Haile Selassie I University," 2 June 1967, 7.

III

IN THE SHADOWS
OF
REVOLUTION

8

THE INTELLECTUAL CONTENT
OF THE REVOLUTION

This chapter summarizes the role that the university played in the 1974 revolution that fundamentally altered the traditional sociopolitical, cultural, and economic arrangements of Ethiopia. It is the thesis of this chapter that, without the prolonged, systematic, and concerted political activism of the university students (and later the secondary school students and the teachers' unions), the revolution would have been postponed and its consequences would have been much less profound. Unfortunately, the revolution and its aftermath exposed the naivete of its proponents. The forces that undermined and finally brought down the old order were pathetically unable to propose a viable replacement. The result was an oppressive, insecure military regime that went through the motions of adopting the programs advocated by the student movement but, in the end, brutally excluded the revolutionary leaders from power.

The revolution emerged from the tension between the traditional conventions of power, on the one hand, and the emergence of new institutions, on the other. How the different institutions, concepts, and personalities supporting them interacted, and the university's role in crystallizing various views into a coherent political platform are critical to understanding the intellectual content of the revolution.

Tradition and Alienation

Ethiopia's traditional institutions consisted primarily of the Ethiopian Orthodox Church, the absolute monarchy, the nobility, and, particularly in this century, the person of the reigning monarch who was the head of the ecclesiastical, civil, military, and judicial institutions. Although the throne was most often inherited, the monarchs often fought contenders to secure it and maintained their power through vigilance. The power and influence of the reigning monarch was defined by the sheer personality, intelligence, stamina, willingness to use power, and ambition of the individual. In other words, the occupant of the throne defined the parameters of the monarchy and not the other way around. On the other hand, the new institutions, such as the parliament, a paid and regulated military, secular educational systems, a constitution, and secular laws were twentieth-century imports which were struggling in the post-World War II period to find their places in the Ethiopian milieu.

At the head of these conflicting traditions and institutions stood the late Emperor Haile Selassie I who ruled the country for over fifty years before he was forcibly removed in September 1974. With one leg in the past and the other in the future, Haile Selassie clung to outmoded conventions, values, and attitudes at the same time that he sought reform. For some time many thoughtful people believed that he might succeed in bringing Ethiopia to the mainstream of modernization without the loss of its soul in the pursuit of material well-being. Unfortunately, he failed. His tenacious refusal to share power in a rapidly evolving world resulted in catastrophe for the emperor, his family, and the institutions and values he represented.

Following the Ethio-Italian war, public education expanded and alienation set in—not only between students and political authorities, but also between parents and their children, and religious leaders and the younger generation. Since this was, for all practical purposes, the first generation schooled in a secular setting, the traditional religious values with their emphasis on obedience, loyalty, and deference to authority were questioned and found wanting. However, there were no other secular ethical values acceptable to the new generation to replace the old, and the educated youth began to act as rudderless ships thrown out on a stormy sea of political uncertainty. In the process, they challenged and ultimately destroyed the pillars of traditional sociocultural institutions, conventions, and values.

The emperor always believed that the schools could be relied on to produce technocrats who were supportive of and dependent on his leadership. He had often told young people that it was "Our hope that you, like your fathers, will work hard to serve Us and Our country." To emphasize the importance he attached to this hope, he retained the portfolio of the Minister of Education for long periods in the 1940s and 1960s. It may have been reasonable for the emperor to assume that the schools could effectively socialize youth to be loyal and unquestioning subjects of authority. Many other societies had also thought so in earlier times, but alas, times were rapidly changing and Ethiopian centers of education increasingly became foci for disaffection and alienation.

Reasons for Alienation

The education system is a subsystem of society and does not operate in isolation from other social institutions. Therefore, in Ethiopia, as elsewhere in the world, the student movements, their orientation, form, and directions, were mediated primarily by the social conditions and political environment of the society at large. This generalization does not minimize the importance of internal institutional problems such as the inadequate quality of instruction, overcrowded classrooms or dormitories, unsanitary cafeteria systems, inadequate library or laboratory facilities, and the like.[1] These are important ingredients for effective educational experiences and success in future careers, but they are secondary compared to the other national issues mentioned above.

The postwar generation of students was the first to be exposed to public secular education. Not sharing similar educational experiences, immediate families were unable to comprehend, let alone provide guidance to, their offspring. In essence, alienation and disaffection from home and family had already taken place by the time the child set foot at the school doors. Understandably, most parents had profound faith in the power of schooling without necessarily understanding it. But the more they learned, the more the children began to appreciate for the first time that their education was earning them membership in an elite group vis-á-vis the rest of their society.

The gaps between the old and the young became almost impossible to bridge—the educated, altruistic, articulate, politically untested juvenocracy, on the one hand, attacking the strong-willed, power-wielding gerontocracy on the other. Of course, this intergenerational conflict is universal.[2] What was new in the Ethiopian context was its timing (while adult literacy was still less than 5 percent) and the extremely small proportion (less than 1 percent) of the younger generation that assumed the awesome task of challenging the establishment.

A third dimension, which was not necessarily a cause of alienation but contributed to it, was that, contrary to the social belief in fate and a feeling of powerlessness in relation to nature and those in power, the young people in school were learning that one can, alone and in cooperation with others of similar concerns and interest, bring about favorable change by forcing the issues against those in positions of authority. In other words, instead of their traditional roles of obedience, submission, and willingness to bear, however heavy, the burden willed by fate, students were learning that many problems are man-made and can be altered by the people whose lives are affected. The educated youth learned to become increasingly self-assertive and politically conscious, in spite of the fact that the schools were not at liberty, due to political censorship and intimidation, to teach civic or current history involving the existing regime and political order.

205

As Robert Grey has noted, beginning in the mid-1960s, even eighth-grade students were cooperating with one another and organizing themselves to achieve certain student goals. They sent student delegations to the headmaster, the local governor, or the police to complain about unjust treatment. In the process, they learned that collective action could result in the removal of unwanted teachers or headmasters; in the improvement of classroom conditions, and the like. This kind of political thinking and action was even more significant at the senior high school levels and became dramatic at the university. Unlike any previous Ethiopian generation, educated young people of the 1960s were taking political action and getting some positive results despite the adamant disapproval and even active opposition of their elders.

At least in the case of Ethiopia, political consciousness was a function of (1) level of education—the higher the grade, the more politically conscious students became; (2) urbanism as opposed to ruralism (due to their relatively easy access to political personalities, institutions, and information, students in urban areas such as Addis Ababa and Asmara became more politically conscious and active than their counterparts in the rural schools); and (3) age, which often corresponds to level of education (older students were more politically knowledgeable and more willing to become involved in the political process).

In the 1960s and 1970s almost all of Ethiopia's senior secondary schools were located in Addis Ababa, Asmara, or in the twelve other provincial capitals. At the university level, all but two of the twelve or more colleges were located in Addis Ababa where parliament, the royal palace, and the headquarters of the church were less than three blocks away from the main campuses. In addition, Addis Ababa, as seat of the Organization of African Unity (OAU), the United Nations Economic Commission on Africa (UNECA), and many international agencies and embassies, provided excellent opportunities for students to become attuned to the complex international situation.[3]

There were other factors that contributed to political awareness and activities. In 1962, when the U.S. Peace Corps program was initiated, some four hundred volunteers were assigned to Ethiopia, most of them as classroom instructors. Though they were young, inexperienced, and unfamiliar with the Ethiopian cultural milieu, these young people were idealistic and willing to work harder than their regular Indian or Ethiopian professional colleagues. Inside and outside the classroom, these young foreign teachers were enthusiastically involved with their students' educational activities. This perception of the Peace Corps lasted into the late 1960s, when the volunteers were increasingly seen as an arm of the U.S.

government, which at that time was criticized for supporting the Haile Selassie regime. As a result, the volunteers were asked to leave. Nonetheless, the volunteers made significant contributions in imbuing secondary school youth with the ideals of freedom of thought, and expression and the need for a representative government.[4]

Another important factor in the creation and expansion of political awareness was the establishment of the Ethiopian University Service (EUS) program in 1965 (see chapter 6). The program required students to serve, mostly as teachers, in rural Ethiopia for one academic year between their third and fourth years of college. Over time, the program afforded excellent opportunities for the university students to impart their political views to their students. Teachers preached the gospel of change and revolution. Students listened and believed. The fire was lit.

Those who gained entrance to the university were relatively tough—intellectually and physically. They were also motivated to achieve, as evidenced by their passing the rigorous school leaving examinations. At the college level they were exposed to an unprecedented liberty to think, speak, and act in cooperation with their peers on university as well as national issues. Their cumulative experiences, acquired during schooling, growth to maturity, and exposure to a college atmosphere which encouraged open discussion, gave the students additional impetus to boldly identify themselves with the oppressed masses of the country.

As the 1960s approached, the mood of the nation was forced to shift. Since the 1940s, the government and its officials had become sufficiently rich from the spoils of war and, as they became increasingly confident that their rule was unassailable, corruption and nepotism became well-entrenched in the public domain. Those in power began to feel they had much to protect and little to gain from continued progress.

Still, the schools continued to expand, and colleges were founded. At first, the teaching staff—predominantly expatriate and not always well-screened during recruitment—were instructed not to interfere in internal politics. This admonishment was largely unnecessary; most of the teachers had little interest in or knowledge of Ethiopian values or social institutions. It was easier for them to teach the history and sociology of Europe and North America. Due to official censorship, materials on Ethiopia were either unavailable or boring.[5]

Most of those enrolled in the secondary schools and colleges had already concluded that it was impossible to influence the traditional entrenched oligarchy in a positive manner.[6] This feeling of powerlessness vis-á-vis the national realities led rapidly to significant feelings of alienation. The system of sixth, eighth, and twelfth grade national examinations, which screened out students who were not allowed to proceed to the next levels was another source of alienation. The twelfth grade school leaving examination (ESLCE), for example, screened out up to 80 percent of the matriculants. Some of these students might have been recruited by other subuniversity institutions, but most of them were left out in the cold, untrained for suitable employment anywhere. Traditionally, the public sector was the largest employer, but the bureaucracy had swelled to more than full capacity. Hence, the prospect of gaining admission to the coveted civil service ranks became increasingly dim.[7] Some were absorbed by the various branches of the armed forces but, as the military ranks swelled, their dissatisfaction grew proportionately.

Education and contact with the outside world also had more subtle effects. It is certain that schooling, even in its less-than-ideal form, imbued youth with concepts of social justice, equality, and critical thinking, for even before the sources of alienation mentioned above had manifested themselves, postprimary students had expressed concern for their country's economic and social plight.

Early in the current century, a new consciousness was becoming apparent among the educated elite. One such graduate, Professor Afework, who was living abroad, began to articulate in a very informed and sensitive manner the plight of the Ethiopian farmer vis-á-vis the wealthy feudal lords and soldier-oppressors.[8] He returned to Ethiopia during the occupation period and continued to criticize the feudalistic policies of Haile Selassie's government, policies which he thought were condemning the masses to a slow death. Another critic, Negadras Gebre-Hiwot Baykedagn, took the existing administration to task and admonished the Ethiopian people to wake up from sleep.[9]

Before the war in the 1930s, a small group of educated military and civilian elite had established an association known as *Jeunesse d'Ethiopie* which published a newspaper. Its primary function seemed to be to consider the government's attempts at modernization. One of the group's members, a graduate of the London School of Economics and future minister of finance, addressed his young colleagues by saying: "We young Abyssinians are in duty bound to our country, we are the bridge the Emperor has thrown across the European culture. . . . We have to pay for our own studies out of our own pocket and then work for the state for nothing."[10] But Yilma Deressa, the author of this statement, and the Habte Wold brothers, Aklilu and Akalework, saw their roles as complementing the efforts of the emperor and never in contradiction to them.

Following the war, the political maturation of college students was greatly facilitated by a number of exogenous factors including the introduction of foreign teachers and learning materials, as has already been pointed out. However, in hindsight, the most significant single factor was the arrival of young people from English-speaking African countries. During the 1958 Conference of Independent African Countries in Accra, Ghana, the emperor promised to provide two hundred scholarships to students from these countries. These young people from east and west Africa were both elated by Ethiopia's centuries-old political independence and, at the same time, startled by the strict censorship and lack of political freedom. They told their Ethiopian counterparts about struggles in their respective countries to attain full freedom and equality. No doubt the Ethiopians drew analogies to local conditions. Shortly thereafter, students tried to defy official censorship by reading in public and organizing student associations without consulting college or government authorities. These initiatives aroused official misgivings, even concerned annoyance, but more dramatic events soon intervened.

The Gathering Political Cloud

Suddenly, the attention of the awakening college students was focused on two brothers, Germame and Mingistu Newaye. The former was a graduate of Columbia University in New York, with an M.A. degree in political science; the latter, a major-general in the Imperial Body Guard, was a graduate of the Military School at Holetta in Shewa province. In December 1960 the Newaye brothers led a military coup d'etat while the emperor was in Brazil on a state visit. Although it failed, the attempt was daring for both its audacity and foolhardiness. Germame committed suicide rather than surrender. The general was wounded, but recovered sufficiently to stand trial. He was convicted and hanged in public. As the coup attempt was in progress, students in Addis Ababa were mobilized to march in public support of the Newaye brothers. That event, perhaps more than anything else, turned the tide of student radicalism once and for all. Upon the emperor's return, the students were made to publicly apologize in writing to the emperor, but neither the students, the emperor, nor the people of Addis Ababa forgot on which side student opinion lay.

Not long after the coup attempt, the dormitory and boarding facilities of the University College of Addis Ababa were dismantled; students were provided a monthly allowance of Birr 50 (U.S. $25) to cover room and board, which they were to arrange for themselves. With this new policy, the government hoped to deprive students of the opportunity to get together to talk, plot, or annoy the authorities. However, the plan did not have the intended effect.

If anything, it heightened student frustrations and encouraged them to greater action.

As for the general public and the armed forces, the coup demonstrated that both the emperor and his government were not invincible and exposed the glaring faults of the regime to public scrutiny. The saga of the Newaye brothers became a standard rallying point for the student movements. The general's statement moments before his death, that the torch he had started would continue to burn for generations to come, seemed to be prophetic.

The consolidation of several colleges under a central administration (Haile Selassie I University) in 1961 further facilitated student cohesion and radical political activism. Students continued publication of *News & Views*, which in the mid-1960s merged with *Struggle*. The two student unions, University Student Associations of Addis Ababa (USAAA), and the National Union of Ethiopian University Students (NUEUS)—the latter embracing the Gondar and Alemaya, as well as the Addis Ababa colleges—became agencies for information gathering and dissemination. Their audiences included both school children and the general public. Political activism was further enhanced by very liberal (for Ethiopia) Faculty Council legislation that became operational in 1966. The legislation established detailed, complicated, but thorough provisions regarding lawful student, faculty, and staff conduct, privileges, and responsibilities. When students violated university rules, they had the right to be heard by a university tribunal and the right to counsel. This legislation, totally alien to Ethiopian concepts, contained provisions supportive of the central university's mission: building an open, just, and democratic community of people governed by civility and law instead of personality. Once the document was accepted by the Board of Governors and became operational, the student unions took full advantage of it.

Viewing themselves as the uncorrupted, pure in heart, the Messiah of the oppressed masses, the youth pressed on to battle. Using the concept of academic freedom, they organized public demonstrations in favor of land reform, abolishment of concentration centers for the poor or maimed, and government and economic reforms. The responses of the government were hesitant, unsure, or sporadic. Student governments often appeared to be much better organized for political action than was the national government. At any rate, students seized upon many social issues and organized demonstrations with or without the requisite permits to march through the city.

The student leaders became increasingly convinced that they were the vanguard of the oppressed people and that it was their responsibility to carry the educated elite's burden to research and expose the numerous weaknesses of the *status quo*. As time went on, they used any pretext to arouse confrontation. For instance, every year from 1966 through 1974 there was at least one student strike or demonstration. The following particular incidents are described in some detail to illustrate the escalation of the conflict:

In the spring of 1968, the HSIU faculty women, nonfaculty Ethiopians, and non-Ethiopians organized a benefit fashion show featuring European styles made from locally manufactured materials. Some of the women were to model miniskirts, which were in vogue in many parts of the world. When USAAA leaders heard of the plans, they protested and sought cancellation of the event. The students came to me in my capacity as dean of student services to explain the grounds for their opposition. The fashion show, they said, was expensive bourgeois entertainment and debased Ethiopian cultural values. Although I did not share their reasons for opposition, my position was that it would be better to cancel or postpone the show in the interest of campus tranquility. However, the vice-president, with the support of some faculty, expressed the view that the scheduled events were purely educational, did not violate decorum or any established law, and that student union leaders had no business interfering with the educational activities of other groups within the university community. They felt strongly that acquiescence to student pressure would weaken the administration's position vis-á-vis future student demands.

On the evening of 29 March 1968 the two vice-presidents, a couple of other people, and I met in Ras Makonnen Hall to prepare for the inevitable confrontation with students during the fashion show the following day. It was reasonably clear that students would organize a demonstration in the Sidist Kilo main campus. It was also likely that they would use physical force to either prevent fashion show participants from attending or disrupt the activities once they began. In light of these expectations, the police and security officers of the city were informed and asked to concur in an agreement that outlined the steps that would be taken and the roles the police and security people would play if the university guards were called on to handle the situation. The agreement document emphasized the university's intention to do everything possible to persuade students not to interfere, but if it failed, the police were permitted to restrain students from carrying out their threats. The business vice-president hand-carried the papers to both the police and security headquarters. At about midnight he returned to report that they had agreed to follow the suggested steps. Meanwhile, our committee had drafted a notice to be distributed that night to all students urging them not to disrupt legitimately scheduled university functions. This notice bore my signature.

211

On 30 March, at 1:00 P.M., students began to assemble in front of Ras Makonnen Hall. Most of the university administration officers were inside the building. Together with some immediate associates, I pleaded with the assembled students to disperse. At about 2:00 P.M., as guests and participants were arriving, the students pelted them with eggs and stones. This prompted the police, who had been standing outside the gates, to disperse the students with high-powered water cannons and tear gas. Subsequently, two truck-loads of students were arrested and taken away to a prison camp in the western part of the city.

The fashion show, or the "miniskirt episode" as it came to be known, proceeded, but I did not see it. For the second time in the history of this young university, outside security personnel had been called in. The aftermath of that afternoon's episode was eerie and depressing. The beautiful spring afternoon sunlight pierced the imposing former palace buildings. I felt it symbolically reflected my thoughts and feelings at that moment—a dash of hope that dialogue, civility, and compromise between the old and the young, between government and the educated elite, between teachers and students, was possible.

Throughout the incident, Kassa Wolde Mariam, the university president, was indisposed. The vice-president for business affairs, Wubshet Dilnesahu, served as the main link between the university and the government. In the afternoon, Wubshet carried the news of what had happened to the emperor, who had, of course, been fully briefed on the plans and developments of the drama, and who was at the national stadium watching a soccer match that afternoon. At about 5:00 P.M., Wubshet reported to the university officers that the emperor had approved the police measures. Later in the evening, the university president appeared, and he too supported the actions.

Subsequently, the Addis Ababa university campuses were closed. On 1–3 April students demonstrated against the university closure and for the release of their detained comrades. As was to become customary following periods of clashes, protests, and the like, on April 9 the emperor ordered the university reopened. Students resumed classes soon after. The detained students were released. The school year ended in June as scheduled.

Almost a year later to the day, students rioted in the streets of Addis Ababa. This time the secondary school students of the city joined the demonstrations. Among other things, the students demanded the replacement of the minister of education, Akalework Habte Wold; an increase in the education budget; abolishment of the small fee students paid for matriculation examinations; a cut in extravagant expenditures for embassies, banquets, and official

212

entertainment; a slashing of ministerial salaries and traveling allowances; and the expulsion of U.S. Peace Corps personnel and Indian lecturers. In all, there were twelve points in their demands: ten were directly related to national political issues and two were related to the university (demands for examinations and for tuition fees for those whose parents were wealthy).

On 7 March 1969 the emperor appeared on national radio and television. He looked tired and infirm. His hands visibly shook. He stuttered and repeated phrases or lines as he read his prepared text, which was an appeal to parents and elders to encourage the younger generation to support and abide by the traditional conventions and values of Ethiopia. Perhaps for the first time, Haile Selassie looked and acted as though he had seen better days; it was time, perhaps past time, that he depart and let someone be in charge of Ethiopian politics. Things were falling apart at an accelerated rate while the emperor gazed out from this palace uncomprehendingly. One of the amazing spectacles in this sphere of national life was that the establishment always placed the blame on others rather than looking inward to critically examine their own doings or otherwise attempt to understand the students' point of view. They seemed to be prisoners of their own upbringing, experiences in power, or expectations; once one is in power one has to project an image of authority by making all decisions or claiming the credit for all decisions. In Ethiopian culture, compromise is a sign of weakness; taking advice from one's "subjects" or subordinates, let alone from children, is inexcusable. Power and authority can only be projected and maintained by maintaining an image of toughness (intellectually and physically) and detachment. One is not necessarily liked or respected for being warm, compassionate, close to the people, or revealing normal human frailties. The ruler must appear to be beyond the vicissitudes of life that afflict other mortal beings. This aura of might and invincibility was no doubt communicated effectively to Haile Selassie for he was groomed from his early years by his father, as well as by his relative and mentor, Emperor Menelik II.

As far as I am aware, no definitive biographical study of Haile Selassie I exists. The few incomplete attempts are by non-Ethiopians who had limited access to him as a person and lacked reliable sources of information.[11] No Ethiopian scholar has attempted to write a biography of Haile Selassie. His own autobiography, in two volumes, does not shed much light on his inner thoughts, struggles, or triumphs.[12] He tells us primarily what we should expect him to say—no revelations, no surprises. It is, therefore, difficult to fully understand him. The few exceptions to this lack of insight about Haile Selassie occurred rather late in his life. In June 1973 an article appeared in the *Chicago Tribune* based on an interview that the famous Italian journalist Oriana Fallaci had with the emperor at his palace in Addis Ababa. The interview was conducted in French, we are told, without the intermediary of the customary translator from Amharic. This may be why the views expressed come closer to the essence of his personality. If we take his expressions literally, and there is no reason why we should not, we get a clearer perception of him and of the attitudes that shaped his views and political policies vis-á-vis the educated youth.

When asked what he thought of the new disconnected generation of young students, Haile Selassie responded:

> Young people will be young people. You can't change the uncouth manners of the young. Besides, there is nothing new in that. There is never anything new under the sun. Examine the past: you will see that the disobedience of the young has occurred all through history. The young don't know what they want.
>
> They can't know it because they lack experience, they lack vision. It is for the head of state to show the young which path to tread and to punish them when they revolt against authority. It is up to Us. But not all the young are wicked and only the most irreducible culprits must be punished unbendingly. The others must be reduced to reason and then permitted to serve their country.

When asked if he would punish them even to the point of death, he replied: "[T]he death penalty is just and necessary for disobedience for instance. . . . Because it is in the interest of the people. . . . We can't abolish that [death penalty]. It would be like renouncing punishment for those who dare to defy authority."

As far as his own youth was concerned, he intimated to Fallaci that he was very serious, very diligent, and very obedient. If he were sometimes punished, it was because he was not spending much time amusing himself or playing games with others. He was also punished for studying too much.[13]

As for the emperor's relationship with his own family, not much is known outside the immediate family circle because, traditionally, royal personalities were never a proper subject for public scrutiny or discussion. One thing we do know is that Haile Selassie's oldest son, the former crown prince, was terrified in the presence of his father. Haile Selassie indulged some of his grandchildren when they were very young; for example, the children of the Late Prince Makonnen. However, it is known that as they grew to adolescence they all came to detest him. One was imprisoned for his daring audacities. In recent conversation, a highly educated Ethiopian, who grew up in Haile Selassie's palace and held several important cabinet posts, intimated to this author that once you were a child in the royal household, "Janhoy" (His Majesty) wanted you to remain perpetually a child and resented one's maturation to independence.[14]

John Spencer, an American lawyer sent to Ethiopia by the U.S. government, was in a position to observe Haile Selassie from 1935 onward. As the emperor's foreign policy advisor, he noted that Haile Selassie had a dual personality. On the personal level he could be generous, thoughtful, gentle, and was often willing to render favors without expecting recompense. To a point, he was also loyal and forgiving. As a monarch, however, he was scheming, devious, egotistical, remorseless, selfish, grasping, and suspicious. According to Spencer, Haile Selassie's oldest daughter was the only family member who was totally devoted to him. To the others, he had all-seeing eyes and employed informants to keep tabs on their activities. At times he was indulgent and domineering, probably more feared than loved by the younger generation. "Yet, to the end the emperor was dogged by the dislike of the elites which no amount of personal favors could alleviate."[15]

Spencer adds that he seldom observed anyone who genuinely liked or respected the emperor, even among the sycophantic cabinet officers with whom he surrounded himself. He puts it this way: "His egotism and tactics nourished approbation among the aristocrats, and Haile Selassie's awareness of their dislike led to negativism, such as delay in designating his heir, emulating Louis XV: 'Aprés moi le deluge.' "[16]

Obviously, the emphasis on symbol, convention, and tradition rather than substance, and the emperor's distrust of others who showed the slightest inclination to question or challenge the status quo were dominant factors in his dealings with the young, educated generation. We are led to conclude that Haile Selassie believed the responsibilities of youth to be obedience, conventional thinking, serious labor, and conformity. In his world view there was no room for deviation from the well-beaten, "tried and true" path. The products of the schools were to function within the political parameters and traditional conventions as he defined them. This attitude is in direct conflict with what schooling tries to achieve—continual examination, analysis, and criticism of the existing order. Haile Selassie's formula failed to incorporate the vision of a progressive Ethiopia, led and supported by the inquisitive mind. This was a major factor in his downfall and Ethiopia's present turmoil.

Even as the educated young people intensified their political struggles, observers of the Ethiopian scene continued to complain that the Ethiopian intelligentsia was corrupted by the allure of the establishment's power and money. These observers maintained that radicalism ended when individuals were recruited into the civil service. One such frequent observer, who was in Addis Ababa during the trial of Mengistu Newaye and who paid a return visit only a few years later, found that some of the promising radicals who had once thought revolutionary changes were imminent were singing a different tune. Now they were praising the wisdom of His Majesty and observing that democracy was inapplicable in the Ethiopian context. The observer, Peter D. Smith, wrote:

> This was the voice of the older order, speaking through its new recruit, this domesticated revolutionary. Every year the Emperor sends a batch of these new young men to study in Europe or America, but he is careful whom he chooses. . . . After two or three years they come home, full of advanced ideas and needing a job. . . . The young men sit around for a few months, drinking coffee and complaining about the regime, until jobs are arranged for them. The most talented are given something with a high-sounding title and little responsibility. . . . In any case, no decisions of any importance are taken except by the Emperor personally. He is 70 and ailing, but he still cannot bear to delegate authority; in Ethiopia it is regarded as a sign of weakness. In such a climate the bright young lights soon grow dimmer, and the suffocating conventionality of Ethiopian life does the rest. Some foreign observers believe that the hope of change lies with these young intellectuals, but I do not think so. Change there must be, more than anywhere in Africa.[17]

Smith's observation of things as they existed then was correct, but fortunately his prediction proved wrong. Although it could be argued that the revolution, when it occurred, did not come from the ranks of those who held high office, it does not follow that it could have been effective without their assistance.

Eventually, political radicalism permeated the elementary and high schools—including those in rural areas. A number of factors contributed to the spread of radical ideas, but perhaps the Ethiopian University Service students, who began working as teachers in 1965, were most influential. As they took the gospel of college radicalism into the country, these articulate young people were received enthusiastically by secondary school students, to the dismay of local government authorities and parents. Some were thrown out, but most succeeded in completing a year of service.

Perceiving the weakness of the regime and their own relative strength, student activists became more daring and bold in the late 1960s. Their efforts were augmented by growing support from organized labor, the Ethiopian Teachers Association, and even the rural people. During one of many demonstrations held in 1968, police arrested several hundred students for violations. En route to the detention center, one of them, Demeke Zewde, age 20, was killed—some say by other demonstrating students who were trying to reach the police convoy. This was the first in a series of killings; upheaval and violence were destined to continue for some time.

On the night of 28 December 1969 a momentous event transpired. As he was leaving the home of a girlfriend in the late evening, Telahun Gizaw, 29, the president of USAAA and half-brother of one of the emperor's sisters-in-law, was gunned down by unknown assailants a few meters west of the main university campus in Addis Ababa. He was taken to a nearby hospital where he died shortly afterwards. The students immediately concluded that the government was responsible. The government security forces issued categorical denials. The next morning, university and high school students retrieved Telahun's body from the hospital to hold a funeral service. This act conflicted with government plans to fly the body to Tigrai province, Telahun's birthplace. A contingent of the Imperial Bodyguard, fully armed, arrived on campus. The students did not relent. The long, hot day progressed, with slogans and speeches by the student leaders urging the soldiers and others to support the students' efforts. The stalemate lasted throughout most of the afternoon. At about 3:30 P.M. the soldiers opened fire; four students were killed and at least five were wounded. Telahun's body was retrieved by the government and flown out of the city. By 5:00 P.M. the students scattered; the campus had become a ghost town. At the same time, Ethiopians who were studying abroad occupied Ethiopian embassies to demonstrate their solidarity with comrades at home.[18]

As the confrontations escalated, the government made no attempt to discover what lay at the root of the problem. It appeared that the authorities had concluded that since the students' demands could not be met (or if they were met, the government would no longer exist), the only way to cope was through the use of brutal force. Meanwhile, the students scattered throughout the city to peddle their revolutionary ideas.

As the 1960s drew to a close, the staff, faculty, and administration of the university became increasingly polarized within the institution. As the process of Ethiopianization of the faculty progressed, academic power devolved upon the largely inexperienced but determined Ethiopian faculty members—almost all of whom were under forty years of age. Most had completed work for advanced degrees in Western Europe or North America and were therefore recent returnees. The Board of Governors, on the other hand, was controlled by senior government officials, mostly of the pre-World War II generation. At the national level, of course, the political leadership was firmly in the hands of the older generation who had come to power following the 1941 return of national independence. These gaps in age, education, experience, and political orientation created problems of communication and understanding within HSIU itself.

The Ethiopian University Teachers Association (EUTA), which was established to serve the professional interests of its membership, came to be perceived by the government as a den of political scheming. The younger academicians, who considered the EUTA dormant and inept, proceeded to form their own association, the Ethiopian University Teachers Forum, whose membership was highly exclusive (by invitation only) and whose political orientation was radical. The members of this organization considered any campus-based organization immune from outside interference. Their political activities were primarily national in concept and application. An attempt by the Ministry of Interior to regulate the activities of these associations by requiring them to register their charters increased the antagonism. At the same time, other factions within the university emerged. Nonteaching university personnel, for example, began to perceive the academicians as an elite group that drew relatively high salaries and enjoyed many privileges while they, the nonteaching staff, languished.

Among the faculty, almost everyone sympathized with student politics. However, there were disagreements on how deeply the faculty, as a group, should become involved in national politics. The degree of direct individual political activity in concert with the student movements varied: the younger members encouraged the students and became actively involved; most of the older faculty counseled moderation and sought deliberate, steady means to achieve political change.

These misperceptions of roles, petty jealousies, and the like within the university community created a climate of uncertainty and apprehension. However, these differences were relatively minor compared to the national malaise. Though their preferred means of affecting change varied, the national issues united almost all segments of the university community. Time and again the government tried to stifle the political activities of university faculty and professional staff. Efforts at suppression succeeded occasionally, but eventually the government was unable to control them. Still, the vanguard of campus political activities remained the students themselves. By 1969 student opinions were becoming solidified into political platforms. In addition to their previous demands for land reform, free and universal education, the abolishment of corruption and the like, they became increasingly sophisticated and adept in their abilities to arouse and draw the masses of people to their side and weaken the establishment. They began to publicize their solutions to the "nationality" issue—ideas that they had been arguing in their small cells for a long time. For instance, in the 17 November 1969 issue of *Struggle*, a student publication, there appeared two pieces on this subject—one an editorial and the other a long article by one of the more articulate exponents of the radical movement, Walelign Makonnen.[19] The editorial, titled "Purge of the Feudal Legacy," and the article supported the various attacks on the government, including the series of skyjackings of Ethiopian Airlines planes. They also supported cultural and linguistic independence for the various Ethiopian nationalities, including secession from the union, if necessary, and called on the people to prepare for the inevitable armed struggle. As might be expected, this sent a jolting message to the regime. The student positions were becoming clearer, more coherent, and more respectable among the heretofore doubting public.[20]

This surge of student activism and militancy was given an additional opportunity to manifest itself on another occasion: the 1972–73 famine. This was not the first event of its kind in the history of Ethiopia. The difference this time was that as the government tried to routinely ignore or gloss over the issues, the students, along with some of their instructors, resisted. They held public rallies at the Addis Ababa campuses, forewent their breakfasts for a period of three months so that the money saved could go to help the famine victims, and otherwise tried to dramatize the plight of the famine victims.

The exposure of the famine, during which an estimated 200,000 people perished, the energy crisis, the labor unrest—all these forces facilitated the revolution that swept the country at the beginning of 1974. Left alone, the Haile Selassie government might have fallen as a result of its own moral and political bankruptcy. The student movement accelerated its demise. However, when the government collapsed the student leaders were not sufficiently organized to fill the vacuum. The two succeeding civilian governments were never able to represent the spirit and tempo of the new national mood. When the military stepped in, hesitantly and cautiously at first, they were surprised that the student and labor movements did not follow enthusiastically. They soon learned that the students and their colleagues wanted a "civilian people's government," and on this point the military and the civilian radicals parted company.

As participants in the student movement watched the devolution of political power into the hands of the military, they became bewildered and disheartened. L. S. Feuer's comments on the Russian student movement a half century earlier aptly described the Ethiopian students' predicament in 1974-76:

> By 1917, the student movement had lost its historic opportunity to promote a rational social evolution in Russia. Its idealism had for several decades been so intermixed with the apotheosis of destruction, its political consciousness had been for so long dominated by generational struggle, that it was emotionally disarmed when the Bolshevik party . . . put into practice what the students so long had preached.[21]

The student intellectuals had brought the socialist ideas to the workers, but Lenin insured that that was their last act as free intellectuals. "From then on, a discipline was to be required to which student movements were incapable," Feuer said.[22] Soon afterward, Lenin's interest in the student movement diminished to the vanishing point.

Meanwhile, cognizant of the political power of the organized student body and mindful of how formidable the students could be, the *Dergue* (committee), as the ruling junta came to be known, promoted the idea of a development mobilization which entailed sending postprimary students and their teachers to a two-year period of rural service. The plan itself was hastily conceived, poorly organized, and clumsily implemented. When, after considerable hesitation, the students arrived in the rural areas, they proceeded immediately to initiate radical ideas regarding land distribution, court and police procedures, and the like. There were conflicts with the new government authorities. Some young people lost their lives in the process. Eventually, after a two-year service period, the students returned to Addis Ababa and other urban centers where full-blown conflicts developed between the leftist radical civilians (comprised mostly of students and the intelligentsia) and the military. During the ensuing "white terror" and "red terror" campaigns, which are discussed in chapter 9, thousands of students were tortured and killed.[23]

In the end, many of the ideas and platforms espoused by the Ethiopian students became guiding policies for the new government. Land reform measures, the nationalization of large industries and commercial establishments, the concept of cultural and linguistic freedom and independence, and a number of other ideas, were all rallying points. Members of the valiant student associations may not have liked the expropriation of their ideas, but they could take some comfort in that the ideas for which they fought were not altogether lost. They paid the price of being educated, of being conscious. To them also goes the glory of having fought well and worthily.

Conclusion

The educational models imported into Ethiopia were expected to provide the cultural, political, and economic leaders of this ancient and hitherto tradition-bound land. The political leadership responsible for the inception and implementation of a university concept hoped to produce educated people who would use their knowledge and technical skills for the advancement of the nation within restricted parameters conforming to the self-interest of the existing regime.

However, once exposed to the ideals of egalitarianism, justice, and democracy, the students began to question the legitimacy of the power structure vis-á-vis the mass of the people who were ignorant and poverty stricken. Acting upon this realization, students, supported by their teachers and an increasingly sympathetic public, through word of mouth, public demonstrations, unions, and publications, began to voice their grievances on behalf of the poor and powerless peasantry. The government's increasingly harsh repression was matched by the increased determination and stridency of the students in their efforts to oppose the regime by any and all means at their disposal.

Eventually, when the government fell without a single shot being fired, the students and intellectuals were not prepared to fill the huge political void. Finally, slowly, hesitatingly, a committee (*Dergue*) of junior officers drawn from the various branches of the armed forces came together to form a government. In line with the momentum established by the students, the *Dergue*'s ideology and policies were leftist, radical, and fundamental. The traditional political and religious institutions, together with their conventions, were fundamentally and irreversibly destroyed or unrecognizably altered. The transformation was profound, the replacement uncertain, the process painful. The Ethiopia of pre-1974 was no more. The new Ethiopia is still evolving.

Notes

1. Desta Asayehgn has shown, for instance, that at the high school level, the alienating factors in the Ethiopian context included student perceptions that they were not involved in decisions affecting their education, mass failure of students in national examinations, lack of access to prestigious educational institutions, and diminished employment opportunities after schooling. "Student Alienation: A Study of High School Students in Ethiopia" (Ph.D. dissertation, Stanford University, 1977), 113–24.
2. See L. S. Feuer, *The Conflict of Generations* (New York: Delacorte Press, 1968), 28–29. For theoretical positions that may help explain generational conflicts, refer to Otto Klineberg, et al., *Students, Values,*

and Politics: A Cross-cultural Comparison* (New York: The Free Press, 1979), 1–6; Margaret Mead, *Culture and Commitment* (New York: Columbia University Press, 1978), 1–132.

3. For further elucidation, refer to Robert D. Grey, "Education and Politics in Ethiopia" (Ph.D. dissertation, Yale University, 1970), 173, 190–93, passim.
4. For an analysis of the American Peace Corps contributions, see Gary D. Bergthold and David C. McClelland, *The Impact of Peace Corps Teachers on Students in Ethiopia, Human Development Foundation* (Peace Corps Contract—P.C. 80-1531, Task Order 2, (Cambridge, Mass.: Human Development Foundation, December 1968), 1–150.
5. See R. Greenfield, *Ethiopia: A New Political History* (New York: Frederick A. Praeger, 1968), 320.
6. See Desta Asayehgn, "Student Alienation: A Study of High School Students in Ethiopia."
7. The author remembers that in 1968, during one of his senior psychology classes, he mentioned the dim prospects of employment in the civil service. The anxiety and hostility this precipitated, on the part of the students, was almost incomprehensible.
8. R. Greenfield, *Ethiopia*, p. 313. Perhaps out of desperation or complete alienation from the Haile Selassie government, Professor Afework became an editor of an Amharic daily in Addis Ababa, under the Italian regime.
9. Ibid., 315.
10. Ibid.
11. Leonard Mosley, *Haile Selassie, Conquering Lion* (Englewood Cliffs, N.J.: Prentice-Hall, 1964); Christine Sanford, *Ethiopia Under Haile Selassie* (London: J. M. Dent & Sons, Ltd., 1946). A number of biographical works exist in Amharic but, due to political repercussions as well as conventions, they may not be objective or insightful enough to be of scholarly value.
12. Haile Selassie, *My Life and Ethiopia's Progress*, trans. Edward Ullendorff (London: Oxford University Press, 1976).
13. Oriana Fallaci, "Journey into the Private Universe of Haile Selassie," *Chicago Tribune*, 24 June 1973, sec. 2.
14. The man, now living abroad, may wish to remain anonymous.
15. John Spencer, "Haile Selassie: Leadership and Statesmanship," *Ethiopianist Notes* 2, no. 1 (1978): 31.
16. Ibid., 31–36.
17. Peter Duval Smith, "No Dawn in Ethiopia," *New Statesman* 65 (March 1963), 456.
18. There were rumors that monies from outside sources were aiding student activities. The Libyan government was one of those suspected. Previously, the Ethiopian Foreign Ministry had announced that three Czech diplomats and two Soviet correspondents were expelled for their connections with student activities. For further information, refer to Peter Schwab, ed., *Ethiopia and Haile Selassie* (New York: Facts on File, 1972), 132–34.

19. Walelign Makonnen, a Wollo-born Amhara, eventually graduated from college, but was killed in the early 1970s with six or seven other young people as they presumably attempted to skyjack an Ethiopian Airlines jet.
20. For a fuller analysis, see the author's article, "Emerging Issues of Ethiopian Nationalities: Cohesion or Disintegration," *Journal of Northeast African Studies* 2, no. 3 (1980–81): 69–75.
21. Feuer, 49.
22. Ibid.
23. See Amnesty International, "The Military Government's Red Terror Campaign," AI Index: AFR 25/14/78, 1–7. Of student involvement and contributions during the revolution up to 1978, see Norman J. Singer, "Ethiopian Human Rights," *Proceedings of the Fifth International Conference on Ethiopian Studies*, ed. Robert Hess (Session B, 13–16 April 1978, Chicago, Illinois), 663–75; and Marilyn Hall Biassa, "Civil Military Elite Interaction in the Ethiopian Revolution," *Proceedings of the Fifth International Conference on Ethipian Studies*, ed. Robert Hess (Session B, 13–16 April 1978, Chicago, Illinois), 771–81.

9

CRISES OF IDEOLOGY
AND ACCOMMODATION

Emperor Haile Selassie's intransigence, coupled with the disorganization of the student movement, the trade unions and intelligentsia, led to wrenching national turmoil and a power vacuum into which the armed forces were inadvertently drawn as the old establishment disintegrated. Writing in the summer of 1975, a year after the fall of the emperor's regime, journalist Colin Legume observed:

> The army takeover of Ethiopia had been entirely unplanned; the soldiers literally stumbled into a position of power for which they were unprepared. What had started in February 1974 as an army mutiny over soldiers' grievances had turned unexpectedly into a revolution which swept the Emperor and his Imperial system, both having outlived their time. By stubbornly clinging to his throne and refusing to arrange for a constitutional transfer of power, Haile Selassie had succeeded in the end only in destroying much of his life's work, probably destroying the royal dynasty, jeopardizing the unity of his country, and leaving behind him instability and the prospect of serious armed conflict.[1]

This was an accurate summary of the events. Fifteen years later in 1990, instability and conflict still prevailed in Ethiopia. In September 1984 the long expected communist party, known as the Workers Party of Ethiopia, was established. Most of the *Dergue* members continued to occupy important positions. The sorry record of political instability, armed conflict, oppression of all kinds, coupled with drought and famine, and the absence of any degree of personal freedom continued to prevail. It is in this new context that educational institutions, particularly institutions of higher learning, must attempt to play a constructive role in the ongoing drama of Ethiopia's social, cultural, and political transformation.

As we have seen, the national university provided students with a protective umbrella under which they were able to conceive, develop, and eventually act upon their political ideologies. From the early 1960s they were, for all practical purposes, the only organized, educated group that was able to challenge the hitherto supposed invincible power of the emperor. As the 1960s progressed, some students from the military academy in Harar and a few members of the Army, Air Force, and other military branches were attending regular courses with other full-time students in Addis Ababa. During this period, public school administrators were also coming to the Addis Ababa campuses to participate, first, in a year-long educational experience, and later, in a series of summer programs designed to upgrade their professional capabilities.[2]

It appears that these educators and soldiers were interested observers of (and possibly participants in) some of the campus-based political activities. When they left the university they no doubt shared what they had learned at the campuses with their colleagues in the schools and the barracks. At the same time, for lack of civilian jobs, many of the newly politicized high school graduates were joining the army, navy, and more significantly, the air force and the engineering corps. The end result of all of this was that before the political leadership became fully aware of its significance, the politicization process was dramatically underway.

For instance, on 11 February 1974 the teachers' association, whose eighteen to twenty thousand members made up the largest professional organization in the country, requested a meeting with the emperor, to which he agreed. In that meeting the teacher representatives not only petitioned for a salary increase and annulment of the recommendations of the Education Sector Review committees (ESR), which the Ministry of Education was ready to implement, but also demanded land reform. This was the first time that a nonuniversity professional association moved beyond its own restricted interests to address larger issues of national significance. Soon afterward, the only national trade association, CELU, began issuing similar demands of national import instead of their usual requests for wage increments to compensate for inflation, government recognition of workers' rights to strike and organize, and the like. The spirit and ideology of the students were firmly established among the urban elite, the trade unions, the teachers' association, as well as the lower strata of the school population.

Following his "divide and rule" policy, the emperor continued to position opposing forces against one another: the Territorial Army against the Imperial Bodyguard and the Air Force against the Paratroopers, for instance. Even senior military officers were positioned so that they could not act in concert. The minister of defense was not on speaking terms with his chief of staff. It was reported that they communicated through third parties or written notes. There were also other subtle but effective efforts to maintain the divide-and-rule strategy. One was a patronage system whereby officers' loyalties were cemented by grants of land, houses, or cash. At court, particular individuals who were favored for the day were deliberately seated in positions of prominence (e.g., next to the emperor). At many banquets, certain types of favorite drinks or foods were taken from the imperial table and served to an officer; often the emperor personally supervised the order of banquet seating arrangements.

An important source of military status and power was graduation from the elitist Harar Military Academy or the Air Force Academy. On the other hand, the graduates of the Holeta School, which usually recruited those with less than secondary education and offered less intensive training, were considered not as important and were treated accordingly. This was, as it later turned out, a fatal mistake, since most of those who assumed power in the *Dergue*, including the chairman and the head of state, were graduates of the humbler institution.

The most radical military groups were located in the air force. By the early 1970s, Air Force officers, who had longstanding links with the student movement and the intelligentsia, formed political cells. Most of these military activists had grown up during the years of student turbulence at the university.

On the other hand, ranking military officers constantly expressed annoyance and impatience with university-student agitation for political and social reform. They thought the real enemies were the secession attempts in Eritrea, which had been ongoing for the previous twelve years, and the struggle with Somalia, which was heavily armed and supported by the Soviet Union, over the contested Ogaden region. Even during national catastrophes such as the cholera threat of 1972, the Wallo drought of 1973–74, and the energy price crisis of 1974, the senior officers remained unconcerned. They admitted that these and other problems were real, but insisted that if the country followed the suggestions of the students and the intelligentsia, Ethiopia as an entity would disintegrate beyond recognition.[3]

The Immediate Issues

The 1974 revolution has been erroneously attributed to a series of army mutinies. This is far from the truth. There had been prior military mutinies and demonstrations. In 1960, immediately following the abortive coup d'etat organized by the Imperial Bodyguard, the army menacingly demanded and received a hefty pay raise. It was reported that if their demands had not been granted the soldiers in Addis Ababa were prepared to take physical action against the government.[4] The difference between the outcomes of the 1960 and 1974 crises was the drastically altered national political climate which was primarily brought about by the continuous propaganda and political action of the university student movement.

On 12 January 1974 the Fourth Army Brigade stationed in Borena, in the southern part of the country near the Kenyan border, complained that its officers were not properly looking after the welfare of the rank and file. It identified specific issues including that (1) the water supply was interrupted, and when soldiers tried to draw from the officers' well they were prohibited from doing so; (2) the food supply was of poor quality and was inedible; and (3) there was corruption among the officers involving food contracts. Led by some noncommissioned officers, the soldiers arrested their officers, including the brigade commander, and asked the emperor to dispatch a higher military officer to investigate the situation.[5] The emperor then made one of his fatal mistakes. Instead of taking forceful measures, he dispatched General Deresse Dubale, the commander of the Territorial Army. Upon his arrival in Borena, the general was immediately detained and treated to the same food and drink that the soldiers had been forced to consume. He soon developed diarrhea. A week later, the commander of the Air Force was dispatched from the capital with the promise that the soldiers' complaints would be thoroughly investigated. The emaciated General Deresse was released. By that time, however, the mutineers had spread news of the episode far and wide among the armed forces.

At about this time, the teachers' union was striking over salary issues, as well as over the Education Sector Review, which set out to drastically restructure the education system to make education accessible to the vast majority of people within the limits of available resources. Among other things, the ESR proposed drastic modifications in the salary structures of school personnel.[6]

On 14 February 1974 students staged public demonstrations in support of the teachers' demands. Soon afterward, they began to attack public buses and other vehicles. This was followed by a series of strikes by the taxi and bus drivers, which effectively paralyzed transportation in Addis Ababa. Even private vehicles moving in the streets were mercilessly stoned. The immediate reason given by the taxi and bus drivers for their strikes was an exorbitant increase in the price of gasoline. Beyond that, it was clear that they were influenced by the increasingly volatile political conditions of the capital.

At about the same time, members of the Army demanded a series of pay raises. When the raises were reluctantly granted by the emperor, the demands escalated and members of the army demanded the resignation and trial of cabinet officers for their alleged incompetence in public office. On 25 February 1974 the entire cabinet resigned, led by Prime Minister Aklilu Habte Wold. On 27 February the emperor announced the appointment of Endalkachew Makonnen, an Oxford University graduate and Minister of Posts and Telegraph, as prime minister. The senate president, Lt. General Abye Abebe, the emperor's former son-in-law, became Minister of Defense.

Endalkachew was an astute, ambitious politician who had been waiting for an opportunity to step into the national limelight. However, he found it extremely difficult to form a cabinet. New political realities demanded that cabinet appointees reflect the plurality of Ethiopian society; that they be free of corrupt, exploitative influences; and that they possess high technical or professional skills.[7] They also had to be acceptable to the armed forces, whose representatives were sitting with Endalkachew as he negotiated procedures and personalities.[8]

Endalkachew's government lasted from 28 February through 22 July 1974. Throughout his brief tenure he struggled to gain control of the situation. While his government lasted, university students adamantly rejected him outright, insisting that he was no different from the personalities he replaced. The armed forces, the teachers' association, and the trade unions demonstrated publicly for his resignation. On 22 July he was forced to resign. He was arrested, and in February 1975 he was executed along with fifty-nine other former senior officials.

Endalkachew was replaced by a fellow Oxford graduate and former friend and colleague, Michael Imru. The son of the late *Ras* Imru, a cousin of Haile Selassie and a radical progressive in his own time, he was respected for his humanity and compassion for the poor. Michael had asserted his independence earlier by resigning his foreign ministry position under Haile Selassie (the first person ever to do so) and had served as ambassador to the United States and to the United Nations. On assuming power in July, he formed his cabinet. Barely two months later, on 12 September 1974, the armed forces dethroned the emperor and assumed power. Michael was retained by the new government as a counselor in political matters.

Thus, the might and aura surrounding the emperor came tumbling down without a single shot being fired in defense of Haile Selassie or against his adversaries. The emperor, after cunningly manipulating power and personalities for such a long time and effectively squeezing out the last drop of will to make decisions or act collectively from all those who had served him—his cabinet, the military officers, and other faithful "subjects"—confronted his young enemies alone at his Jubilee Palace. After the reasons for his removal were read to him by a member of the *Dergue*, he was driven away, amid shouts, jeers, and insults, in a small blue Volkswagen to the southern part of the city where he stayed for nearly a year. The *Dergue* announced that upon returning from medical treatment abroad, Haile Selassie's only surviving son, Merid Azmatch Asfa Wessen, would replace him as king. By March 1975, however, the monarchy was completely annulled.[9]

Many countries in Africa and elsewhere offered Haile Selassie asylum and urged the *Dergue* not to put him on trial. In the words of el Numerei, ruler of the Sudan, "He is not just an Ethiopian; he belongs to Africa." In response to these pleas the emperor is supposed to have said: "I am an old man and I have been in exile once in my life; I've no desire to become an exile again."[10] This debate was soon put to an end when his death was announced on 28 August 1975.[11]

Governing power was transferred fully to the hands of the Provisional Military Administrative Council (PMAC); the popular Army general, Aman Andom, became chairman of the Council of Ministers, the chairman of the *Dergue*, Minister of Defense and Chief of Staff.[12] On 20 December 1974, Ethiopian *hebrettesebawinet* (Ethiopian socialism) was announced. Under the banner of "Ethiopia *Tikdem*" (Ethiopia First), the major goals and programs were spelled out in a document entitled "Program of the National Democratic Revolution of Ethiopia."[13]

Subsequently, the new government undertook a number of important steps that profoundly affected the social and economic structure of Ethiopia. All lands (rural and urban) were nationalized, putting an end to the long vexing inequities and property litigations which contributed to the stagnation of development for the vast majority of the people. Major industrial and commercial establishments were also nationalized in line with the new philosophy of bringing the means of production under state control.[14] These measures brought immediate popularity to the new regime. Whether they were well thought-out and whether they will eventually alleviate the economic burden of the poor and landless peasants is another matter altogether. The military government also established *Yekebele Mahiberoch* (urban associations) and *Yegebere Mahiberoch* (peasant associations).[15] These two institutions were very promising tools for the democratization process. The need for such associations had been rallying points of the student movement, and it seemed that the platforms formulated by the student movement had become the policy of the new government. In a way, this development was disquieting since the students had taken such extreme positions only because the conservative former regime had upheld such diametrically opposite policies.

By taking these radical steps, the PMAC hoped that by building upon the political positions of the students and intelligentsia, they would be able to attract and hold together these hitherto disaffected social elements. They were mistaken. The students, together with the major trade unions (CELU) and the Ethiopian Teachers Association (ETA), appreciated the demise of the old regime. However, they maintained that what was needed was a "peoples' democratic government" composed primarily of civilians. The PMAC disagreed.

The Students

Although the students, in collaboration with the teachers' associations and the trade unions, had played the major role in bringing down the *ancien regime*, in its aftermath they failed to design a viable replacement political institution. As a result, they were crushed by the security forces of the Endalkachew government. It took some time for them to regroup. When the military junta seized power in September 1974, therefore, it did not necessarily snatch the leadership of the revolution from the students and workers; it rejuvenated a political movement that the civilians were unable to sustain,[16] indicating once again that the organizational and technical skills that effectively destroyed the old order were not capable of launching its replacement. The students and the few intelligentsia of the civilian left were handicapped by a number of problems. Among these were an inability, due perhaps to cultural history, to compromise or accommodate divergent viewpoints in the interest of achieving common goals; the composition of the groups' membership itself, which ranged from the most sophisticated politician-professors to college freshmen; and a lack of logistical and communication support.

The PMAC was well aware of the importance of the civilian left wing. It understood from the outset that the Ethiopian student movement, for instance, had always been guided by leftist political ideology. Since this movement destroyed the old order on whose ashes the present regime was founded, and since the knowledge and skills of the intelligentsia were indispensable to the consolidation of its political gains and future, the military tried to court the intellectuals. The quest for military-civilian cooperation proved elusive, however, for at least two fundamental reasons. First, before the revolution, the military and police forces had arrested, dispersed, and even killed student demonstrators and political dissidents. This was a very serious matter as far as the students were concerned and they came to believe that their former oppressors should not profit from the peoples' revolution. Secondly, the student movement did not believe the military would actually initiate and implement meaningful, genuine, revolutionary programs that would benefit the poor majority. Despite these misgivings, of which they were well aware, the military junta still hoped that once their drastic economic and social measures were announced they would be able to attract sufficient support from student and other civilian groups.

Following the revolution, several opposing factions developed within the ranks of the university students—a splintering that derived, in part, from the students' social and economic backgrounds. Ethiopian university students came primarily from urban areas (notably Addis Ababa, Asmara, and Harar), centers of power and opportunity and the locations of the better secondary schools. Successful completion of studies in any of these urban senior high schools qualified students for admission to one of the local colleges or a North American or western European university. Those who studied abroad were exposed to wider ranges of political influence and were more intellectually sophisticated and articulate than were those who remained in Ethiopia. Although almost all of the university students progressively adopted a socialist ideology of development, most of those who went to North America adopted the 1960s concepts of participatory democracy—a version of Maoism. Ethiopian students who had studied in western Europe were more likely to endorse a form of bureaucratic socialism. The ideology of the students in Ethiopian colleges tended to follow the North American pattern. Ultimately, these ideological patterns determined who would side with the military and who would side with the opposition in 1975.

The *Dergue* continued to seek alliances with the progressive elements—the students, professionals, and trade unions. In the fall of 1975, the nominal head of state announced his intention to create a political party of peasants and workers. He appealed directly to students and alumni to collaborate in this endeavor, which he said was the right approach to consolidation of the gains achieved by the revolution. In December of the same year, the government formed a political bureau under the chairmanship of Haile Fida, a graduate of a French university who had recently returned to Ethiopia at the request of the new government after many years abroad. Eventually, the bureau's membership totaled some fifteen people, all of whom were recent returnees from many years in Europe and the United States. They were young and inexperienced (none of them had ever held any meaningful full-time job), and all had been divorced for years from the day-to-day realities of Ethiopia.[17]

The *Dergue*'s creation of the politbureau intensified the opposition of the civilian radicals. The latter group claimed that the decisions of their former colleagues and friends to join the bureau in collaboration with the military were acts of treason. They saw in the *Dergue* Bureau alliance a concerted effort to stifle the promises of the revolution.

Though the *Dergue* wished to include as many of the radicals as possible in the new government, some were reluctant to join. Some of those who joined later defected. The main reasons for their opposition to the military were the radicals' beliefs that the top-down approach to political organization contravened the spirit and intent of the revolution, which was a mass uprising, and that a true political party could only develop from the grassroots level.

By December 1975, the opposition revealed the existence of the Ethiopian People's Revolutionary Party (EPRP) and its official publication, *Democracia*, which had been appearing since 1974.[18] The major issue that divided the bureau and the EPRP was not only ideological. The debates revolved primarily around whether or not a feudal state could be pushed to socialism in one movement. The bureau supporters maintained that a rapid transformation to socialism could be achieved by utilizing the organizational structure and power of the army, and that a planned, democratic transformation would take too much time. Even though the *Dergue* was far from being socialist, it had shown progressive tendencies that the radicals might have expanded by forming an alliance with it. But hard lines were being drawn. The bureau also maintained that, by rejecting the concept of a military-civilian alliance, the EPRP was advocating an anarchist position.

EPRP supporters insisted that there was no shortcut to socialism. They thought that the popular movement that had been manifest since before 1974 had to run its course through a period of unlimited democracy. This would enable the antifeudal, anti-imperial forces to organize. They believed, with some justification, that such a popular movement was actually underway until the *Dergue* brutally arrested student and labor leaders. The *Dergue*, they said, had already indicated its fascist tendencies by its brutal suppression of grassroots movements working toward self-administration and self-sufficiency. According to the EPRP, the military, represented by the *Dergue*, was afraid to permit peasants and workers to organize and arm themselves to protect the gains of the revolution. The bureau and its supporters, they said, were elitists, which was a contravention of the spirit of the revolution. Therefore, any cooperation with the *Dergue* and the bureau was out of the question. The struggle had to continue. Accordingly, the EPRP peoples' provisional (civilian) government was established.

Otherwise, the Political Bureau and the EPRP were in substantial agreement on social and economic goals. Both pledged equality of rights to all religious and ethnic groups; equality of the sexes; and the eradication of poverty, illiteracy, and disease. Both parties advocated job opportunities for all; pension rights for workers; higher salaries, and the nationalization of rural land, industries, and

233

major commercial establishments.[19] They could not agree on whether the military should be included in national governance and on the pace of socialist development.

The Political Bureau steadily accumulated more power by directly associating itself with the *Dergue* and it began to indulge in some precarious political maneuvering. The bureau thought that it could, in a relatively short time, manipulate the *Dergue* to a subordinate position and establish a civilian government similar to the one advocated by the EPRP without risking the good will of the military.[20] The EPRP, in the meantime, proceeded to organize support by creating cells in the schools, trade unions, and colleges. As usual, it continued to attract large followings among the student body, the middle class, and the radical intelligentsia.

However, it was clear that the Political Bureau enjoyed the more advantageous position. It had the support of the national government and access to all segments of society. As a bureau set up to establish organizing committees and peasant-worker parties, it was able to establish branch offices in the many hundreds of districts and subdistricts and staff them with MEISON (All Ethiopia Socialist Movement) supporters controlled by the bureau. The bureau was also in charge of the new political school set up to indoctrinate civilians and military officers regarding the emerging socialist political realities, and it had almost unlimited access to the public media and other forums which were beyond the reach of the EPRP.

In 1976 the EPRP leadership adopted a very drastic and, as it later turned out, fatal solution to its frustrations. It organized and armed groups of people to launch an urban guerilla warfare campaign, eventually called the "white terror," against the *Dergue*, the bureau, and their supporters. The second-ranking official in the bureau's hierarchy, Fikre Merid, was assassinated in broad daylight in the middle of Addis Ababa as he sat in his car. A number of other civilian and trade union leaders who supported the bureau were also killed. On the night of 23 December 1976, the chairman of the *Dergue,* Mengistu Haile Mariamo, eluded an assassination attempt.

At this stage of the revolution, the slogan, "Ethiopia *tikdem yalminim dem*" (Ethiopia first without bloodshed) became obsolete. The government, in concert with the Political Bureau, launched a counterattack—the "red terror"—to oppose the "white terror."

What ensued, during 1977 and 1978, was a nightmare. With the government's encouragement and active support, the militia, the police, and the armed forces carried out a program of indescribable terror and destruction against real or imagined EPRP members and supporters. Children as young as nine years old were arrested, interrogated, tortured, or murdered—often for minor offenses such as reading propaganda materials scattered in the city streets. Others were shot in the streets or at home while their families watched in horror. Most of the victims were schoolchildren, high school and college students. Many thousands perished.[21]

What was left of the EPRP and its supporters moved to the northern part of the country. They tried to regroup and fight back; however, they were never successful in the armed struggle against the bureau or the government. Eventually, the EPRP as a political organization virtually disappeared from the scene.

During the "red terror" campaign, the *Dergue* became aware that the Political Bureau and its MEISON supporters were using the purge against the EPRP to entrench their political fortunes. Indeed, there were reports that the bureau chairman, Haile Fida, and his associates had used the purge to eliminate their real and imagined enemies in a move to assume power. Once the *Dergue* realized this, it turned its fury against the bureau members. In the process, as they attempted to flee the city, several were killed and others were captured and imprisoned.[22]

Most surviving members of the EPRP, MEISON, and their supporters, escaped to neighboring African countries, to Europe, North America, and the Middle East. For many of those apolitical but educated individuals who remained in Ethiopia, day-to-day existence continued to be a life-threatening situation. An estimated 3,500,000 people, including some of the most highly educated Ethiopians of their generation, fled to safety. Indeed, the most valuable Ethiopian export since 1975 has been its highly educated, highly skilled citizenry—an export the country can ill afford.[23]

After a palace shootout in February 1977 which resulted in the murder of the second postrevolutionary head of state, General Teferi Bante (who had replaced another murder victim, General Aman Andom), and at least five of his associates, Lt. Colonel Mengistu Haile Mariam, a graduate of the Holeta Military School and first vice-chairman of the *Dergue* since September 1974, emerged as the dominant political figure. By then the membership of the *Dergue* had been reduced, through execution, imprisonment, or defection, to almost half its original number of 120.

In order to satisfy external pressures and quell internal expectations, a central committee was set up to organize a socialist political party. Its membership was drawn primarily from the armed forces, though it included some civilians loyal to Mengistu. Contrary to official rhetoric, the central committee included no representation from the peasants or trade associations. Freedom of assembly, expression, and association was banned, as were the student union movements and the trade and teachers' associations. As far as political freedom was concerned, Ethiopia returned to square one. Instead of expanding civilian participation as it had promised to do, the *Dergue* increasingly placed soldiers in almost all provinces, districts, and subdistricts as governors or watchdogs of the *Dergue*'s interests. The civilian opposition forces were no longer a threat. The *Dergue* controlled everything and permitted no one to dare utter even mild criticism.

Institutional Survival

In the aftermath of the struggle for supremacy, the *Dergue* feared that the national university might once again shelter and nourish threatening ideas that could eventually challenge its power. The members of the *Dergue* were mostly grade school and short-term technical school graduates who deemphasized the importance of formal education.

The educational system, the university in particular, was blamed for accomplishing "more harm than good" in the past. The system was criticized for being academically oriented, examination centered, and elitist. The graduates of the system were harangued for being self-centered, of bourgeois mentality, consumers, and exploiters. The entire educational system was blamed for corrupting Ethiopian cultural values, for creating wealthy individuals while the masses remained destitute, and for encouraging class structure in society. This criticism became so heated, and the anti-intellectual climate became so intense, that it was advisable for individuals who were suspected of being educated to hide their identities if possible.[24]

Unfortunately, among the forces behind such inflammatory statements were some members of the intelligentsia who, for one reason or another, had their own grievances against the university. These people insisted that the "revolution should not stop at the gates of the university," meaning that the university should not be allowed to shelter those whose ideas differed from the political ideology of the day.

In response to this antiacademic ferment, the new university leadership made a shrewd political move. The president approached the *Dergue* leadership and suggested that the thinking of the university community might be influenced by dialogue and education. This, he proposed, could best be achieved by sending faculty members to socialist countries for short visits. The idea was accepted.

No one could guarantee, of course, that once the faculty left the country they would return, but the risk was considered worthwhile. Some forty people were selected for the first experiment. Before being sent abroad, however the *Dergue* insisted that, in case they fled or refused to return, potential replacements would have to be identified. Replacements were selected by discipline and level of qualifications. On the journey to and from the USSR, great pains were taken to make sure that no opportunities for escape were provided. The flights, hotel accommodations, and even the routes they were to take were carefully planned. Finally, to the relief of all concerned, all the participants returned home after several weeks in the Soviet Union. Several other faculty trips were subsequently undertaken with progressively less concern that the participants might defect.[25] There is no way to know how exposure to Soviet thinking might have influenced the Ethiopian academics. But for the time being, it saved the university from invasion or worse. Prudent, imaginative leadership protected the university from the worst of the political excesses.

Within the university, however, political tensions arising from continued factionalism between teaching and nonteaching staff, senior and junior academic staff, students and other members of the community, and supporters of the *Dergue* and those who opposed it, persist to this day. No doubt, these tensions have taken their toll on the productivity of university teaching and research.

Change and Continuity

The new political philosophy designed to provide direction for all major national endeavors including higher education was embodied in two basic documents. The first, "Ethiopia *Tikdem*" (Ethiopia First), was declared on 20 December 1974. Ethiopia *Tikdem* "means *hebrettesebawinet* (Ethiopian Socialism), which means . . . equality; self-reliance; the dignity of labor; the supremacy of the common good; and the indivisibility of Ethiopian unity."[26] The second basic document was known as the *National Democratic Revolution Program*. It highlighted the design of the national agenda as follows:

> The objective of the national democratic revolution is to liberate Ethiopia from the yoke of feudalism and imperialism and to lay the foundations for the transition to Socialism. . . . Towards this end, and under the leadership of the working class and on the basis of the worker-peasant alliance and in collaboration with the petty bourgeois and other anti-feudal, anti-imperialist forces, establish a people's democratic republic in which the freedom, equality, unity and prosperity of the Ethiopian people is ensured, in which self-government at different levels is exercised and which allows for the unconditional exercise of human democratic rights. To this end, there will be an educational program that will provide free education, step by step, to the broad masses. Such a program will aim at intensifying the struggle against feudalism, imperialism and

bureaucratic capitalism. All necessary measures to eliminate illiteracy will be undertaken. All necessary encouragement will
be given for the development of science, technology, the arts
and literature. All the necessary effort will be made to free the
diversified cultures of imperalist cultural domination from their
own reactionary characteristics.[27]

This basic document of the revolution provided for a socialist,
presumably classless state led by the proletariat majority, consisting of peasants, workers, and their alliances. This philosophy was,
of course, in direct opposition to the policies of the previous government, under which the national university was established.

The most important single policy document regarding higher education that has emerged from the postrevolutionary regime provided
for the creation of a national higher education commission. The
concept, however, was by no means new. The 1972 Education Sector Review recommended such an organization in response to the
growing number of higher education institutions and the need to
coordinate or regulate their activities.[28] Prior to that, in 1968, the
Presidential Commission of the Haile Selassie I University suggested
a similar measure.

Like these earlier proposals, the commission established by the
military government was designed to coordinate and regulate the
activities of all postsecondary institutions rather than directly influence the goals, approaches, or missions of individual institutions
of higher learning. The commission was to assume some responsibilities of the Ministry of Education, such as accreditation of nongovernment postsecondary institutions not directly controlled by
the national university system, and coordination of the activities
of existing and future institutions of higher education.

In its preamble, the proclamation establishing the commission
redefined the mission of higher education to include the improvement of the material, educational, and cultural well-being of the
oppressed masses. The specific objectives were to (1) teach, ex-
pound, and publicize socialism and formulate methods to carry out
these functions; (2) produce the national work force required by
overall national plans; (3) conduct research and studies on the needs
of the country in general and on the increase and distribution of
production in particular; (4) explain, disseminate, and try to implement the results of these studies; (5) educate and prepare competent professionals and technicians to serve the population; (6)
provide for the necessary refresher programs for workers; and (7)
in cooperation with government and mass organizations, make
every effort to develop and enrich the country's culture, free from
"imperialist influence and reactionary content."[29]

As far as its organization was concerned, the commission had a council and a secretariat, or office. The council was made up of the ministers of Education (chairmen), Agriculture, Health, and Industry; the commissioners of Planning and Science and Technology; and five others appointed by the government. The secretariat of the commission was headed by a commissioner of Higher Education appointed by the government. As executive officer, he was in charge of the day-to-day activities of the commission. The commissioner was also a member of the council and was its secretary. All in all, there were twelve council members. The functions and powers of the council generally corresponded with those of the former Board of Governors which it replaced, though the power of the council was greater both in scope and intent. The former university board included an elected representative of the alumni, a position that was excluded from the new council. This was very ironic since the new government professed its intention to involve all segments of the national community in its governance. It is possible, of course, that the fact that the last alumni representative was arrested and imprisoned for presumably siding with the civilian opposition to the *Dergue* influenced the decision to do away with alumni representation. Also interesting was the fact that neither the teachers' association or trade unions, nor any of the mass organizations such as the peasant, *kebele*, youth, or women's associations, had representation on the council. In this case, as well as in a number of other organizations, such as the Committee to Elect the Political Party, membership was drawn exclusively from the military and civilian elite.

The responsibilities of the former chancellor or vice-chancellor (which had been exercised by the emperor or his designee) were transferred to the council. In practice, however, Colonel Mengistu, chairman of the *Dergue*, presided at commencements and other functions just as the emperor had done under the previous regime. In the meantime, the charters of the national university system and the other colleges remained operational, pending the issuance of substitute regulations by the commission. In other words, although a number of responsibilities and functions provided under the old charters were transferred to the commission, the new proclamation did not do away with the older charters, and presumably most of the colleges and universities continued to operate under the old provisions.[30]

It was anticipated that the creation of the commission would enable some of the twelve or so colleges or faculties of the national university, including those located outside Addis Ababa, to establish their own distinctive charters. So far, however, the university has remained an umbrella administrative organization and, through the respective deans, the coordinator of administrative, curriculum, and budgetary activities for all colleges. Although the military government altered some of the structures of higher education, most of the changes were proposed before 1974, and those that were not did not grow from deliberate plans to bring about substantive reform that would reflect the profound changes in social, economic, and political conditions.

After a period of uncertainty following the overthrow of Emperor Haile Selassie, the institution that had borne his name from 1961 to 1974 was renamed Addis Ababa University.[31] In addition, three former technical schools or research institutes were elevated to junior college status. The Gondar campus was expanded from an undergraduate public health college to a full college of medicine equivalent to its counterpart in Addis Ababa. The former Arts Faculty was reconstituted under a new name—the College of Social Sciences—and expanded to incorporate the former College of Business Administration, the School of Social Work, and the Departments of Political Science, Geography, and Economics. Some of its own former units were transferred to other colleges. The former Faculty of Education was renamed the College of Pedagogical Sciences. Ironically, at a time when concerted efforts to accelerate the preparation of school teachers were as critical as ever, its functions were diluted. Teacher training was delegated to several other colleges, although some minimal core courses were still offered by the College of Pedagogical Sciences. A new Institute of Language Studies was established to offer instruction in Ethiopian and foreign languages, literature, linguistics,and theatrical arts. All these units, except the two-year colleges and the College of Medicine, offered the equivalent of four-year undergraduate programs leading to a B.A. or B.S. degree. The total number of colleges, including two-year colleges and the Division of Continuing Education, grew to sixteen.[32] In addition, there were six research institutes: the Agriculture Research Center, the Institute of Development Research, the Educational Research Center, the Institute of Ethiopian Studies (with its museum), the Geophysical Observatory, and the Institute of Pathobiology.

One of the most elusive problems in Ethiopia—as elsewhere in the Third World—has been the question of equity in access to educational opportunities, particularly higher education. The better high schools are located in the few large cities. Since most of the people live in rural areas and those who can afford to send their children to the better schools are the politically and financially powerful, and since university admission is primarily based on successful passes on national examinations, college students have usually come from the upper social classes. The new regime addressed this issue by assigning quotas based on population to the high schools, with a lower threshold for those from rural schools. For the most part, however, students admitted on such criteria, who had never before seen a laboratory or an organized library, encountered serious language problems and were unable to survive the unfamiliar world of the urban colleges. Many failed, and the experiment was discontinued with the tacit admission that until the quality of the rural schools was improved the problem of unequal access to colleges would remain intractable.

The new government also attempted to shorten the time required for undergraduate program completion from the regular four years to three years. The rationale was that this would accelerate fulfillment of national high-level work force requirements, reduce investment per student, and spread opportunities to a larger number of qualified students. However, given the relatively low quality of the high schools, especially in the English language (the language of instruction in the colleges, including science-technology instruction), it was found that the full four-year period at the university level could not be reduced if the undergraduate degrees were to have any value at all. This experiment was also discontinued.

In recent years the academic community has come under increasing pressure to accept more sweeping reforms. Radical measures to alter the political orientation, curricula, and approaches of higher education to conform to the new political philosophy have been proposed. However, most of these measures have not been implemented. Where they have taken place they have been subtle and limited to a class or unit. There is no reason to doubt that such pressures will continue to be exerted in the foreseeable future.[33] As far as general policy directions are concerned, a recent paper of the government broadly indicates:

> the need to bring about a radical change in the atmosphere of learning in institutions of higher education so that the social functions of these institutions is emphasized rather than individual motivation . . . so that high level manpower formation reflects the needs for practicality and an emphasis on science and technology. The higher education institutions also have a fundamental role to play in providing an increasingly relevant output from research activity.[34]

One of the most unfortunate phenomena of the postrevolution era is the exodus of many highly skilled and educated professionals from Ethiopia. Nobody has accurate statistics (some say a total of three and a half million) by category, but at this writing, wherever one travels across the globe one is likely to encounter educated

Ethiopians in important positions in the academic or business world. Within Ethiopia, higher education has suffered most from this exodus. Before the revolution, 75 percent of the academic staff of the national university were Ethiopians—a level of achievement that was hailed for its quality and quantity. Now, some colleges, such as the Agriculture College, are staffed by foreigners (in this instance, East Germans). In many other colleges 50 to 80 percent of the teaching staff is composed of recent graduates with a first degree. Expatriate faculty members from the Soviet Union, Yugoslavia, East Germany, and some west European countries are common. Sixty percent of the foreigners are from the Soviet Union or east European countries.[35]

A number of other problems persist. While the number of students seeking admission is increasing at a tremendous rate, the resources to accommodate these growing demands have not been forthcoming. The classroom, library, dormitory, cafeteria, and health facilities are overcrowded beyond imagination. Due to the unsettled internal and external political conditions, and the need to maintain a large standing army to defend against external aggression and maintain internal security, there are no plans to significantly expand the facilities and equipment of the colleges in the near future.[36] Since it is politically impossible to reduce the annual admission rates, the quality of instruction and research will continue to suffer tremendously.[37] In the meantime, the provisional government is putting more emphasis on expansion of the formal and informal aspects of primary education and improving adult literacy; higher education does not seem to be a priority.

As things stand today, only a small percentage of those who complete secondary education and seek admission are admitted to institutions of higher learning. In 1981, for instance, 75,000 students sat for the national matriculation examination (ESLCE), but only 3,000 were admitted to the four-year colleges; perhaps another 2,000 were admitted to other postsecondary institutions. In subsequent years, the number seeking admission will increase while the capacity of the colleges will remain relatively static. The situation is, once again, ominous. Most of the high school graduates have not been equipped with salable skills, job opportunities in the public sector are not available, and only a few can afford to emigrate. Ethiopia may be restocking its store of social dynamite.

Local or nationwide student organizations are nonexistent. It is not surprising that one of the military government's first proclamations included a strong clause prohibiting unauthorized assembly, expression, or strikes: "It is hereby prohibited, for the duration of this Proclamation, to conspire against the motto "Ethiopia *Tikdem*" to engage in any strike, hold unauthorized demonstrations or assemblies, or engage in any act that may disturb public peace or security." To this end, a military tribunal was established to try those who transgressed this law and others, and "judgment handed down by the Military Court shall not be subject to appeal."[38] This proclamation was a clear recognition of the power of the student movement, and an unequivocal warning that the military would not tolerate dissidence.

For now, at least, the students seem to be exhausted. As a group they have no opportunity to sound a battle cry. They appear to be paying more attention to questions pertaining to their careers. How long this campus tranquility will last, no one can say. It is likely that, in the absence of other galvanizing challenges which could engage the attention and energy of youth, such tranquility, based on fear or threat of force, will prove short-lived. When and if students and the enlarged, politicized intelligentsia regroup to address national or university issues, the kind of political response they will encounter cannot be predicted. Tolerance or accommodation are highly unlikely.

That the Ethiopian revolution has resulted in fundamental political, social, and cultural transformation cannot be doubted. For good or ill the old institutions are gone; their replacements are struggling to find a niche in Ethiopian soil. In the process, high prices have been paid by all sectors of Ethiopian society. Perhaps the greatest cost of all has been incurred by the educated elite. Institutions of higher learning, limited as they were by many factors, played a significant role in Ethiopia's social transformation. Their potential for change is well understood by the present rulers. Whether this recognition will inspire or inhibit continued support for their full development remains to be seen. In a profoundly altered Ethiopia, it is not clear how the university will be viewed politically.

Notes

1. Colin Legume, *Ethiopia: The Fall of Haile Selassie's Empire* (New York: Africana Publishing Co., 1975), 3.
2. There were other less significant associations among the armed forces which had some political significance. However, most were motivated by the immediate interests of the membership or were positioning themselves to assume power after the emperor was gone. See Legume, *Ethiopia: The Fall of Haile Selassie's Empire*; 31–32.
3. Here the officers had in mind the students' platform which actively espoused granting freedom of choice in government to the various "nationalities," including Eritrea. The military emphasized Ethiopia's vulnerability to external attack, primarily from Somalia and some Arab countries through Eritrea, as well as from several national minorities

within Ethiopia. These were constant themes advanced by high military and civil officials when they wanted to condemn the student political platforms and activities. Yet it was obvious that aside from trying to strengthen the defense forces, these officials were blind to or unwilling to address the basic economic and political forces that lay at the foundation of most of the structural weaknesses that made the country vulnerable to external aggression or internal subversion.

4. Since that time, a large segment of the army was stationed outside Addis Ababa—in Nazareth, Jimma, and the like.

5. It is a sorry state of affairs that the senior military and civilian officers seldom traveled to the different regions of the country to learn and observe first hand the conditions of the people. When they did they were accompanying the emperor. As members of the retinue, their purpose was to provide a gesture or aura of dignity and respectability rather than to learn first hand about the conditions prevailing in the particular regions. The late Prime Minister Aklilu Habte Wold stated at his trial that he and his colleagues had clear instructions not to leave Addis Ababa unless the emperor ordered them to do so—which seldom happened. Thus, even the prime minister was alien to the Ethiopian realities as represented by the vast majority of people living in rural areas.

6. The recommendations of the Education Sector Review were very informed and enlightened. The problem was that no practicing teachers were involved in the conception or planning exercises. In addition, once the study was completed, the Ministry of Education did practically nothing for a long period of time to sell it to the practitioners as well as the general populations. See Teshome Wagaw, *Education in Ethiopia: Prospect and Retrospect*, 183–97.

7. I was awakened early on a Saturday morning and urgently summoned to Endalkachew's office. I was rushed to his presence without even shaving, whereupon I was asked if I would consider accepting the portfolio of Minister of Education. I declined for the simple reason that I did not feel that Endalkachew represented the political mood of the country at that time. In spite of his technical qualifications and motivation to succeed, he was tainted by being intimately associated with the previous government; he was a die-hard aristocrat; and during the many years he enjoyed senior positions, he was never known as one who stood for the principle of justice or equality on behalf of the Ethiopian people. I felt his desire to rule did not necessarily qualify him to be in that position. Subsequent events proved me right.

8. The representatives of the Air Force and the Army urged Endalkachew to be unafraid of raiding the university for the best qualified people for cabinet posts. They said that the academics could be replaced by foreigners. Some useful information regarding military-student alliances is provided by Marilyn Hall Baissa, "Civil-Military Interaction in the Ethiopian Revolution: The Role of Students," 771–82.

9. Actually, he was never crowned king; the monarchy was abolished in March 1975. The proclamation establishing the provisional military

government was proclamation No. 1, Maskerem 2, 1967 (12 September 1975). The order deposing the emperor was No. 2.

10. For the debate on the fate of the emperor, see Colin Legum, *Ethiopia: The Fall of Haile Selassie*, 47–51.
11. How he died remains shrouded in mystery. The government alleged that he died of natural causes following a postoperative relapse. There is, however, circumstantial evidence that he was killed. To this day, nobody outside the inner circles of the ilitary knows where he was laid to rest.
12. Although he had all these titles, he was never a member of the *Dergue* (the inner circle of the armed forces committee which made all the important decisions).
13. "Program of the National Democratic Revolution of Ethiopia" (April 1976).
14. The two measures that provided for ownership of rural and urban lands were "Proclamation to Provide for the Public Ownership of Rural Lands," *Negarit Gazeta*, no. 23 (28 April 1975), and "Proclamation to Provide for Government Ownership of Urban Lands and Extra Houses," *Negarit Gazeta*, no. 47 (26 July 1975).
15. "Urban Dwellers Associations Consolidations and Municipalities Proclamation," *Negarit Gazeta*, no. 104 (1976), and "Peasant Associations Organization and Consolidation Proclamation," *Negarit Gazeta*, no. 71 (1975).
16. A useful analysis of this phenomenon is presented in Marina Ottaway and David Ottaway, *Ethiopia: Empire in Revolution* (New York and London: Africana Publishing Co., 1978), 100–12.
17. The earlier assertions by this author that the Ethiopian youth rejected their past based on default or ignorance rather than reasoned and critical analysis are sustained.
18. Since 1972 there had been a student underground political party known as "The Crocodile." Whether there was a direct link between this and the EPRP cannot be ascertained.
19. It seems that in actuality the two groups did not wish to accommodate even the minor differences arising from real hatred of the military even though they were former fellow students and colleagues. For further analysis on this, see Ottaway and Ottaway, *Ethiopia: Empire in Revolution*, 115–27.
20. Ibid., 123.
21. Due to the expulsion of foreign correspondents and the reluctance of Ethiopian exiles to talk, data regarding the extent of political murder and imprisonment is incomplete. Norman J. Singer indicated that in Addis Ababa alone, during the first three months of 1977 following the initiation of the "red terror" campaign, four to five thousand young people were murdered and more than thirty thousand were imprisoned and inhumanely tortured by the military and *kebele* representatives. See his work, "Ethiopia: Human Rights, 1948–1978," *Proceedings of the Fifth International Conference on Ethiopian Study*, ed. Robert L. Hess (Chicago: University of Illinois at Chicago Circle, 1978); 672–76. Amnesty International gave a much higher

figure: see its report, "Human Rights Violations in Ethiopia," 14 December 1977 (AFR 25/97/77). For an eyewitness report, refer to Mesfin Bekele, "Prison Conditions in Ethiopia," *Horn of Africa* 2, no. 2 (April–June 1979): 4–11.

22. The bureau chairman, Haile Fida, was one of those imprisoned. In 1980 it was rumored that he was one of the fourteen political prisoners executed that year.
23. See Ethiopian Government, *Ethiopia Profile* 1, no. 3 (March 1982): 9. This number seems to include graduates of postsecondary schools, such as technical and vocational schools. This author's 1969 study showed that the total number of people who had been exposed to some form of university education both within and outside the country totaled about 11,000.
24. See, for example, the Amharic language daily, *Addis Zemen* (New Era, Ginbot 7, 1967 [17 May 1975]).
25. For their safety, my sources remain unidentified.
26. "Ethiopia *Tikdem*: The Origins and Future Direction of the Movement," 20 December 1974 (mimeographed).
27. Military Government of Ethiopia, "Programme of the National Democratic Revolution of Ethiopia," April 1976.
28. See the report of "Task Force 13" of the Ministry of Education's *Education Sector Review* (Addis Ababa: Ministry of Education, August 1972).
29. Ibid.
30. Two universities have been in operation for the past two decades, namely the semi-private University of Asmara and the Addis Ababa University. The latter is an umbrella for some twelve colleges and faculties and has one charter and one set of executive officers with a dean at the head of each college.
31. By giving it this name instead of calling it "Ethiopian University," the authorities wished to deemphasize the supremacy of one university over the other existing or future institutions of higher learning.
32. For more detail, refer to "Basic Facts and Information" (Addis Ababa University, January 1979). Recently, the government has established an institute for the study of social science independent of the national university. Whether or not this is another step to bypass the university remains to be seen.
33. Personal interview by the author of AAU faculty at the University of Lund, Sweden, 26–29 April 1982 (names withheld for security reasons).
34. Government of Ethiopia, "Education and Economic Development in Socialist Ethiopia" (Paper prepared for the Conference of Ministers of Education and those responsible for Economic Planning of African Member State, Harare, Zimbabwe, 23 June to 3 July 1982), 18.
35. See the Amharic daily, *Addis Zemen* (Hamile 13, 1973 [22 July 1981]).
36. The estimated strength of the regular armed forces was 50,000 before the revolution. At that rate, it was consuming the largest budgetary allocation of any single government function. Since the revolution that figure has increased to over 250,000—a fivefold increase—

devouring financial and human resources and leaving very little for other activities such as education.

37. It is unimaginable that another revolution may occur for this reason.
38. Ethiopian Goverment, ''Proclamation to Provide for the Establishment of a Provisional Military Government of Ethiopia,'' no. 1 (15 September 1974), Articles 8 and 9.

AFTERWORD

As this study shows, institutions of higher learning—through their major clientele, namely students, faculty and alumni—played significant roles in the processes that ultimately and fundamentally transformed a traditional society. We also saw how these forces, which played such vital roles in bringing about the demise of the old orders, were unable or unwilling to influence the direction and emergence of effective democratic replacements of the destroyed realities.

In form, if not in substance, institutions of higher learning have expanded and changed to conform to the post-1974 realities. As spelled out in a 1977 proclamation, one of the major tasks of these institutions is "to teach, expand and publicize socialism and formulate methods to carry out these functions."[1] In addition to teaching and preparing qualified personnel for the country's developmental needs in accordance with the national plan, and the carrying out of research and studies the institutions are charged "to make every effort to develop and enrich the country's cultures free from imperialist influence and reactionary content." For this latter task they are to seek the cooperation of existing government and mass organizations. The same proclamation also created a Commission of Higher Education whose functions include the assumption of responsibilities formerly held by the chancellor, vice-chancellor, and the Board of Governors.[2] Whereas in the old charter governance membership included representatives of the alumni and the church, in the current charter all of the membership is drawn from the ranks of heads of ministries (cabinet members) or others appointed by the government. Although not explicitly ruled out, there is no stipulation for including representatives from the various mass organizations.[3] This omission seems incoherent in view of the fact that this government claims to support involvement of the proletariat and peasants. Be that as it may, the CHE is charged with formulating broad policies regarding staffing, budgeting, as well as admissions, graduation, and curricula. In addition, the CHE is entrusted with the administration of a number of the newly created technical and vocational junior colleges in cooperation with the appropriate ministries (agriculture, commerce, and education). The semiprivate Asmara University is now under the government umbrella.

Since 1974, a number of former technical, vocational, and agricultural high schools, as mentioned above, have been elevated to junior college status and a few new ones have been created. The stated purpose for creating these institutions is to prepare a middle-level skilled work force for the country's development needs, and perhaps also to alleviate the huge demand for high school graduates to enter tertiary institutions. In addition, a former teacher training school at Kotebe in Addis Ababa has been raised to a full four-year, degree-granting college. It seems likely that in due time some of the others will also develop into chartered, degree-granting regional or national colleges and universities. Seven of these specialize in agriculture, four in technology, four in teacher training, and one in commerce. As indicated above, some of these colleges fall under the administration of CHE, the rest fall under the umbrella of Addis Ababa University. This arrangement creates considerable confusion and some duplication of effort.[4]

Curricula

In general, policy announcements referring to the need and direction of curricula and program reforms were made explicit. During the 1974–76 period when students, staff and faculty were sent on *Zemetcha* (a rural campaign to teach people about the new developments), some teachers stayed behind to formulate curricula, teaching materials, and to plan for research and further studies. In 1977 the AAU Senate established a committee whose responsibilities included the identification, coordination and facilitation of curricula and research of the various college activities. Although its tasks seem to include the act of controlling faculty initiatives, the committee might have some useful purpose along the intended lines. As an extension of the legally mandated call for a "thorough application of the principles of Marxism-Leninism to the programmes of higher education,"[5] many teaching staff members were sent on short-term visits to socialist countries to familiarize themselves with socialism theory and practice in higher education. Seminars and conferences were conducted within Ethiopia. Faculty and staff attended orientation classes at the school for political education at Yekatit Square. The result thus far is reflected in the reorganization of the common programs of the freshman courses. The founding of an Institute of Language Studies in 1977, to concentrate on the question of the many local languages, might be considered part of the curricula reform. However, one must constantly bear in mind that the confused nature of what is or is not relevant in the current environment of political uncertainties inevitably ends up intimidating faculty and students and inhibiting active initiative. This leads to the following of the party line proclaimed by the regime in power (since 1987 a political party) to make sure one's position is safe and secure. To the extent that this position is taken by faculty and staff alike, the inevitable result will be dullness and stagnation, which in turn ultimately nullifies the purpose of higher education in national development.

Other problems that continue to evade solutions are found in the areas of selection and placement of students in the various programs. Due to the rapid expansion of the lower grades, enrollment and graduation rates from grade 12 level are growing faster than could be absorbed by the labor market and admissions to tertiary institutions. For instance, in 1982 the number of graduates from the twelfth grade was 36,000 while the maximum intake of all colleges was only 12,000. Further, the number of grade 12 graduates has swollen to 92,000 by the addition of secondary school graduates from previous years who had not made it to the colleges but were ''retaking'' the Ethiopian School Leaving Examination (ESLCE). The dilemma, being political as well as human and economic, is how to resolve this tremendous mismatch between politics, expectations, and the ability of existing institutions to absorb these cohorts.[6] Given the current policy trends of the country this problem of mismatch will be even more exasperating in the future.[7] The continued conscription of young people into the armed forces and the periodic *Zemetchas* (campaigns) that take young people to the rural areas are, at best, stop-gap measures and, at most, wasteful of precious human resources.

Another mismatch is between the motivation and qualification of the individual student entering any of the colleges and the kind of program these colleges are able to offer. But problems of this type are relatively mild compared to other, larger problems.

Educational facilities and opportunities have for too long been not only limited but unevenly distributed among the urban and suburban, male and female, and the different ethnic or religious groups within Ethiopia. Due to historical and cultural reasons, people living in the Addis Ababa-Shewa, Asmara-Hamassen, Hararge, and Wollega regions have, as a rule, fared much better when it comes to the amount and quality of educational opportunities.

These regions have the highest density of populations, are relatively better industrialized, and enjoy higher representation of powerful people in government. Although there are some differences, the remaining ten regions or provinces have suffered from poor and inadequate educational provisions. Also, on the whole, the participation rate of females (although very low across the board) is very much behind that of males and is more apparent in the less advantaged regions. The result is that people from the favored regions are overrepresented in the institutions of higher education. In addition to the concerns for fairness and justice, these imbalances constitute political and economic pitfalls as well. The need to share national resources and to distribute skills requisite to development equally among the regions is imperative. As indicated, debates and efforts to redress these problems, such as improving the quality and number of learning institutes of affected regions, and initiating a system of admission quotas to higher education have been ongoing for at least the last twenty years.[8]

Improving educational provisions for all regions and subregions is a good goal and perhaps one has to look there for a lasting solution. However, it requires not only time and additional resources but also political support; it is not certain that any of these are available in sufficient supply. The quota system tries to take into account the number of people living in a region, the number of students who sit for the ESLCE, etc. Based on this, the quota system tries to address the problem by providing for differentiated college admission standards based on geographic location. For instance, whereas students from the less-favored regions would be admitted to degree programs with a 2.0 grade point average (GPA) as measured by the ESLCE, those from the advantaged areas would be required to get a score of 2.5 or above. For admission to subdegree programs, the GPA would be 1.4 instead of 2.0, and so on. This was tried for a year in the late 1960s, but it became so controversial that it was suspended. It was reintroduced in the late 1970s and remains controversial.

With respect to making access to educational opportunities more equitable, the quota concept may be sound, but making it work is problematic and fraught with programmatic and political problems. The main arguments against this practice center around the ability of students to benefit from university programs when they are ill-prepared at the lower levels. University teachers bitterly complain that they are wasting too much instructional time catering to unprepared students at a time when classrooms are bursting at the seams. Attrition among participants increased, which ultimately led to questioning the fundamental wisdom and utility of this policy.[9] As a result, implementation of this policy is declining, and the central problem remains unresolved. Establishment of the several junior colleges may alleviate part of the problem, but other problems may emerge, such as the perpetuation of inequality along the lines of degree and diploma programs for people living in the various regions.

Since assignments are highly centralized in Addis Ababa, the practice thus far has been to assign students to programs based on their grade point averages and the availability of spaces at the various tertiary institutions. No consideration is given to the interests and aspirations of the student. Knowing that this may be his/her only chance, the student tries to stick it out. It seems that this policy would contribute to learning-teaching problems and attrition. Finally, it is doubtful whether the student would be able to contribute fully to development in an areas that he or she was unqualified for, not interested in, or from which he/she is unable to benefit fully.[10]

Staffing and Finance

From the creation of the colleges in the 1950s and throughout the 1960s the recruitment of qualified academics proved to be very challenging. During the first decade practically all faculty and administrative staff were drawn from overseas—Canada, the United States, United Kingdom, Israel, etc. At the same time, systematic efforts were made to provide indigenous people with overseas scholarships sponsored by the national government in cooperation with bilateral and multilateral aid-giving agencies. As a result, by 1973 most of the colleges and departments had attained an average of 75 percent Ethiopianization.[11] The administrative staff was almost all Ethiopian nationals. Although the rapid promotion of relatively young and inexperienced people created some problems, anyone visiting the colleges after mid-1966 could not help but be impressed favorably with the enthusiastic vigor and dedication with which the business of the colleges was carried out.[12] With the maturity of this corps of professionals, it was thought, the futures of both the colleges and Ethiopia were in good and secure hands. Now, nearly two decades later, one can categorically say that these optimistic expectations have evaporated. The teaching staff has expanded from about 500 in 1972 to 1,026 in 1982, including the junior college staff; 46 percent (469) hold the B.A. or B.S. degree. 24 per cent (242) hold the master's degree. 21 percent (214) have a Ph.D. or its equivalent, and 9 percent (96) have less than the first degree. If we take the three major universities, i.e., Addis Ababa University, Asmara University, and Alemaya Agricultural University where most of the Ph.D. holders are concentrated (32 percent of the total faculty), we find that the majority of terminal degree holders are expatriates—Russians, other East Europeans, and some from the United Kingdom.[13] Among many other things these data indicate how badly the ranks of the highly qualified, prominent Ethiopian faculty have been eroded. Obviously they are a significant part of the estimated 3.5 million people who left Ethiopia for economic and political reasons.

Further faculty development and overseas training have been plagued by lack of resources, the decline of international or bilateral support for such activities, and the high rate of nonreturnees once training programs are completed (about 60 percent fail to return to Ethiopia at the conclusion of their studies).

In addition, the existing instructional staff is overworked, under-paid (no change in salary structure since 1972), highly regulated, and not surprisingly—demoralized.[14] Since the preparation of quali-fied personnel is a time-consuming process and those in the pipe-line are few, the shortage of staff is likely to get progressively worse. Although the new graduate school at the AAU, which offers a master's level program in certain disciplines, may help some, it will be in-adequate to meet both the numerical and qualitative needs.

Yet another problem of central importance to academic life is the opportunity and freedom to exchange ideas, opinions, and research results among faculty and students as well as with the outside world. Multiple outlets such as seminars, forums, workshops, and confer-ences, as well as journals, magazines, and publishing houses are es-sential if these activities are to be carried out. These provisions were in the developmental stage in the 1960s. Lively discussions and de-bates over ideas took place in a generally healthy climate for intellec-tual and aesthetic expression. There were also problems with the political authorities as outlined in chapters 8 and 9, but over the last two decades most of these activities have ceased. There is no faculty union worthy of the name, and very few publications by staff members. The lively and useful student unions, together with their publishing organs, no longer exist. The present political authori-ties apparently think that the forces that helped to bring about the 1974 changes are no longer needed. The campus climate is dull and stifling. The government seems satisfied with docility on the col-lege campuses, maintained by threats of force and severe coercion if breached. As one of their publications put it, "In strong contrast with the situation prior to 1974, the higher education system has oper-ated since the revolution without any disruption to the study pro-grams . . . there is no conflict of objectives leading to protest and disruption."[15] Speaking of the political and social climate of Ethiopia in general, and the colleges in particular, a distinguished African po-litical scientist observed that "Ethiopia is the most regimented society in Africa."[16] One cannot go any further along the scale of oppression.

What a painfully underdeveloped country such as Ethiopia needs, among other things, is the effective marshaling of all resources to help the population get enough to eat and wear, and to alleviate dis-eases and untimely death. Instead, present practices of government, more so than in the past, give priority to control and regimentation as a means of securing and staying in power indefinitely.

The question of budgetary allocation for the tertiary educational system has always been a problem, not only in terms of adequacy of amount but in timely development and availability. The budgets are still derived from three sources: government allocation, foreign aid and loans, and small fees for certain activities from students. In the last decade, funding from external sources to help tertiary education decreased to almost nothing.[17] On the whole, most of the students pay very few fees, if any. In most instances expenses covering tuition, room and board, textbooks, and the like are supplied by the national treasury.

Over the period of 1976–77 to 1982–83, taxation by the government increased substantially and the expenditures went up from 21.5 percent to over 31 percent. For instance, in 1976–77 the total government expenditure was 1.465.7 billion Birr.[18] Over the seven years to 1982–83 it grew to 3.220.2 billion Birr or double what it was in the base year. Over the same period, 1976–77, higher education's share was 45 million Birr. Over the following few years it actually decreased, indicating a shift in resource allocation to national security areas, and by 1982–83 it amounted to 60 million Birr. It is apparent, then, that in light of inflation and despite the increased income of government, higher education was barely able to maintain itself.[19] This is surprising when one considers that total enrollment at these institutions has nearly doubled since 1974.

In the face of the mounting economic and political crises, the increasing pressures brought on tertiary institutions to keep their doors open and to admit an ever-increasing number of young people may indicate that the quality of higher education will continue to deteriorate in the foreseeable future. Unless immediate drastic action is taken to arrest and eventually reverse the trend, the value of higher education will become almost meaningless. In this eventuality, the country may pay the high price of prolonged poverty, underdevelopment, and the absence of fundamental human rights. Over the last decade and half, reason and dialogue concerning the many ills of society have been replaced by unexamined political dogmas, sloganeering, and aimless series of *zemechas* (campaigns) of all sorts. The principles and ideals the institutions of higher learning were created for have been effectively subverted. Consequently things are falling apart and the center is not holding. Once again drastic change for the better seems not only imperative but urgent as well. Change will come, the question is who will be the catalyst this time round and with what result.

Notes

1. Proclamation No. 109 of 1977, Article 3 (1), "A Proclamation to Provide for the Administration of Higher Education Institutions."
2. The proper word here may be "reactivated" rather than "created" since such a commission was envisioned long ago.
3. Although there is representation of mass organizations in the AAU Senate, this is not true in the CHE, the highest policymaking organ of postsecondary institutions.
4. "Ethiopia: Tertiary Education and National Development" (Paris: UNESCO, 1983), 45–52.
5. "Twenty Years of Experience in the Reform, Redirection, and Expansion of Education: The Case of Ethiopia" (Addis Ababa, Ministry of Education, 1982), 99.
6. "Ethiopia: Tertiary Education and National Development," 141–142.
7. In spite of a deliberate policy to expand the lower grades at the expense of secondary level education the number of ESLCE graduates is rapidly growing.
8. See my article, "Access to Haile Selassie University," *Ethiopia Observer* 14, no. 1 (1971): 31–46.
9. "Twenty Years of Experience," 185–86.
10. Addis Ababa, Ministry of Education (1982), 50, 57; "Ethiopia: Tertiary Education," 141–44.
11. Summerskill, 111–18.
12. I had arrived in Addis Ababa on 11 September 1966 after an absence of twelve years. I was surprised and favorably impressed with the number and conduct of former classmates and friends then holding important positions as deans of colleges and department heads. Commitment to the rapid reconstruction of Ethiopia was clearly evident.
13. Refer to "Ethiopia: Tertiary Education," table 50; and Summerskill, 114.
14. "Ethiopia: Tertiary Education" (UNESCO, 1983), 47–48. 55–59 and table 50.
15. "Twenty Years of Experience," 57–58.
16. This statement was made to the author in the fall of 1984 by Ali A. Mazrui.
17. A policy was developed in 1968 to charge students from well-off families. It was politically unpopular and was dropped. A loan system was suggested in 1972, but was never implemented.
18. Birr = US $0.40.
19. See "Tertiary Education," 18–26, and Annexes 8–15.

GLOSSARY

Abun	Head of the Ethiopian Church
Abyssinia	Another name for Ethiopia
Aksumite Kingdom	The ancient kingdom of Ethiopia centered in the city of Aksum
Aqwaqwam	Religious dance
Amhara	The culturally dominant ethnic group in Ethiopia
Aleqa (Aleka)	Chief; head of a parish or head teacher
Bahitawi	Eccentric monk; a monk who lives in voluntary isolation from others for purposes of achieving superior religious life; a hermit
Birr	Ethiopian currency, equal to approximately US$0.40
Blatengeta	Honorary title for a learned man who also occupies a high political position
CELU	National Trade Union
Debtera	A deacon or cantor of the Church
Dergue	Literally, committee; the military junta which ruled Ethiopia between 1974 and 1987
Dervish	A sect or an Islamic faith from the Sudan which invaded western Ethiopia in 1887
E.C.	Ethiopian Calendar: the Ethiopian year (Julian calendar) consists of thirteen months; each of twelve months has thirty days and Pagumen, the thirteenth month, has five days (six in Leap Year). The year begins on September 11 and ends in August. From September through February it is seven years behind the Gregorian calendar, and from January through August

257

it is eight years behind. The months of the year and their Gregorian equivalent are as follows:

Maskerem	September
Tikimt	October
Hidar	November
Tahisas	December
Tir	January
Yekatit	February
Megabit	March
Miazia	April
Ginbot	May
Sene	June
Hamle	July
Nehasse	August

Pagumen	A five-day (six in Leap Year) month at the end of the year
Etchegue	Administrator of the Monasteries (or monks)
EPRP	Ethiopian Peoples Revolutionary Party
EUTA	Ethiopian University Teachers Association
Gasha	A unit to measure land; gasha is equivalent to 100 acres
G.D.	Gregorian Calendar
Ge'ez	The ancient language of Ethiopia still in use in liturgical services
Lij	Literally, child; used with a proper noun it signifies a title of courtesy given to a person of noble birth or rank; equivalent to an esquire
Liq	Scholar; one who excels in any branch of scholarly endeavor
Liqe-Kahinat	Chief of the clergy
Liqe-Siltanat	Full professor; chief scholar, or one who excels over other scholars
Liqawint	Very learned persons, professors
MEISON	All Ethiopian Socialist political party
NEUSA	National Ethiopian University Student Association
PMAC	Provisional Military Administrative Council

Qine	Ge'ez poem
Tergum	Translation; interpretation
UNECA	United Nations Economic Commission for Africa
USAAA	University Students Association of Addis Ababa
USAID, Point IV foreign or Technical Cooperation Administration	Agency of the US Government through which foreign aid is channeled
Zema Bet	House (school) of singing (music)
Zemcha	Campaign

NOTE: In the bibliography, names of Ethiopian authors appear first name first as is the custom in that country. Authors who have published extensively outside of the country and are known by their last name might be listed in the non-Ethiopian format, i.e., last name first.

BIBLIOGRAPHY

Articles

"Africa and the UN University." *Africa,* no. 105 (May 1980): 67–70.

Ajayi, J. F. A. "African Universities and the African Tradition." *East African Journal* 8, no. 11 (November 1971): 3–8.

Aklilu Habte. "A Brief Review of the History of the University College of Addis Ababa." *University College Review* (Addis Ababa, Spring 1961): 25–33.

Aklilu Habte, Mengesha Gebre-Hiwet, and Monika Kehoe. "Higher Education in Ethiopia." *Journal of Ethiopian Studies* 1, no. 1 (1963): 3–7.

Ashby, Sir Eric. "A Contribution to the Dialogue on African Universities." *Universities Quarterly* 20, no. 1 (December 1965).

Ashby, Sir Eric and Mary Anerrson. Universities: British, Indian and African: A Study in the Ecology of Higher Education. Cambridge: Harvard University Press. 1966.

Biobaku, S. O. "Africa's Needs and Africa's Universities." *West African Journal of Education* 7 (June 1963): 61–63.

Choudhury, S. D. Roy. "College of Engineering and Technical School." *Ethiopia Observer* 1, no. 7 (1957): 213–16.

Chojnacki, Stanislaw. "A Survey of Modern Ethiopian Art." *Sonderausgabe* (Addis Ababa, 1973).

Court, David. "The Experience of Higher Education in East Africa: The University of Dar es Salaam as a New Model?" *Comparative Education Review* 11, no. 3 (October 1975): 193–218.

Dillon, Wilton S. "Universities and Nation-Building in Africa." *Journal of Modern African Studies* 1, no. 1 (March 1964): 75–89.

Educational Journal Bulletin No. 1. Addis Ababa: The University College Education Students' Association (UCESA), 1954 E.C.

Educational Journal Bulletin No. 2. Addis Ababa: The University College Education Students' Association (UCESA), 1954 E.C.

Educational Journal Bulletin No. 3. Addis Ababa: The University College Education Students' Association (UCESA), 1954 E.C.

Fallaci, Oriana. "Journey into the Private Universe of Haile Selassie." *Chicago Tribune,* 24 June 1973.

"The First Ten Years of the Public Health College." *Menen* 9, no. 9 (1965): 30–32.

Giel, R., and J. N. van Luyk. "A Follow-up of 1066 Freshmen at Haile Selassie I University." *Journal of Ethiopian Studies* 8, no. 1 (January 1970): 21–30.

Gillete, Arthur. "The Ethiopian University Service: A Novel Approach to Student Development Work." *UNESCO Features,* nos. 509–10 (1967).

Gillett, Margaret. "Symposium on Africa: Western Academic Role Concepts in Ethiopian University." *Comparative Education Review* 7, no. 2 (October 1963): 149–51.

Girma, Amare. "Higher Education in Ethiopia: A Report on Haile Selassie I University. M. Kehoe, Reply." *Journal of Higher Education* 33, no. 7 (1963): 398–400.

Greenfield, Richard David. "Afro-Ethiopia: A Note on the Current State of Higher Education and University Research in Ethiopia." *Mekerere Journal* 8 (Kampala, 1963): 1–15.

Haile Fida. "Do We Need a University?" *UCESA Educational Journal* 2 (Addis Ababa, 1964): 16–18.

Haile, Gabriel Dagne. "Education Magic in Traditional Ethiopia." *Ethiopian Journal of Education* 4, no. 2 (June 1971).

Han, Lee-Min. "A Historical Sketch of the Public Health College and Training Center, Gondar." *Ethiopia Observer* 10, no. 3 (1966): 199–203.

Hess, Robert, ed. *Proceedings of the Fifth International Conference on Ethiopian Studies.* Chicago: University of Illinois at Chicago Circle, 1978.

Kalimuzo, F. K. "The Triple Role of the University." *East African Journal* 8, no. 10 (October 1971): 2–4.

Kehoe, Monika. "Higher Education in Ethiopia, A Report on Haile Selassie I University." *Journal of Higher Education* 33, no. 9 (December 1962): 475–78.

Klassen, Frank. "Teacher Education in Ethiopia." *School and Society* 91 (February 1963): 96–98.

Knowles, L., Jr. "History of the Peace Corps at the Business College of Haile Selassie I University." *Ethiopia Observer* 9, no. 1 (1965), 42–45.

Korten, David C. "Evidence of an Important Social Change in Ethiopia: Motivations and Career Objectives of Students Studying in the Haile Selassie I University, College of Business Administration." *Business Journal* 2 (College of Business Administration, HSIU, April 1965): 7–15

Korten, David C. and Frances F. Korten. "Ethiopia's Use of the National University Students in a Year of Rural Service." *Comparative Education Review* 10, no. 3 (October 1966): 482–92.

———. "The Impact of a National Service Experience upon Its Participants: Evidence from Ethiopia." *Comparative Education Review* 13, no. 3 (October 1969): 312–24.

Kramer, Roberta C. "Teacher Training in Ethiopia." *Ethiopia Observer* 9, no. 1 (1965): 37–38.

Krzeczunowicz, Jerzy. "Ethiopian Legal Education: Retrospection and Prospects." *Journal of Ethiopian Studies* 1, no. 1 (1964): 68–74.

Legesse Lemma. "The Ethiopian Student Movement 1960–1974: A Challenge to the Monarchy and Imperialism in Ethiopia." *Northeast African Studies* 1, no. 1 (1979): 31–46.

Leys, Colin. "The Role of the University in an Underdeveloped Country." *Journal of Eastern African Research and Development* 1, no. 1 (1971): 29–40.

Lipset, S. M. "University Students and Politics in Underdeveloped Countries." *Minerva* 3 (1964): 15–56.

Mathews, Z. K. "African Awakening and the Universities." *Overseas Quarterly* 3 (September 1962): 77–79.

"The New Faculty of Law." *Menen* 8, no. 1 (1963): 23–24.

Nicol, Davidson. "Politics, Nationalism and Universities in Africa." *African Affairs* 62, no. 246 (January 1963): 20–28.

Ogot, B. A. and T. R. Okhiambo, eds. "East African Brain Power." *East African Journal* (August 1965): 3–44.

Ottaway, Marina. "Social Classes and Corporate Interests in the Ethiopian Revolution." *Journal of Modern African Studies* 14, no. 3 (September 1976): 469–86.

Pankhurst, E. Sylvia. "Imperial College of Agriculture and Mechanical Arts." *Ethiopia Observer* 1, no. 10 (1957): 312–17.

———. "The Institute of Building Technology." *Ethiopia Observer* 1, no. 11 (1957): 370–71.

Paul, J. C. N. "Fourth Annual Report from the Dean, 1966–1967 (1959 E.C.)." *Journal of Ethiopian Law* 4, no. 1 (1967): 21–31.

"Post-Secondary Vacation Course for Teachers." *Educational Torch* 1, no. 1 (1951 E.C.): 41.

Plant, Ruth. "The Ancient and Medieval Architecture of Tigre Province in the Light of Present Evidence." In *Proceedings of the Fifth International Conference on Ethiopian Studies,* edited by Robert L. Hess. Chicago: University of Illinois, 1978.

Ranger, T. O. "Students and the Nation." *East African Journal* 4, no. 2 (May 1967): 3–8.

Smith, Peter Duval. "No Dawn in Ethiopia." *New Statesman* 65, no. 1672 (29 March 1963): 456–58.

Solomon Inquai. "What Kind of a University?" *Dialogue* 1, no. 2 (1968): 35–39.

Southall, Robert. "Federalism and Higher Education in East Africa." *East African Specials,* no. 1 (1974).

Tesfaye Kabtihimar. "Higher Education in Ethiopia." *Ethiopian Mirror* 1, no. 2–3 (1963): 5.

Teshager Wube. "The Wandering Student." *University College of Addis Ababa Ethnological Society Bulletin,* no. 9 (July–December 1959): 52–60.

Tickaher Hailu. "Is the Junior College Idea Useful for Ethiopia?" *Dialogue* 2, no. 1 (1968): 37–40.

Tilahun Gamta. "That Education at All Levels is the Basis for Any Country's Development." *UCESA Educational Journal,* no. 2 (1964): 3–8.

"The University College of Addis Ababa." *Ethiopia Observer* 2, no. 6 (1958): 195–207, 210–13.

"University College of Addis Ababa Examination Papers." *Ethiopia Observer* 2, no. 6 (1968): 213–14.

Wagaw, Teshome G. "Access to Haile Selassie I University." *Ethiopia Observer* 14, no. 1 (1971): 31–46.

———. "Education During the Fascist Occupation." *Ethiopian Journal of Education* 1, no. 3 (March 1974).

————. "Emerging Issues of Ethiopian Nationalities: Cohesion or Disintegration." *Journal of Northeast African Studies* 2, no. 3 (1980–81): 69–75.

————. "A Follow-up Study of the 1961 Addis Ababa Education Conference of African States: Implications for Ethiopia." *Dialogue* 3, no. 2 (1971): 41–56.

————. "The Participation of Youth in Ethiopia's Rural Development." *Rural Africana,* no. 30 (Spring 1976): 75–86.

————. "Youth Participation in Ethiopia's Rural Development." *Rural African* 30 (Spring 1976).

Wagaw, Teshome G., and Darge Wole. "Teachers and Directors Speak Out About School Problems." *Ethiopian Journal of Education* 4, no. 2 (1971): 43–67.

Books and Monographs

Ababe Ambachew. "The Influence of Higher Education on the American Society and Its Implications for the Role of Higher Education in Ethiopia." Ph.D. dissertation, Ohio State University, 1962.

Abebe Ghedai. "Some Characteristics and Motivational Patterns of University Continuing Education." Ed.D. dissertation, Syracuse University, 1977.

Agricultural Education and Research at Haile Selassie I University. Seminar Report, Haile Selassie I University, April 1969.

Aklilu Habte "Factors Affecting the Development of Universities in Africa: A Case of Ethiopia." Paper presented at the Conference on the Role of a University in a Developing Country, Addis Ababa, 1967. Mimeographed.

————. *A Forward Look: A Special Report from the President.* Addis Ababa: Haile Selassie I University, September 1969.

Aklilu Habte, and Edouard Trudeau. "Project for a School or Institute of Education of University College of Addis Ababa." Addis Ababa: Haile Selassie I University, 1962. Mimeographed.

Ashby, Sir Eric. *African Universities and Western Tradition* Cambridge: Harvard University Press, 1964.

————. "Investment in Education. A Report of the Commission of Post-School Certificate and Higher Education in Africa." Lagos: The Government Printers, 1960. Mimeographed.

Ashby, Sir Eric, and Mary Anderson. *Universities: British, Indian and African: A Study in the Ecology of Higher Education.* Cambridge: Harvard University Press, 1966.

Assazenew Baysa. "Ethiopia." In *The Recruitment and Training of University Teachers.* Ghent: Unternational Association of University Professors and Lecturers, 1967.

Beeby, Clarence Edward. *The Quality of Education in Developing Countries.* Cambridge: Harvard University Press, 1966.

Bent, James Theodore. *The Sacred City of the Ethiopians.* London: Longmans, Green, and Co., 1896.

Bergthold, Gary D., and David C. McClelland. *The Impact of Peace Corps Teachers on Students in Ethiopia.* Peace Corps Contract—P.C. 80–1531

Task Order 2. Cambridge, Mass.: Human Development Foundation, December 1968.

Bjerkan, Ole-Christian. "Plans, Targets and Trends in Ethiopian Education." Ph.D. dissertation, University of Maryland, 1970.

Blaug, Mark. "Report of the Exploratory Employment Policy Mission in Ethiopia." Addis Ababa, 1974. Mimeographed.

Bloom, Michael. "Planning Education in Ethiopia—A Critical Analysis of the Education Sector Review." A Harvard paper, 1974.

Branson, Bruce W., et al. "Report of Visiting Committee for the Faculty of Medicine, HSIU." Addis Ababa, 1966. Mimeographed.

Brembeck, Cole S., and John P. Keith. *Education in Emerging Africa: A Select and Annotated Bibliography.* East Lansing: Michigan State University, n.d.

British Library, The. *The Christian Orient.* London: British Museum Publications Ltd., 1978.

Broberg, Bertram, et al. *Report on Technical Education for Haile Selassie I University.* Addis Ababa, March 1969. Mimeographed.

Brown, Robert Lane. "A Resume of Attitudes of Ethiopian Students." Addis Ababa: Haile Selassie I University, Faculty of Arts, 1968.

Burney, L. E., R. A. Moore, and R. M. Walker. *Report of the Advisory Group on Medical Education to the President of Haile Selassie I University.* October 12, 1962. Mimeographed.

Buxton, David R. *The Abyssinians.* London: Thames and Hudson, 1970.

Calloway, A., and A. Musone. *Financing Higher Education in Nigeria.* Paris: UNESCO, 1968.

Carr-Saunders, Sir Alexander M. *Staffing African Universities.* London: Overseas Development Institute, 1963.

Central African Council. *Report of the Commission on Higher Education for Africans in Central Africa.* Salisbury: Central African Council, 1953.

Clapham, Christopher S. *Haile Selassie's Government.* New York: Frederick A. Praeger, 1969.

Cowan, L. Gray, James O'Connell, and David G. Scanlon, eds. *Education and Nation-Building in Africa.* New York: Frederick A. Praeger, 1965.

Cox, David R. "Principles of Learning for Teachers." Addis Ababa: Artistic Printer, 1968.

de Kiewiet, C. W. *The Emergent African University: An Interpretation.* Washington, D.C.: American Council on Education, Overseas Liaison Committee, 1972.

Demoz, Abraham. "The Problem of Quality in Higher Education: A Case Study." Paper presented at the Conference on the Role of a University in a Developing Country, Addis Ababa, 1967. Mimeographed.

Dolan, Eleanor F. *Higher Education in Africa South of the Sahara: Selected Bibliographies, 1945–1961.* Washington, D.C.: American Association of University Writers Educational Foundation, 1961.

Doresse, Jean. *Ethiopia.* New York: G. P. Putnams, 1959.

Education Sector Review Conference. "Final Report—Agricultural Education." In *Collected Papers,* vol. 3. Addis Ababa, 1971.

———. "Final Report." In *Collected Papers,* vols. 1, 2, 3. Addis Ababa, 1972.

————. "Symposium—Summary of the Discussions Held in Africa Hall from January 16–19, 1972." In *Collected Papers,* vol. 2. Addis Ababa, 1972.

Emmerson, Donald K., ed. *Students and Politics in Developing Nations.* New York: Frederick A. Praeger, 1968.

Ethio-Swedish Institute of Building Technology. *Annual Report: 1959–1960.* Addis Ababa, 1960.

Fafunwa, A. Babatunde. "The Growth and Development of Nigerian Universities." Overseas Liaison Committee Paper No. 4. Washington, D.C.: American Council on Education, April 1974.

————. *A History of Nigerian Higher Education.* London: Macmillan and Co., Ltd., 1971.

Geddes, Brecher, et al. *Physical Development Plan for Haile Selassie I University.* Addis Ababa, 1970.

Gilkes, Patrick. *The Dying Lion: Feudalism and Modernization in Ethiopia.* London: Julian Friedmann Publishers, 1975.

Ginzberg, Eli, and Herbert A. Smith. *A Manpower Strategy for Ethiopia.* USAID/Ethiopia, 1966.

Girma Amare. "Education and the Conflict of Values in Ethiopia. A Study of the Socio-Moral Problems Arising out of the Introduction of Modern Education in Ethiopia." Ph.D. dissertation, Southern Illinois University, 1964.

————. "A Review of a University in the Making: Past Experiences and Future Expectations." Paper presented at the Conference on the Role of a University in a Developing Country, Addis Ababa, 1967.

Goldthorpe, J. E. *An African Elite: Makerere College Students, 1922–1960.* Nairobi: Oxford University Press, 1965.

Grey, Robert. "Education and Politics in Ethiopia." Ph.D. dissertation, Yale University, 1970.

Haile Selassie I. "Address by His Imperial Majesty, Chancellor, on the Occasion of the Graduation of 1969, College of Agriculture," Alemaya, 1969. Mimeographed.

Haile Selassie Belay. "A Comparative Analysis of Higher Education in Agriculture and a Proposed Plan for Further Developing the System in Ethiopia." Ph.D. dissertation, Cornell University, 1964.

Haile Selassie I University. "Assessment of Accomplishment, 1961–1965 E.C." Addis ababa, 1973. Mimeographed.

————. "Consolidated Legislation of the Faculty Council of the Haile Selassie I University." Addis Ababa, 1967. Mimeographed.

————. "Consolidated Legislation of the Faculty Council—Revised to July 1, 1968, except for Title V." Addis Ababa, 1968. Mimeographed.

————. "Consolidated Legislation of the Faculty Council of the Haile Selassie I University." Addis Ababa, 1973. Mimeographed.

————. "Convocation Celebrating the Founding of Haile Selassie I University, Monday, December 18, 1961." Addis Ababa: Artistic Printing Press, 1965.

————. *Haile Selassie I University: The Last Decade.* Addis Ababa: Artistic Printers, 1972.

————. "Interim Report of the Development Committee to the Faculty Council, December 1965." Addis Ababa, n.d. Mimeographed.

————. "Outline Guide to the Central Business and Financial Administration and Planning Services." Addis Ababa: Haile Selassie I University, Office of the Vice-President for Business and Development, 1969. Mimeographed.

————. "A Preliminary Study of Certain Aspects of Haile Selassie I University." Addis Ababa, 1964. Mimeographed.

————. "The President's Annual Report 1968–69 and Faculty Reports." Addis Ababa, 1968–69. Mimeographed.

————. "Statute on Academic Rank, Tenure, Salaries and Academic Responsibility and Freedom." Addis Ababa, 1964. Mimeographed.

————. *Twentieth Anniversary of Higher Education in Ethiopia.* Addis Ababa: Artistic Printers, 1971.

————. "University Policies and Procedures." Addis Ababa, 1966. Mimeographed.

————. "University Procedures and Academic Regulation 1970–71." Addis Ababa, 1968. Mimeographed.

————. "University Statute of the Faculty Council Establishing a Program of Ethiopian University Service." Addis Ababa, 1966. Mimeographed.

————. Haile Selassie I University, Advisory Committee on Higher Education. *First Report of the Advisory Committee on Higher Education to His Imperial Majesty Haile Selassie I, Chancellor of the University.* Addis Ababa: Commercial Printing Press, 1966.

————. *Second Report of the Advisory Committee on Higher Education to His Imperial Majesty Haile Selassie I, Chancellor of the University.* Addis Ababa: Commercial Printing Press, 1971.

————. Haile Selassie I University, Department of Sociology. "Report on the Social Situation of Haile Selassie I University Students." Addis Ababa, 1970. Mimeographed.

————. Haile Selassie I University, Extension. "Information Bulletin, 1962." Addis Ababa, 1962. Mimeographed.

————. Haile Selassie I University, Faculty of Education. "Annual Report of the Dean of the Faculty of Education." Addis Ababa, 1967. Mimeographed.

————. "Conference on Elementary School Administration, 29 August-4 September 1965." Addis Ababa, 1965. Mimeographed.

————. "Expansion Project for Faculty of Education Haile Selassie I University, Secondary School Teachers Training Programme." Addis Ababa, 1964. Mimeographed.

————. "Innovation in Teacher Education." Report of the Addis Ababa Conference of African Teachers Education Association, 25 March-1 April 1972. Addis Ababa, 1972. Mimeographed.

————. Haile Selassie I University, Faculty of Law. "Report of the Dean for the Year 1956 E.C. (1963–64 G.C.)." Addis Ababa, 1964. Mimeographed.

————. "Report of the Dean of the Faculty of Law for the Academic Year 1964–65 (1957 E.C.)." Addis Ababa, 1965. Mimeographed.

————. "Report of the Dean of the Faculty of Law for the Academic Year 1964–65 (1957 E.C.)." Addis Ababa, 1965. Mimeographed.

————. "Report of the Dean of the Faculty of Law to the President for 1958 E.C. (1966–67 G.C.)." Addis Ababa, 1966. Mimeographed.

————. Haile Selassie I University, Faculty of Medicine. "Present State of the Faculty of Medicine, 11 October 1965." Addis Ababa, 1965. Mimeographed.

————. Haile Selassie I University, Faculty of Science. "Faculty of Science Bulletin 1967–68." Addis Ababa, 1967. Mimeographed.

————. "School of Pharmacy 1965–66." Addis Ababa, 1965. Mimeographed.

————. "Statistical Training Centre: Prospectus." Addis Ababa, 1966. Mimeographed.

————. Haile Selassie I University, Laboratory School. "Director's Report, Prince Bede Mariam Laboratory School, 1969–70, HSIU." Addis Ababa, 1970. Mimeographed.

————. Haile Selassie I University, Office of the Academic Vice-President. "HSIU Leadership Seminar: A Summary of Proceedings." Nazareth (Ethiopia), 1971. Mimeographed.

————. "Annual Report 1969–70." Addis Ababa, n.d.. Mimeographed.

————. Haile Selassie I University, Office of the Dean of Students. "Report on Student Support, presented to Dr. Aklilu Habte, President of HSIU, by Office of the Dean of Students." Addis Ababa, 9 May 1969. Mimeographed.

————. Haile Selassie I University, Office of Public Relations. "The Ethiopian University Service: An Inspiration of Genius." Addis Ababa, 1966. Mimeographed.

————. "Ethiopian University Service Handbook." Addis Ababa, 1966. Mimeographed.

————. "Ethiopian University Service: Student Manual." Addis Ababa, 1970. Mimeographed.

————. *This Is Haile Selassie I University.* Addis Ababa: Artistic Printing Press, 1964.

————. Haile Selassie I University, Office of the Registrar. "Enrollment Statistics of Haile Selassie I University, 1963–69." Addis Ababa, 1969. Mimeographed.

————. "Number of Graduates from Haile Selassie I University by Country and Field of Studies to Date." Addis Ababa, n.d. Mimeographed.

————. "Number of Other African Students Enrolled in Institutions of Higher Learning in Ethiopia between 1958–68." Addis Ababa, n.d. Mimeographed.

————. Presidential Commission on Planning, Reorganization and Consolidation of Academic Programs of the University. "Final Report." Addis Ababa, 1968. Mimeographed.

————. Haile Selassie I University, Theological College. "Report of a Consultation on Theological Education, January 16–17, 1970." Addis Ababa, 1970. Mimeographed.

————. "Seminar on Theological College." Collected Papers. Addis Ababa, 6 January 1970. Mimeographed.

————. Haile Selassie I University, Ministry of Education. "Educational Administration Conference: Final Report. 15 July–22 July 1963." Addis Ababa, 1963. Mimeographed.

Haile Wolde Mikael. "The Problems of Admission to the University through School Leaving Certificate Examination." Addis Ababa: Haile Selassie I University, Faculty of Education, 1969. Mimeographed.

Hanna, William, and Judith L. Hanna. *University Students and African Politics.* New York: Africana Publishing Co., 1975.

Hanson, John Wagner, and Geoffrey W. Gibson. *African Education and Development Since 1960: A Select and Annotated Bibliography.* East Lansing: Institute for International Studies in Education and African Studies Center, Michigan State University, 1966.

Henderson, Algo D. *Policies and Practices in Higher Education.* New York: Harper and Row, 1960.

Herskovits, Melville. *The Human Factor in Changing Africa.* New York: Alfred A. Knopf, 1962.

Ike, V. Chuckwuemeka. *University Development in Africa: The Nigerian Experience.* Ibadan, Nigeria: Oxford University Press, 1976.

Imbakom Kalewold (Aleka). *Traditional Ethiopian Church Education.* New York: Teachers College Press, Columbia University, 1970.

Imperial Ethiopian College of Agriculture and Mechanical Arts. *Bulletin, 1961–62.* Addis Ababa: HSIU, 1961.

International Association of Universities. *Report of a Meeting of Heads of African Institutions of Higher Education,* Kartoum, 16–19 September 1963. Paris: International Association of Universities, 1964.

International Seminar on Inter-University Co-operation in West Africa. *The West African Intellectual Community: Papers and Discussions,* Freetown, Sierra Leone, 1961. Ibadan, Nigeria: Ibadan University Press, 1967.

Jones, Reginald L. "The Prediction of Academic Performance at Haile Selassie I University: A Summer of Studies," Technical Report. Addis Ababa: Haile Selassie I University Testing Centre, May 1973.

Jones, Thomas Jesse. *Education in East Africa.* New York: Phelps-Stokes Fund, 1926.

Klineberg, Otto, and Marisa Zavalloni. *Nationalism and Tribalism among African Students.* Paris, The Hague: Mouton, 1969.

Klineberg, Otto et al. *Students, Values, and Politics: A Cross-Cultural Comparison.* New York: The Free Press, 1979.

Koehn, Peter H. "Political Socialization and Political Integration: The Impact of the Faculty of Arts, Haile Selassie I University." Paper prepared for the Interdisciplinary Seminar of the Faculties of Arts and Education, Haile Selassie I University, Addis Ababa, 1972. Mimeographed.

Korten, David C. *Planned Change in a Traditional Society.* New York: Frederick A. Praeger, 1972.

Korten, David C., and Frances Korten. "A Novel Education Program for Development: Ethiopia's Use of National University Students in a Year of Rural Service." Addis Ababa, 1965. Mimeographed.

————. "Proposal for Revision of the Curriculum of the College of Business Administration." Addis Ababa: Haile Selassie I University, 1964.

La Follette, Robert. *Reconnaissance Study of Haile Selassie I University.* USAID/Ethiopia, 1963 and 1964.

Legesse Lemma. "Political Economy of Ethiopia 1875–1974: Agricultural, Educational and International Antecedents of the Revolution." Ph.D. dissertation, University of Notre Dame, 1980.

Legume, Colin. *Africa: The Year of the Students.* London: Rex Collins, 1972.

Levine, Donald N. *Wax and Gold: Tradition and Innovation in Ethiopian Culture.* Chicago: University of Chicago Press, 1965.

Lowe, J., N. Grant, and T. D. Williams, eds. *Education and Nation- Building in the Third World.* Edinburgh: Scottish Academic Press, 1971.

Lyons, Charles H. *To Wash an Aethiop White.* New York: Columbia University Press, 1975.

Macpherson, Margaret. *They Built for the Future; A Chronicle of Makerere University College 1922–1961.* Cambridge: University Press, 1964.

Madsen, Harold S. "Coping with English Language Transition Problems at Secondary and University Levels in Ethiopia." Addis Ababa: Haile Selassie I University, May 1970. Mimeographed.

Mahiteme Selassie Wolde Meskel (Blatengeta). *Zetire Neger.* Addis Ababa: Berhanina Selam Printing Press, 1942 E.C.

Marcus, Harold G. *The Life and Times of Menelik II: Ethiopia, 1844–1913.* Oxford: Claredon Press, 1975.

———. *Haile Selassie I: The Formative Years, 1892–1936.* Berkeley: University of California Press, 1987.

Markakis, John. *Ethiopia: Anatomy of a Traditional Polity.* Oxford: Clarendon Press, 1974.

Markakis, John, and Nega Ayele. *Class and Revolution in Ethiopia.* Nottingham, England: Spokesman, 1978.

Mathew, David. *Ethiopia: The Study of a Polity, 1540–1935.* London: Eyre and Spottswoode, 1947.

Matte, Lucien. "History of University College of Addis Ababa." An outline submitted to the Board of Governors on 24 January 1955. (Copy in Haile Selassie I University Public Relations Office file.)

———. "Projet de College. A Report Given to the Vice-Minister of Education." Addis Ababa: Haile Selassie I University, 1949. Mimeographed.

Mazrui, A., and T. G. Wagaw. "Towards Decolonizing Modernity: Education and Culture Conflict in Eastern Africa." *The Education Process and Historiography in Africa.* Paris: UNESCO, 1985.

Mjoku, E. "The Relationship between University and Society in Nigeria." *The Scholar and Society.* Bulletin of the Committee on Science and Freedom, 13 (Manchester, 1959): 82–86.

Mogus Tesfa-Tsion, et al. *High Level Manpower Demand and Supply Analysis with Particular Reference to the Field of Business.* Addis Ababa: Haile Selassie I University, College of Business, July 1967.

Mulugeta Wodajo. "Government and University Relationship and its Implication to University Autonomy." Paper presented at the Confernce on the Role of a University in a Developing Country, Addis Ababa, 1967.

Negewo Beyene. "The Impact of University Education on the Formation of Political Attitudes: Sources of Negative Political Attitudes of Ethiopian University Students." Ph.D. dissertation, Stanford University, 1977.

Netherlands Economic Institute. *The Financing of Higher education in Africa*. A report prepared for the Conference on the Development of Higher Education in Africa. Paris: UNESCO, 1962.

Odumosu, Peter I. *Government and University in Developing Society*. Nigeria: University of Ife, 1973.

Oklahoma State University. "Oklahoma State University in Ethiopia: Terminal Report, 1952–1968." Stillwater: Oklahoma State University, 1969.

Ottaway, Marina, and David Ottaway. *Ethiopia: Empire in Revolution*. New York and London: Africana Publishing Co., 1978.

Ozanic, Ivanka. "Ethiopian Schools of Nurses." In *Nursing in Ethiopia*, 24–28. Addis Ababa: Ethiopian Nurses Association, 1962.

Paulos Tzadua (Abba), trans. *Fetha Negest*. Faculty of Law, Haile Selassi I University, Addis Ababa, 1968.

Pankhurst, E. Sylvia. *Ethiopia: A Cultural History*. Woodford Green: Lalibela House, 1955.

Peter, Yehuda. "Engineering Education in Ethiopia." Addis Ababa: Haile Selassie I University, Engineering College, 1967. Mimeographed.

Presidential Commission on Graduate Programs. Preliminary report. Addis Ababa: Haile Selassie I University, June 1970. Mimeographed.

Prewett, Kenneth, ed. *Education and Political Values: An East African Case Study*. Nairobi: East African Publishing House, 1971.

Quarmby, Andrew, and Dian Quarmby. "The Ethiopian University Service." Geneva: International Secretariat for Volunteer Service, 1970.

Rubensen, Sven. *King of Kings, Twedros of Ethiopia*. Addis Ababa: Haile Selassie I University, 1966.

———. *The Survival of Ethiopian Independence*. London: Heineman Educational Books, 1976.

Samaan, Wahib I. *Guidance and Counseling at the Higher Education Level in East Africa: A Case Study Prepared for UNESCO*. Paris: UNESCO, 1974.

Sanyal, B. C., J. H, Case, P. S. Dow, and M. E. Jackman. *Higher Education and the Labour Market in Zambia: Expectations and Performance*. International Institute for Educational Planning. Paris: The UNESCO Press, 1976.

Sasnett, Martene, and Inez Sepmeyer. *Educational Systems of Africa: Interpretations for Use in the Evaluation of academic Credentials*. Berkeley: University of California Press, 1966.

Scanlon, David G., ed. *Chruch, State and Education in Africa*. New York Teachers College, Columbia University Press, 1966.

———. *Traditions of African Education*. New York: Bureau of Publications, Teachers College, Columbia University Press, 1964.

Sloan, Ruth, comp., and Helen Kitchen, ed. *The Educated African*. New York: Frederick A. Praeger, 1962.

Summerskill, John. *Haile Selassie I University: A Blueprint for Development*. Addis Ababa: Haile Selassie I University, 1970.

Sutherland, Sir Gordon. *Ethiopia: Science Policy and Scientific Research at Haile Selassie I University*. Paris: UNESCO, March 1969.

Taddesse Tamrat. *Church and State in Ethiopia, 1270–1527*. Oxford: Clarendon Press, 1972.

Taggart, G., R. Clodius, and J. Hanson. *Memorandum: Issues Raised for Consideration by Haile Selassie I University's Planning Task Forces and in the Preparationof its Five-Year Plan.* American Council on Education, Overseas Liaison Committee, 19 August 1973.

Thompson, Kenneth W., and Barbara R. Fogel. *Higher Education and Social Change: Promising Experiments in Developing Countries.* Vol. 1. New York: Frederick A. Praeger, 1976.

Thompson, K.W., B. R. Fogel, and H. E. Danner, eds. *Higher Education and Social Change: Promising Experiments in Dveloping Countries.* Vol. 2. New York: Frederick A. Praeger, 1977.

Trimingham, John Spencer. *Islam in Ethiopia.* London: Oxford University Press, 1952.

Trudeau, Edouard. *Higher Education in Ethiopia.* Montreal, Canada, 1964.

Ullendorff, Edward. *The Ethiopians: An Introduction to Country and People.* London: Oxford University Press, 1960; 2d rev. ed., 1965.

University College of Addis Ababa. "Some Notes on the Development of the University College of Addis Ababa." Document prepared by the College, now in Addis Ababa University Registrar's Office, n.d.

University of Utah Survey Team. *Higher Education in Ethiopia: Survey Report and Recommendations.* Salt Lake City: University of Utah, 1959–60.

Wagaw, Teshome G. "The Burden and Glory of Being Schooled: An Ethiopian Dilemma." *Proceedings of the International Colloquium on Growth, Equity, and Self-Reliance—Challenge of the 80's.* Lome, Togo: Club d'Afrique, 1984.

———. "The Challenge of Education in Africa's Transformation." *Commemorative Volume of the Twelfth Internatioal Conference on the Unity of the Sciences,* New York: ICUS Books, 1984.

———. *Configuration of Education and Culture: An African Experience.* Ann Arbor: University of Michigan Program of Adult and Continuing Education (ERIC Document Reproduction Service No. ED 250 239), 1984.

———. "The Cultural Context of the Dilemma of Skill Formation in Africa." *Conference Papers of the Fourth World Conference on Cooperative Education.* Edinburgh: International Cooperative education Association, 1985.

———. *Education and Cultural Change in Black Africa: A Regional Case Study.* Institut de Sciences l'Educacion, Laboratoire de Psycho- Pedagogie, University de Caen, 1982.

———. "Education for National Integration." *Education Sector Review.* Addis Ababa: Ministry of education and Culture, August 1971.

———. *Education in Ethiopia: Prospect and Retrospect.* Ann Arbor: The University of Michigan Press, 1979.

———. "Educational Determinants of Modernization: Problems of Skill Transformation." *Proceedings of the Fourteenth International Conference on the Unity of the Sciences.* New York: ICUS Books, 1985.

———. "Ethiopia: System of Education." *The International Encyclopedia of Education.* Oxford, New York: Pergamon Press, 1985.

———. "An Evaluation Survey of High-Level Manpower Output and Development to Meet Critical Needs in Social Development." Addis Ababa:

United Nations Economic Commission for Africa, 1970. Mimeographed.

―――. "High-Level Manpower Development and Utilization in U.A.R." Addis Ababa: United Nations Economic Commission for Africa, 1970. Mimeographed.

―――. "The Importance of EArly Years of Emotional Development." *The 1973 Dag Hammarskjold Seminar on the Dilemma of Quality, Quantity and Cost in African Child Care.* Addis Ababa, 5 May 1973.

―――. "Multiplicity of Holidays in Ethiopia: Their Possible Effects on the Psycho-socioeconomic Development of the Country." Paper prepared for the Interdisciplinary Seminar on the Faculties of Arts and Education. Addis Ababa: Haile Selassie I University, Faculty of Education, 1971. Mimeographed.

―――. *A Pilot Field Study of Child-Rearing Practices in Rural Ethiopia.* Addis Ababa: Haile Selassie I University Press, 1974.

―――. *Report on Student Support.* Addis Ababa: Haile Selassie I University, Office of the Dean of Students, 9 May 1969.

―――. "Some Notes for the World of Work in Ethiopian Tradition." Paper presented to the annual Historical Society of Ethiopia Conference. Addis Ababa, 1971. Mimeographed.

―――. "The Unfulfilled Role of Higher Learning Institutions in Africa's Economic Development." *Proceedings of the International Colloquium on Growth, Equity, and Self-Reliance—Challenge of the 1980s.* Lome, Togo: Club d'Afrique, 1984.

Wagaw, T. G., and A. Mazrui. "Education et Diverste Culturelle in Afrique Noire: Une Etude Regionaliste." In *Historie Mondial de l'Education,* edited by G. Mialeret and J. Vials. Institute de Sciences l'Education, Laboratoire de Psycho-Pedagogie, University de Caen, 1981.

Ward, F. Champion, ed. *Education and Development Reconsidered.* New York: Frederick A. Praeger, 1974.

Ward, F. Champion and Barbara Fogel. *Higher Education and Social Chance.* 2 vols. New York: Frederick A. Praeger, 1976, 1977.

Wedemeyer, C. A., R. D. Goodman, and J. K. Balbir. *Evaluation of Extension at the Haile Selassie I University, Addis Ababa.* Paris: UNESCO, 1973.

Weele, A. H. ter. "A Comparison of Education Financing in Ethiopia, Kenya and Tanzania." Addis Ababa, 1973. Mimeographed.

Wrinkle, William L. "The Improvement and Expansion of Ethiopian Teacher Education." Addis Ababa: Ministry of Education and Fine Arts, 1953. Mimeographed.

Yesufu, T. NM., ed. *Creating the African University.* Ibadan: Oxford University Press, 1973.

Government Publications

Ethiopia, Imperial Air Force. "The Training in IEAF: The Technical Schools." In *UJoin the Air Force.* Addis Ababa: Berhaninna Selam Printing Press, 1967.

Ethiopia, Imperial Ethiopian Government/United Nationa. *School of Social Work: Bulletin 1961–1962.* Addis Ababa: Artistic Printers, 1961.

Ethiopia, Imperial Ethiopian Government/United Nations. *School of Social Work: Bulletin 1961–1962*. Addis Ababa: Artistic Printers, 1961.

Ethiopia, Ministry of Education and Fine Arts. *Haile Selassie I University Committee Report: Technical and Agricultural Education*. Addis Ababa, 1952.

————. *Minutes of the Meeting of the Committee on Technical Training and the Proposed Imperial College of Engineering, 28 March 1950*. Addis Ababa, 1950.

————. "Plan for Technical Education for Ethiopia." Prepared by Mikael Mesgenna, Addis Ababa, 1965.

————. *Recommendations Made by the Conference on Teacher Training Education Held at the Ministry of Education and Fine Arts on 21–23 March 1963*. Addis Ababa, 1963.

————. *Report of the Conference of Directors of Teacher Training Institutions Held at the University College of Addis Ababa in July 1961*. Addis Ababa, 1961.

————. *Teacher Education in Ethiopia*. Addis Ababa: Department of Teacher Education, 1965.

————. *Teacher Training Institutes*. Addis Ababa, n.d.

————. *Technical and Vocational Education in Ethiopia*. Addis Ababa: Division of Technical and Vocational Education, 1966.

————. *Vocational and Technical Education Today and Tomorrow*. Addis Ababa: Department of Vocational and Technical Education, 1964.

Ethiopia, Ministry of Education and Fine Arts, and Haile Selassie I University. *Conference on Teacher Education*. Addis Ababa, 1969.

Ethiopia, Ministry of Pen. *Negarit Gazeta* 13, no. 13 (1954). General Notice No. 185. Charter of the University College of Addis Ababa.

————. *Negarit Gazeta* 20, no. 8 (1961). General Notice No. 284. Haile Selassie I University Charter.

————. *Negarit Gazeta* 19, no. 19 (1968). Order No. 52. University of Asmara Charter.

Netherland's Economic Institute. *The Financing of Higher Education in Africa*. Report prepared for the Conference on the Development of Higher Education in Africa. Paris: UNESCO, 1962.

United Nations, Economic Commission for Africa. *Final Report: Conference of African States on the Development of Education in Africa, Addis Ababa, 15–25 May 1961*. Paris: UNESCO/ED/181, 1961.

————. *Report of an Evaluation Survey of University Level Manpower Supply and Demand in Selected Countries*. Addis Ababa, 1970.

United Nations Educational, Scientific, and Cultural Organization. *The Development of Higher Education in Africa*. Report of the Conference on the Development of Higher Education in Africa, Tananarive, 3–12 September 1962. Paris: UNESCO, 1963.

————. *The Financing of National Plans of Education, Review of Recent Trends in Expenditure for Education in Africa*. Paris: UNESCO/AFMIN/5, n.d.

————. "Working Party on Higher Education, 1967." Serial no. 1105, Annex 5. Paris: UNESCO, 1967.

United States Agency for International Development. *The University of Utah Project in Ethiopia.* Logan: University of Utah Printing Service, 1967.

United States-Ethiopian Governments. "Agreement for a Cooperative Education Program between the Government of the United States of America and the Imperial Ethiopian Government." Addis Ababa, May 1952.

United States Operations Mission to Ethiopia. *Report on the Organization and Administration of the Ministry of Education and Fine Arts.* Addis Ababa: Cooperative Education Program Press, October 1954.

INDEX

The Development of Higher Education and Social Change

Series Editor: Harold Marcus
Production Editor: Julie L. Loehr
Design: Lynne A. Brown
Copy Editor: Dawn Martin
Proofreaders: Loretta Crum, Kristine M. Blakeslee

Text composed by Lansing Graphics in 10½ pt. Garamond Book and Garamond Book Italic.

Printed by Thomson-Shore on 55# Glatfelter Natural and smyth sewn in Roxite B Linen